Faces in the Firelight

FACES in the FIRELIGHT

New Zealand folk song & story

Phil Garland

Martin
with many thanks
for your support.
Best wishes
Phil Garland

STEELE ROBERTS
AOTEAROA NEW ZEALAND

Cover design by Lynn Peck, Central Media; upper photo Gilbert Van Reenen, photo of Phil Garland by Trevor King. Graphic on page 1 by Nikki Slade Robinson.

We gratefully acknowledge the assistance of the Price family in supporting the publication of this book, and thank Janette Munneke, Kate Stephenson and Jude Watson for production assistance.

Thanks to the Alexander Turnbull Library (ATL) for many images reproduced in the book. Other images are from the author's or publisher's collections. Please let us know any additional attribution, information or other amendments for future editions and posting on our website.

National Library of New Zealand Cataloguing-in-Publication Data:
Garland, Phil, 1942-
Faces in the firelight / Phil Garland.
Includes bibliographical references and index.

ISBN 978-1-877448-70-6

1. Folk music—New Zealand—History and criticism.
I. Title.
781.6200993—dc 22

Steele Roberts Ltd
Box 9321, Wellington, Aotearoa New Zealand
info@steeleroberts.co.nz • www.steeleroberts.co.nz

CONTENTS

PREFACE

THIS BOOK IS THE CULMINATION of years of study, field collection, research and making music. It is based on the workshops, instructional performances and teach-ins I have presented over the last forty or more years at folk festivals, clubs, universities and folklore conferences throughout New Zealand and Australia.

My main wish in writing such a book is to stimulate interest in our national folk heritage. I want people to realise that despite its relative youth, New Zealand does have a vibrant and exciting heritage, which is reflected in our oral history, music, songs, backblocks rhymes, home-grown yarns, stories and verse. Few Kiwis ever get to hear them or even know they exist, thanks in part to an ongoing cultural cringe which manifests itself in the broadcasting media's seeming reluctance to play anything that smacks of a unique local identity. The majority of radio and television media, and the education system to a lesser extent, steadfastly refuse to believe that audiences want to hear or learn about our cultural heritage, yet my performing experience refutes this notion. People constantly ask me where they can listen to Kiwi songs and why they are never played on the radio. The answer from the commercial radio stations is often the same: "It doesn't fit our format" or "Nobody wants to hear these songs, they're not commercial enough." This reluctance to acknowledge our musical heritage amounts to criminal neglect on their part, for these attitudes only foster public discomfort with our cultural heritage. If interest in our country's heritage grows as a result of this publication, I will be more than satisfied.

I cannot claim that everything of cultural interest and importance is included within, but there is certainly plenty of material to sink your teeth into. I look forward to the time when Kiwis travelling overseas, asked to sing an appropriate song at an important social occasion, will be able to find something more suitable to launch into than a garbled version of 'Po Karekare Ana', the 'Ka Mate' haka or the oft-heard Chesdale cheese commercial:

> We are the boys from down on the farm, we really know our cheese
> There's much better value in Chesdale, it never fails to please.
> Chesdale slices thinly, never crumbles, there's no waste,
> Chesdale cheese, it's finest cheddar, made better."

I gratefully acknowledge the help and support I have received from individuals and organisations throughout New Zealand and Australia, while engaging in my lengthy and often painstaking search for Kiwi folklore and music.

Firstly I'd like to thank the New Zealand Folklore Society and National Folk Foundation for their financial assistance and support over the years, and David De Santi, Kiwi Pacific Records and Roger Steele for believing in me and having the courage to publish and record my work. It would be remiss of me not to acknowledge those whose pioneering work paved the way and offered inspiration … Rona Bailey, Les Cleveland, Neil Colquhoun, James Cowan, Frank Fyfe, Elsie Locke and Herbert Roth.

I offer special thanks to all those people and groups (too numerous to mention) who have demonstrated belief in the existence of New Zealand's folk heritage and offered information, support, encouragement and in some cases, financial assistance. My heartfelt thanks and appreciation go to all my informants, supporters and contributors, some of whom are no longer with us. I thank Declan Affley, the Alexander Turnbull Library, John & Sue Allan, Graeme Anderson, Shirley Andrews, Banks Peninsula Folk Club, Alan Brady, Les Brady, Warwick Brock, Michael Brown, Roger Buckton, Canterbury Museum Library, Canterbury Public Library, Canterbury University Folk Club, Peter Cape, Joe Charles, Jim Delahunty, Roger Dick, Warren Fahey, John Flynn, Vin Garbutt, Mike & Margaret Garland, Jim Geddes, Roger Giles, Don Grady, Mike Harding, Dave Hart, *Heritage* magazine, the Hocken Library, Dennis Hogan, Christine Hunt, Oliver Hunter, Hugh Isdale, Charles Jemmett, Ian Johnston, Trevor Johnston, Dave Jordan, Larry Lacey, John A Lee (especially in Chapter VI 'Swags to Riches'), AL Lloyd, Jocelyn Logan, David Loomes, Hugh McDonald, Gordon McIntyre, Ian McNamara, Colin MacNicol, Phillip Maxwell, John Meredith, Tony Miles, Will Millar, Heather Mitchell, Mitchell Library (National Library of Australia), Peter Morgan, National Folk Foundation, Graeme Nesbit, John Newsham, Otago University Folk Club, Jack Perkins, Radio New Zealand, Martyn Wyndham Read, Brian Ringrose, Sam Sampson, Roy Sinclair, Sharyn Staley, Television New Zealand, Dusty Spittle, Danny Spooner, John Stafford, Jim Sullivan, Rudy Sunde, Tod Symons, Victoria University Folk Club, Murray Vincent, Robyn Willams, Graham Wilson and Max Winnie.

I am eternally indebted to their friendship, talent, support and inspiration.

For permission to quote works or excerpts, special thanks to Roy Abbott for 'And When They Dance'; Colin Amodeo for Coll Cameron's 'Blow the Brothers Down'; John Archer for his Kiwi folksong website; John Baxter and the James K Baxter estate for 'By the dry Cardrona'; Joan Botting for poetry by her father, Tod Symons; Neil Colquhoun for his pioneering work, background information and his book *New Zealand Folksongs*; Martin Curtis for 'Gin and Raspberry'; Grant Dawson for 'Barrett's Shanty'; Raewyn Flygel for Cecil Winter's 'The Star Hotel', 'The Mill' and 'A Bloke You Useter Know'; Peter Gross for 'Kauaeranga Kauri'; Helen Henderson for 'The Ballad of Minnie Dean'; Robert Hoskins for information and lyrics from his book *Goldfields Balladeer*; Gladwen McIntyre for the works of Peter Cape; Willow Macky for 'Thames', 'Te Harinui' and 'Song for Captain Cook';

Ross McMillan for several poems; Robyn Matheson for the works of her father, Joe Charles; Paul Metsers and Sagem Music for 'Hooray for the Swag and the Shiner', and 'Song for Captain Cook', and to Paul and Topic Records for 'Farewell to the Gold'; Alwyn (Hop) Owen for 'The Charleston Drum'; Allen Shaw for his research and the song 'You Don't Get Over Me'; Tony Simpson for an unemployment verse from 1932 and the yarn 'Keeping the wolf from the door' from *The Sugarbag Years*; Bill Worsfold for 'Fields of the Gum', 'Crossing the Kaipara Bar' and 'Farewell to the Gumfields'; and Dave York for 'A Rousie's Life'.

Attempts were made to contact all known copyright owners of songs and other material used in this publication, and I sincerely apologise if anyone has been inadvertently omitted or overlooked. Please advise the publisher so that any amendments can be made in future editions and posted on their website.

Finally, thanks to my loving partner Jan Wilson for her understanding, nurturing, critiques and constant support.

Phil Garland
May 2009

Music is often part of Kiwi social occasions. Here friends and family farewell a soldier leaving for the Middle East in World War II.
Photo by Bert Snowden; ATL PAColl-0785-1-011-01,Ca August 1940

PROLOGUE

A DIFFERENT DRUM

IT HAS ALWAYS BEEN MY BELIEF that I had a fairly normal childhood, growing up in the Christchurch suburb of Opawa, but as I recall events that shaped my life, it now seems anything but normal.

My earliest memories are of being aboard a sailing boat in Auckland harbour (my parents later told me I was only 18 months old), and waving a flag whilst seated on my father's shoulders during a parade down Auckland's Queen Street — this was apparently the Victory parade after World War II and I was three and a half years old. On both occasions we were probably in Auckland to visit my mother's sister Marjorie, who lived at Freeman's Bay. Mum had been born Ruth Tully, in Carterton, and eventually took up nursing at Cook Hospital in Gisborne, where she met my father Humphrey Garland on one of his visits to the north.

I began my schooling at Opawa School in 1947, where I regularly had my left hand strapped by the teacher, who was trying to make me use my right hand instead. I have been a leftie all of my life in everything I do — except when learning to play

Garland family homestead at Hillsborough.

Phil aged 6, at home; At 7, waiting for a tram in Cathedral Square; Sea cadet, aged 14.

guitar, for that was how the book said it was done. My journey to school took me past the home of a local larrikin and bully, who regularly attacked me as I passed by. Consequently I was very unhappy with my lot.

My father, who had been a chorister in the Christchurch Cathedral choir, made arrangements for me to attend Cathedral Grammar School and I moved to this seat of learning at the tender age of seven. I would travel daily by tram to Kilmore Street and walk the remaining half mile or so to school — returning the same way I'd come. Within six months of being there I had put on considerable weight and blown up into a little barrel. Family and friends put it down to me being happy with life, although I do recall being involved in a couple of schoolground fist fights with anyone who made adverse comments about my size. One of the masters noticed my unhappiness about being called Fatty by my peers and christened me Tubby, which I seemed perfectly willing to accept for some reason. I became known as Tub or Tubby throughout my school career.

I joined the church choir at St Mark's, just across the road from our house, and thoroughly enjoyed every opportunity to sing. The first time I was asked to sing solo in church my knees knocked and my face felt as red as a beetroot, but I came through the exercise intact. I grew up with classical music around me and both my mother and father used to sing occasionally at home. Dad would sometimes play the piano in our front room, displaying a very nice touch indeed. I enjoyed his playing and often wished that he would play more frequently, but his time always seemed very precious. He was the chief engineer with Davis Gelatine, in charge of the workshop and on call 24 hours a day. Whenever trouble occurred or machinery broke down, Dad would be called out to oversee the repairs. After gaining his engineer's certificate he had done an apprenticeship with the Christchurch Tramways Board and during the 1930s Depression even helped drive trams on the city to Sumner route.

When I was nine I was enrolled to learn piano at school, but lasted only a year or so because I always found practice a chore and wanted to be outside playing sport with my mates. It did teach me to read music, however, which would stand me in good stead later on.

Despite changing schools I was still harassed by my larrikin nemesis whenever our paths crossed, and I longed to get my own back. Meanwhile I had become a pretty good swimmer, having taught myself at the local pool. I competed with other lads to see who could swim furthest underwater and only a few of us ever managed to hold our breaths the full length of the pool. A couple of times I even did a length and a half, of which I was extremely proud. One day I noticed my tormentor at the baths, obviously unable to swim, spending his time harassing kids in the shallow end. I hit on a novel revenge — I would swim underwater, take his legs out from under him, and continue on my way. This didn't totally satisfy me, however, because he didn't know it was me. I decided to walk up to him and duck him under, then run like hell while he chased me until I dived into the deep end. He couldn't follow because he couldn't swim. This happened a few times until he

Serenading my mum;
Dad waters the roses.

Singing at a church dance in 1958, aged 16.

realised he couldn't win and a truce was called. He gave me no more trouble.

The time came to move on to secondary school and along with two dozen schoolmates from Cathedral Grammar, I found myself at Christ's College. Immediately on arrival all new boys had to learn the school haka and be auditioned for the chapel choir. Older boys warned us not to get involved with the choir because it would take all our spare time and we'd have to come back to school twice on Sundays to sing at the services. When it was my turn to sing for the master in charge, Robert Field-Dodgson, I did my best to sing off key and only ended up in the school choir.

Later in the year, when we were rehearsing selections from Edward German's *Merrie England* to perform at the end of year prizegiving, Bobby Field-Dodgson called on all those boys who had sung the same pieces during their last year at Cathedral Grammar to demonstrate the music. Naturally I was one of these. I was standing at the end of the line right beside Bobby and when the performance was over he said "Garland, I want to see you later."

Worried sick, I wondered what I'd done wrong. After everyone had gone he asked me why I wasn't in the chapel choir, to which I replied "I have no idea, sir." He then told me that he wanted me to sing 'O Peaceful England' as a soloist at the prizegiving.

The thought of singing alone in front of the whole school and their parents scared me half to death. The day eventually dawned and I sang my heart out before the assembled crowd and felt quite good about it all. Mum told me later that Dad was slumped in his seat until I started to sing, when he sat bolt upright, puffing out his chest with pride. He was talking to Bobby later and told him why I never made it into the chapel choir. Bobby took it well and years later informed me that I was still the only non-chapel choir boy to ever sing solo in such a school production. He followed my musical career with interest and became quite supportive over the years. My band and I were presenting a barn dance for the Canterbury Folk Festival at Diamond Harbour in 1981 and as we finished our set I turned round to find Bobby Field-Dodgson standing there listening to us. He said "I was up the hill when I heard the music and thought it was the Garlands performing, so I came down to listen." My brother Mike was in that band and continues to perform with me today. It was good to see Bobby again after all those years.

My friends and I used to bike to school and when wearing our black and white striped caps would cop cheek in the form of "Blackballs are cheap today, cheaper than yesterday", along with the occasional physical attack from other school kids. We learnt to cope with it pretty well, although every now and then a few scuffles broke out when we refused to take it any longer. We usually acquitted ourselves pretty well. Biking to and from school posed problems, especially in bad weather. It was no fun biking into a nor'west gale, so we'd leave home up to ten minutes early just to make it to school on time. In winter, frosts could take their toll with bikes slipping and sliding on the icy roads. Many a schoolmate ended up with chillblains on a regular basis.

I got into strife in the fourth form when I copped flak from certain sections of the school about my size and the suburb I came from. This affected me so much that I decided to run away to sea. Since age seven I had made up my mind that I wanted to become an officer in the navy and my whole schooling was oriented towards this aim, but things got so bad at college that I just wanted to get away. I set off from home as though I was going to school, but with a change of clothes hidden in my bag. I went straight to the Union Steam Ship office in Hereford Street and booked a berth on that night's ferry to Wellington. I had no plan other than to try and find a suitable vessel that might want to take on a cabin boy. The overnight voyage was uneventful enough, but on arrival in Wellington the following morning I was met by the police and taken to my Aunt Mary's home in Karori to be looked after for the day, before being placed on the ferry back to Lyttelton that night.

Surprisingly I didn't get into too much trouble, but a couple of masters at college kept a close eye on proceedings from that moment on.

Because of my interest in the sea I was able to join the sea cadets instead of having to participate in army cadets for the remainder of my time at school. I went for an eye check as part of a test to determine my suitability to join the navy as an officer cadet and to my utter dismay was found to be slightly colour blind. Red-green defective is not acceptable for anyone wanting to be a deck officer in any of the sea-going services. My whole world was disintegrating around me — I was devastated. I was told that my eyesight defect would enable me to join the army as a spotter, for it meant I could see through camouflage.

Still determined to go to sea, however, I decided to become a purser with the merchant service, and changed my school subjects to suit my intended career. On leaving school I joined the Union Steam Ship Co as an office boy by day and studied accountancy at Canterbury University by night. The shipping firm used to recruit all their pursers from office staff, so I thought it would be a simple step to achieving my aims. Before the year was out, someone had made a decision that no more pursers would be recruited from office staff and I found myself high and dry. What was I to do? I left and got a job as assistant to the accountant at Shaw Savill shipping company. My lengthy dream of going to sea had finally ended.

1959: With my brown *f* hole Antoria guitar.

During my time at Christ's College I heard about a film that had become popular around the world and my interest was aroused to go along to see *Rock Around the Clock*. School rules were quite strict: we had to go everywhere in school uniform, so after obtaining permission I went to see this movie with a schoolmate, Noel Porter. After being brought up in a classical music household I was blown away by rock 'n' roll music and intrigued by all the young folk dancing in the aisles of the Regent Theatre. To my parent's horror I came home humming and whistling a couple of the tunes I had just heard. I desperately wanted to get a guitar, but Mum and Dad were not keen on my new interest so I had to sell my British Commonwealth stamp collection to raise the money for my first guitar.

I was now the proud owner of a brown Antoria (*f* hole model) and I needed lessons. Off I went to Maurice Liebert's studio in Armagh Street and my tuition began. Maurice was certainly a very good guitarist, but wasn't teaching me anything that I wanted to learn. I gave up my lessons after a short time and bought a little skif-rock tutor book and began teaching myself the basic chords. I was soon playing songs like 'Tom Dooley' and some simple rock 'n' roll favourites. I was on my way.

Other fellows at college were also interested in the new music, so the inevitable happened — we formed a dance band. Our first gig was providing the supper extras at a school dance, where we were supposed to play for 20 minutes. The response was so overwhelming that we weren't allowed to leave until we'd done almost 50 minutes. We started performing for other school and church dances, the only drawback being that we had to play dressed in our Christ's College uniforms. Embarrassed, we circumvented the rules by taking our blazers and ties off whenever we could. We practised in the lounge at home and it wasn't until much later that I discovered Dad used to adjourn to the garden shed down the backyard with a book and torch, just to get away from the noise. He never attempted to prevent us from playing the kind of music that he didn't understand.

I played plenty of sport at college, eventually captaining the school 3rd XV as prop, a position where I proudly played a couple of games for the first fifteen. I

Singing with the Saints at the Caledonian Hall, 1961,
and below (second from left), with the Playboys at Spencer Street, 1962.

continued playing rugby for the Christchurch club after I'd left school and both
Dad and my brother Mike used to support me from the sideline. I played cricket
every Saturday afternoon for the 3rd XI, as an opening batsman and medium-fast
bowler. I had a modicum of success with the game, going on to represent Canterbury
schoolboys in our grade. My interest and ability in swimming led me to join the
Sumner surf lifesaving club, earning my bronze and silver medals for lifesaving.

When I left school to start work and study I entered the Joe Brown 'Search for
Stars' talent quest and auditioned solo in the little theatre above Beggs music shop
in High Street. I made it into the heats and resurrected my old school band to

accompany me during the quest. Calling ourselves Phil Garland and the Fortunes, we performed two songs on the night — 'Bluebirds over the Mountain' and 'Boom Boom Baby'. Amazingly we won our heat, beating some well-known names about town in the process. We reached the semi-finals and were part of an impressive line-up on this occasion. We were placed third behind the eventual overall winner, Charles Hikana, and second-placed the Boys, actually Max Merritt's Meteors playing under an alias. Within a short time I received a phonecall from promoter Bart Ball and Pat Neho of local band the Saints, asking me to join them on a regular basis. Despite my guitar work not really being up to scratch, I was kept on as a vocalist, joining Cyril Edwards, who later made a name for himself as Super Cyril around the Christchurch pub scene. There seemed to be only three bands playing regularly around Christchurch in 1960: Max Merritt & the Meteors, Ray Columbus & the Downbeats (later to become the Invaders) and the Saints. We were playing every Saturday night at the Hibernian Hall and it seemed a real den of iniquity to a young fellow fresh from a cloistered existence at Christ's College. Diane Jacobs — later famous as Dinah Lee — was next to join the band, giving us three vocalists on stage. Whenever one of us was singing, the other two would provide backup vocals and clapping to augment the beat. Diane and I became a couple and supported each other's musical ideals. Dad used to transport us to and from performances, never uttering a word against what I was doing.

I spent a couple of years with the Saints at the Hibernian and often performed with them for sponsored stage shows in Christchurch, Timaru and Dunedin. It was not uncommon for me to stagger in to the dance hall some nights after playing

1964: The Dynamics, resident band at the Plainsman, with me at the bottom of the photo.

rugby for the Christchurch club in the afternoon and it soon became apparent that something had to give.

Music won, of course. By now I wanted more control over my music so I left the Saints to form my own band. With Diane Jacobs we became Phil Garland & the Playboys, and began rehearsing. In keeping with the playboy image we dressed in dark suits and Slim Jim ties, quite unlike what was being worn around the traps at that time. Matching Fender electric guitars were all the rage with local bands — the Meteors had a matching set of white Fenders, while the Invaders sported a red set. We opted for pastel green, which really offset the charcoal suits we wore onstage. We played our first audition gig at the hugely popular Spencer Street Dance one Saturday in 1962 and proved an instant success with the crowd, becoming a regular fixture at this dance. We also began playing at the Dolphin Lounge in conjunction with another Spencer Street favourite — the Downbeats. When Max Merritt & the Meteors left the local scene for Auckland, the Playboys were asked to be part of their farewell concert at the Theatre Royal. A similar thing occurred when the Invaders also left for Auckland — the Playboys were truly riding high at the time.

Six months later I had a call from the owners of the Top Twenty Club in Auckland, asking the Playboys to come up north for six weeks. The Meteors were their resident band, but were going on a national tour, and Max had suggested we fill in during their absence. The band was keen, so I asked for time off work without pay and was given the okay. We signed a six-week contract with the Top Twenty, but about a week before we were due to leave the accountant decided he wanted Easter off and I would have to stay on at work. I told him I couldn't, especially after having been given the okay and signing the contract. He just said "Too bad, you have to stay on here in my place!" I resigned on the spot, giving immediate notice, which put the office into uproar. Called into the general manager's office, I was asked to reconsider, but as I was already committed to Auckland and angry with the accountant, I declined. I phoned my father to tell him what I'd done; rock 'n' roll claimed another soul.

We went to Auckland for the six weeks and played our little butts off at the Top Twenty Niteclub in Durham Lane. We would play a two-hour lunchtime stint five days a week and every night from 8 till 1, which meant we had little spare time during our stay. One night the club was visited by Ron Dalton, owner

1962: The Playboys; Phil at right rear. In front is Diane Jacobs, who became famous as Dinah Lee.

of Viking Records, who asked me to record some tracks for him before our time was over. I duly did so, recording a cover of 'Little Band of Gold' bracketed with 'All By Myself Alone'. The musical backings had been purchased from the USA, so I was the only one in the studio for the entire session. As I recall, I liked the B side much better than 'Little Band of Gold' and spent more time perfecting this song, including singing a harmony line as well. To my amazement, my version of 'Little Band of Gold' was listed at number one beside the James Gilreath original on the Coca Cola-sponsored Des Britten Hi Fi Club Hit Parade. My musical career seemed poised to take off.

When the Playboys returned to Christchurch, Diane and I handed in our notices and returned to Auckland to take advantage of the better times around the corner. On my return, Ron Dalton called me into his studio to record a follow-up song. Meanwhile I had been asked to appear on the TV show *Teen '63*, which had Max Merritt & the Meteors as resident backing band. I now made two of the biggest mistakes of my rock 'n' roll life — firstly choosing to sing 'All By Myself Alone' instead of 'Little Band of Gold'. The rehearsals went fine with the cameras only shooting head and shoulders shots of my performance — but when it came to the real thing, they unexpectedly pulled back and started filming me from head to toe. I almost froze in fright, but managed to keep singing. The whole thing was a disaster. Ron Dalton called me in the next day and ripped up my contract, so the follow-up recording was never completed. I continued to live and work in Auckland for the next year, doing the occasional gig around town, but my reputation had taken a bit of a beating. It was an expensive lesson to learn.

Diane's career was taking off as I contemplated returning home for Christmas. We parted amicably and I returned south to find myself looking at more bookings than I could handle. The Christchurch music scene was improving once again as I started doing floor shows around town, often appearing at the Laredo Lounge with my old band the Playboys, who had now become Dave Miller & the Byrds.

After appearing as a guest at the Plainsman club in Lichfield Street I was offered a singing and compering residency there, for up to five nights a week. It wasn't a very stressful job, having to perform two twenty-minute sets Tuesday to Saturday. I had to attend band rehearsals each afternoon, which left mornings free. One day as I was returning home from rehearsals I noticed a Gibson 12-string guitar in the window of Beggs music shop. I strummed a couple of chords on the instrument and, taking a liking to the tone and the full sound it produced, I undertook some research and found it was used in folk music circles by such luminaries as Pete Seeger, Leadbelly and even the Kingston Trio. The more I listened to the music, the more I was captivated, and so began my love affair with folk music. After considerable research and procrastination I decided to buy this guitar, and having spent my life savings on it, needed to learn to play it properly. Obtaining a Pete Seeger guitar instruction book, I spent up to five hours every day teaching myself to play this beautiful instrument.

Before long I was incorporating the 12-string guitar into my late-night set at the Plainsman, singing and playing the likes of 'Drunken Sailor', 'Five Hundred Miles', 'Four Strong Winds' and 'Don't Let the Sun Catch You Crying'. It was here that a group of visiting folkies, led by Warwick Brock (who was to become a great mate and supporter), suggested that I join them at the local folk club on a Sunday night. There I was introduced to a whole new scene, full of Irish songs and unaccompanied sea shanties. I began singing a completely new repertoire with a different audience from that I had become accustomed to. My

1964: Studio portrait for the Plainsman nightclub.

Playing the jug with Band of Hope
jug band, 1968.

early repertoire was mainly American, but when the singer-songwriter trend emerged, I tried my hand at composing. No matter how hard I tried to write and sound American, I was unable to divorce myself from the New Zealand experience. I resolved to accept the situation and tentatively sang my new songs at the folk club, where to my surprise people actually applauded my efforts.

I was hooked on folk music, and further research led to discovering a group called the Song Spinners and traditional Kiwi song. I incorporated more and more Kiwi material into my performances, though still presenting mainly British and Australian material. It wasn't until my big OE in 1965 that my eyes were fully opened to the possible existence of a rich store of song back home. My interest in further research and collecting work was fired and the rest, as they say, is history.

Now the story really begins.

1970: At Nicoberg coffee lounge, Palmerston North.

INTRODUCTION

CHASING A DREAM

THE IDEA OF SEARCHING FOR NEW ZEALAND FOLK SONG came to me while on my big OE in 1965. I was already familiar with the apparently small tradition of Kiwi song from recordings by the Song Spinners and international balladeer William Clauson, and from hearing a 'Roads to Nowhere' documentary on National Radio a couple of years previously. During my travels I attended several British folk clubs and when I returned home I joined the newly formed New Zealand Folklore Society, keen to research our musical heritage more fully.

Frank Fyfe took me under his wing and encouraged me to undertake field collecting work. After reading a couple of relevant publications I was introduced to Rona Bailey, who explained how she had approached her own field research. Soon I hit the road as a 'new chum', with a little financial support from the National Folk Foundation, the Folklore Society, some folk clubs and interested individuals.

I spent the first week holed up in Dunedin's Hocken Library, trawling through early newspapers and publications, all of which yielded a wealth of folk poetry and bush verse. Here I was introduced to David McKee Wright via the pages of the *Otago Witness*, which had published his works in the 1890s before they became more widely known and available in literary form. Other rhymesters and bush poets also submitted their material to newspapers in a similar fashion to 'letters to the editor' today. Over time I have ascertained that several local writers (with no outlets available to them in New Zealand) were first published in the *Sydney Bulletin*, leading to confusion later among Australian folklorists as to their true origins.

I discovered that our folk heritage held a large store of poetry heavily influenced by Henry Lawson, and Banjo Paterson to a lesser extent. This was mainly due to the influx of Australian shearers to this country in the 1890s, heralding the most influential and exciting period in the development of our folk heritage. Here's 'A Bloke You Useter Know', a typical example of bush poetry from the pen of 'Riverina' (CH Winter).

He only lives in fancy, yet you love him passing well,
He's a mate you'll ne'er forget, whose deeds no pen can tell,
Though there were giants on the earth, in days long long ago,
He was a dozen giants' worth, a bloke you useter know.

You're seated in a shanty where the liars congregate,
You simply lie back in your chair and peacefully you wait.
Then when the yarns begin to fail and lose their cheerful flow,
You tell again his fearsome tale — this bloke you useter know.

Or in the shearers' hut at night amongst the other men,
With tallies rising left and right, as big guns 'ring' again,
When someone springs it extra high — two hundred rams or so,
You'll swear you saw it beaten by — a bloke you useter know.

You knew a horse that never shirked a fence of any height,
You knew a collie pup that worked sleep-walking through the night,
(And yarded thus — without a pause — a thousand ewes or so)
The man who owned these wonders was a bloke you useter know.

With rails to rattle, spars to break, unwilling nags to 'send'
With flooded creeks and risks to take and mighty cheques to spend,
With wild man-eating colts to ride and thirsty tracks to go,
There's none can stand a chance beside — a bloke you useter know.

He's really quite imaginary — just a mythologic bloke,
The friend of days of lurid 'bust' and days when you were broke.
And yet you love him and your eyes with real affection glow,
As you his mighty deeds appraise — this bloke you useter know!

From the Hocken Library I moved into Central Otago, where I began collecting in earnest. I had approached local schools, and after explaining my mission to the principal I was permitted to sing a few songs to the children. They were then asked to speak to their families, grandparents, uncles and aunts, etc, and I would return in a week or so to ascertain if they had uncovered anything or anyone of interest. I gained new contacts in this way. The pub was always a good bet for meeting local identities, while a chat with the local policeman or priest also proved beneficial in helping locate the colourful characters I was seeking. Some older folk, however, were more than a little suspicious of my good intentions …

I was looking for a renowned character, fiddler and local dance musician on the outskirts of Roxburgh, who was reticent to talk to anyone lest they were from the Musicians Union and chasing him for back dues. Apparently he'd never been a member the whole time he was playing, 46-odd years, so was suspicious of strangers. When I arrived on the doorstep with the black bag containing the tape-recorder, he must have thought I was a Jehovah's Witness or a union rep.

The front door opened after my knock and I asked the bloke who answered if this was where Alf Woods lived.

"It might be," he cautiously replied.

"Well, do you know if he's home?"

"I don't know," was his reply.

"Listen, are you Alf Woods?"

"Nope!"

"Bullshit," I said with a chuckle.

"Come in, mate," he said.

Alf had been a good fiddler in his day but now played only at church. While we were talking I noticed an old concertina on top of the wardrobe — he was keeping it handy in case someone from the family might show an interest some time. This became a common occurrence in homes I visited; concertinas had been popular in earlier days.

After a fairly unprofitable week in Central Otago, I was invited to appear on Dunedin Television's *Town & Around* programme, where I was interviewed about my collecting mission. On return to Central Otago I was greeted with renewed interest and enthusiasm — my TV appearance had given me a badge of authenticity and people were now only too willing to share what knowledge they had. I didn't find as much material as I had hoped, but perhaps my expectations were unrealistic given the late time factor in searching for previously unheard songs.

Shortly thereafter I arrived in Arrowtown, searching for a song that members of the National Film Unit had heard on one of their visits. Film producer Hugh McDonald had mentioned it to Frank Fyfe, who passed the details on and gave me the names of two possible informants. My first contact gave no assistance, while the other was Davy Dennison, who I found drank at the Goldfields pub. The barman was sure that Davy would be in there that night. While I was waiting for him to arrive I noticed a banjo ukelele (reputedly belonging to him) hanging up behind the bar and I was hoping he might make use of it. When Davy arrived I introduced myself and enquired about the song 'The Life of the High Country Shepherd'. He seemed keen to help, so I asked if he minded my setting up the tape machine to record him singing it. He insisted that I put it away

I met Graeme Anderson, a local identity and member of the Dunstan Trio, in Alexandra in 1969. He was a source of several David McKee Wright songs based on the Otago gold rush.

and said if I wanted to learn the song I'd have to do it orally, the same way as his children had done. Consequently I spent the entire evening singing, chatting and learning the song, all the while consuming copious quantities of whisky. Eventually I staggered back to the camping ground where I was staying, set up the tape recorder and began singing somewhat drunkenly into the microphone around 1 a.m. Fortunately I seemed to have done a good job in remembering it all and this performance remains in Folklore Society archives today.

> It's the life of a high country shepherd
> Resembles the life of a dog,
> In summer you 'frizzle' in sunshine,
> In winter you freeze like a log.
>
> For companions I have only collies,
> Who're continually scratching for fleas.
> And for climbing the slopes of the Coronet,
> I'm considerably gone at the knees.
>
> But give me my stick and snow leggings,
> It's away to the tops I must go.
> Where a few thousand jumbucks are waiting,
> For a chance to get out of the snow.
>
> So give me the life of a squatter,
> Who can sit by his fire at ease,
> Then mortgage his run for a motor,
> And drive out whenever you please.
>
> When climbing the slopes of Mt Aurum,
> You go for a hell of a skid, skid, skid,
> And then you look yourself over,
> To see if you are the full quid.
>
> And after a thorough look over,
> You find that you're only five bob, five bob,
> It's then that you roll up your bluey,
> And look for a government job.
>
> Now when I get my cheque in the springtime,
> It's away to the races I'll go.
> I'll back some old brumby a double,
> And forget all the ice and the snow.

This song had wider local circulation, for in 1990 I was booked to perform in Invercargill and before the evening began I was approached by Colin and Jean MacNicol from Dacre, who were concerned about my having recorded 'The Life of the High Country Shepherd' so wrongly. They had heard my version on National

Radio and were dismayed that I didn't have it correct. (Obviously they had never heard of the 'folk process', whereby songs and stories alter in the retelling and singing.) Colin informed me that the verses had been written by his grandfather, while mustering on Mt Aurum Station, up Skippers Canyon in the 1920s. Colin's father later set them to music using the old tune 'Wrap me up in my Tarpaulin Jacket' in the 1940s and duly named it 'The Shepherd's Song'. The MacNicols handed me the original 'correct' version of the words, which contains more verses with further variations, but the major difference is the addition of a chorus. They asked me to sing it for them that very night, so I obliged. The original chorus reads:

> Oh give me my stick and snow leggings,
>> When the sun strikes those tops I must go.
>> For thousands of sheep they are waiting
>> For a track to get out of the snow.
>> I've my tea by the light of a slush lamp,
>> For I'm up in the morn with the lark,
>> Now if this is not simply a dog's life,
>> For I'm climbing from daylight to dark.

My travels took me all over Otago and on one of my collecting trips I came into contact with delightful Kiwi yarns. In North Otago I heard about a couple of old-timers in the old folks ward at Ranfurly Hospital. I called in and met up with Mick Carr and Harold Read, who shared a room and regaled me with wonderful stories about each other. According to Mick, Harold had been a shearer, a rabbiter, a fencer, farmhand and bullock driver in his time.

It seems one Sunday morning Harold was droving a team of bullocks along the Pig Route and got bogged right outside the local church at Morrisons, just as the congregation were departing from their devotions. The air was blue as bullockies were well known for their colourful language. A new parson had been recently appointed to the district and was unfamiliar with the ways and manners of the bullockies. He stepped towards the wagon, and looking up at Harold said "I say, my good man, you can't talk like that round here — you'll never get to heaven if you do!"

Harold stopped his tirade and looked down at the parson.

"What's bloody heaven?"

The parson was taken aback. "It's a wonderful place you go to after you've died, particularly if you've been good throughout your life."

Harold Read, Ranfurly 1969.

Harold was less than impressed with this response, causing the parson to get flustered and almost fall over his words. "It-it-it's where your soul goes after you die, if you've led a decent, God-fearing life."

Harold looked over the side of the wagon. "What's your bloody soul then?"

The parson was beside himself by now and stammered "tha-tha-that after you die and if you've led a jolly decent life, it-it-it's a little thing inside you that leaves your body and flutters off to heaven!"

Harold looked at him. "It wouldn't get very bloody far round here, a bloody hawk would have it before it'd gone fifty bloody yards!"

This yarn made me realise that there were gems lurking out there, and I still include this story in my on-stage performances today.

My next informant was Ross McMillan, high country farmer and fantastic bush poet of Naseby, who has become a good friend. Something in the *Alexandra News* in 1966 under the *nom de plume* 'Blue Jeans' piqued my interest in his work. Ross is an important contributor to our heritage, doing for New Zealand what Henry Lawson did so admirably for Australia. The only book of poetry in his house while he was growing up was a collection of Lawson's poems, and they have clearly influenced his work.

Writing poetry helped Ross remain sane while trying to cope with increasing family troubles. His wife was struck down by multiple sclerosis, so he ended up nursing her, caring for two young children and running the family farm. This was his lot for some fifteen years before his wife finally succumbed. Maybe because of this difficult period in his life a number of his poems reflect a mix of nostalgia and regret, but humour is never too far away.

When I first recorded examples of his work Ross had an interesting style of performance, reciting poetry underpinned by a very basic guitar accompaniment, reminiscent of the old-timers in the Australian bush, who used concertina or harmonica in a similar fashion. It has been the only example of this style of performance I have come across in New Zealand during my entire collecting travels.

The character of rural pubs changed when later closing hours were introduced, which didn't escape Ross's notice. Here's his poem, 'Country Pub':

They're changing the style of the pubs in the land,
They're trying to make each one look like the Grand.
From Queenstown to Kyeburn it's modern décor,
With wall-to-wall carpet across the bar floor.

There's wining and dining and neon and chrome,
And the comforts are better than those back at home.
While oysters and cray are the counter lunch grub,
To a band or TV in the old country pub.

The high country musterer now takes off his boots
And spurs, and refrains from language that pollutes,
While the tired greasy shearer must first shower and scrub,
Before he can drink in the old country pub.

Old Jackie the rabbiter came in for a drink,
His clothes — blood and guts — bore a terrible stink,
As an escort for blowflies he was the main hub,
And a dog or two followed him into the pub.

But Freddie the publican dropped in a faint,
While a tourist from Sydney turned green with the taint.
So Jack jumped in his jeep and took off for the scrub,
Where he's making home brew in an old copper tub.

Mixed drinking means changes a man cannot flout,
For swilling and swearing and fighting are out.
While spitting or throwing a cigarette stub,
On the floor, is taboo in the old country pub.

The top dressing pilot, the plumber and chips
The pensioner in for a couple of nips,
Will soon need a reference like some high toned club
Before they can drink in the old country pub.

One day Ross was telling me about the coldest places he'd ever been. He was droving a mob of sheep along a mountain track one winter's morning when the dogs started barking and spooked the sheep — one old ewe panicked and slipped on an ice-covered rock before losing her footing and tumbling over the edge of a bluff. Ross rushed across to look over the edge, expecting to see a dead sheep a few hundred feet below, but couldn't believe his eyes.

"The sheep never fell the full distance — it was so cold she froze in mid-air!'

"C'mon, Ross, the laws of gravity wouldn't allow it, mate!"

Ross looked at me. "The laws of gravity be damned, Phil, they was bloody frozen too!"

Yorky Francis was a local high country farmer Ross wrote about and I've subsequently set his poem to music. I finally got to meet Yorky when I was performing in Naseby in 2001 and have since met a couple of his sons, who tell me that we had the old man's character 'dead to rights.'

It seems Yorky was a procrastinator, often leaving things to the last minute. His wife, who was pregnant, finally went into labour, so he thought he'd better do something about it and phoned for the doctor.

The doctor took a couple of hours to get to the isolated station and arrived there just as it was getting dark. He threw his coat and hat on the nearest hook and said to Yorky, "Bring me a bowl of hot water and a lantern, we might need them."

He rushed into the bedroom where the wife was in the last stages of labour.

"It looks like I've arrived just in time. Yorky, hold that lantern up — yes, yes here we are!" The doctor promptly delivered a baby girl and handed her to the proud father.

"Isn't that wonderful, she's done all that work on her own. Hello, hello, I think there's another one coming. Yorky, hold that lantern up again."

"Yes, yes, here we are," as he delivered a baby boy. He handed the child to Yorky and said, "Isn't that fantastic — twins — and she's done all that hard work on her own."

"Hello, hello, I think there's another one coming. Yorky, hold that lantern up again will you?"

"No way, Doc, I reckon the bloody light's attracting them!"

The perfect example of a song with a wide circulation is 'The Dying Bushman'. Rona Bailey collected the song from Jim Case of Kumara, with Angela Annabel also obtaining a version in Waipukurau. The Waipukurau version was relatively close to that given to me by Frank Fyfe, who collected it from an informant in the Wellington region in the early 1970s.

I subsequently recorded it for my *Colonial Yesterdays* album in 1975, so imagine my surprise the next year when a young West Coast bushman, Richard Hart, called in to see me after hearing the recording and sang me a longer version, which he said was still being sung by a younger generation of bushmen on the Coast.

Richard had learned the song from his father, Ken Hart, and was certain there was even more to it. Ken lived in Palmerston North and as Richard was on his way north to visit him, I asked if he could possibly record him singing the song for me. When Richard returned he handed me a tape with a much longer version of the song, performed unaccompanied by his mum and dad together. His father introduced the recording by stating that he had first heard it sung by bushmen in the Otaki area in the early 1930s, and credits their source as a Mr Justice Tom Ongley, who in turn had learned it on the West Coast.

I was over the moon with the results achieved by one simple recording of this great song. In *The Singing Kiwi* I included the three versions of this song for general comparison. I have drawn from the best of these versions to arrive at my current interpretation of 'The Dying Bushman'.

I've knocked around the logging camps, since early boyhood days,
I've seen the famous axe men come and go.
Now my chopping days are over, I shall swing that axe no more,
On the hillsides where the native timbers grow.

Chorus   For my slasher is all rusty and my axe handle's broke,
             I've laid them both behind the whare door.
             For the rata and the rimu have got so mighty tough,
             That I really cannot chop them any more.

I'll no longer tread the tramway in the valley far below,
No more I'll hear the hauler's whistle blow.
As I wander down the track I shall keep on looking back,
Please don't take me from the only home I know.

In all the West Coast bush there was none could chop like me,
And I long again to hear the felling's roar.
Down the valley of the shadow, I'll soon be on the track,
Where I've often seen old bushmen go before.

Now when I sleep that last long sleep, I pray that it may be,
Where the tawa and the matai and the pine,
With the ngaio and the hinau and the koromiko tree,
Grow forever by that lonely grave of mine.

Despite the important work undertaken by earlier collectors and enthusiasts, the huge field of New Zealand folklore and song is still neglected and overlooked by the great majority of folk performers and musicologists. I sincerely hope that this book will go some small way towards helping create a wider awareness of New Zealand's wonderful folk heritage.

I

INHERITORS OF A DREAM

New Zealand's folk music heritage

EUROPEANS WERE VISITING NEW ZEALAND shores well before the 19th century, but not until the 1790s was any sort of continuous contact with the country and its inhabitants made. This was hastened by a developing interest in flax, thought to have a great future in the manufacture of rope for rigging, and kauri timber, earmarked for masts and spars on British naval sailing vessels.

> Come all you jolly seamen bold and listen to my song,
> I'll have you pay attention and I'll not detain you long,
> Concerning of a voyage to New Zealand we did go,
> For to cut some lofty spars to load the *Buffalo*
>
> *Chorus* Cheer up my lively lads, to New Zealand we will go,
>   For to cut some lofty spars to load the *Buffalo*.
>
> The *Buffalo*'s a happy ship, from Portsmouth she set sail,
> With South Australian emigrants, we had a pleasant gale.
> For six long months in Holdfast Bay, our hands did work on shore,
> Building houses for those emigrants, which grieved our hearts full sore …
>
> When at New Zealand we arrived, our hands were sent on shore,
> Our tents were then all pitched well and provided with good stores.
> At six o'clock we all rouse out, then such a precious row,
> Come quick and get your grog m'boys, unto the woods you go.
>
> With saws and axes in our hands, it's through the bush we steer,
> And when we see a lofty tree unto it we draw near.
> With saws and axes we begin to lay the tree quite low,
> Then lop and trim those lofty spars to load the *Buffalo* …

Our ship she is well loaded and for England we are bound,
There's plenty of good rum m'lads and pretty girls abound.
Farewell to Tonga — Mowries and Wyenas also,
They will oftimes wish to see again the happy *Buffalo*.

This ballad, 'The Voyage of the *Buffalo*', appears to have been written during her 1836 voyage to load kauri spars for the return voyage to England and is featured in WH Cheeseman's diary, where he mentions much singing and versifying being done by the crew in the evenings aboard ship.

New Zealand's heritage varies vastly from that of USA and Australia, and there does not appear to have been the same degree of singing by our early settlers. New Zealand colonists were in the main generally drawn from a different class of immigrant, so there were no Pilgrim Fathers — or convict transportation.

Most of the New Zealand colony was planned in advance, in a conscious effort to create a better society. Though significant numbers of early arrivals were drawn

Lydia Myrtle Williams (1857–1938) and members of the Mountfort family having afternoon tea, probably at her home in Napier. Previous page: Lydia and William Williams (who took the photo) at their cottage at Carlyle Street, Napier. Because of their musical ability, they were known as Mr and Mrs 'Banjo' Williams.
Alexander Turnbull Library G25686 1/1; G25685 1/1

from the wealthier middle and upper classes of British society, there were also members of the lower middle and working classes, many brought as labourers. The South Island in particular became home to sons of nobility and landed gentry seeking to continue the family status in the new colony. It is therefore not unusual to find that the most common respectable entertainment was of the drawing room variety and more in keeping with upper middle class status. Consequently before the onset of the gold rushes, there is a relatively small singing tradition, but a much larger tradition of the writing and recitation of poetry, often taking a similar form to 'Home Thoughts from Abroad'.

EMIGRAVIT

Mountain lilies shine, far up against the snow,
And the ratas twine on wooded slopes below.
Rata and clematis sweet as bush may hold,
While honey-loving wild birds kiss the kowhai's cups of gold.
Dear and fair shall all of these henceforth to children be:
But ah! my childhood's flowers are far away from me.
In an English lane where the primrose patches blow,
And the sweet spring rain hangs jewels high and low.

Homely flowers set where our farmsteads rise,
Make an England yet under sunny southern skies.
Lilac scent is blown with wattle on the breeze;
September bids the leaves grow broad on happy English trees;
And apple orchards smile again in sweet familiar show —
But in my heart is mourning for the scenes of long ago.
When the reeds grow high and the cowslips in the grass,
And my young love and I saw the springtime pass.

Homely blossoms grow in our graveyard near the sea,
Where my love lies low with a place beside for me.
Pansy blooms and pinks, the columbine's quaint bell,
Rosemary for remembrance (Pray, love, remember well!)
But ah! my happy ghost must walk, if happy ghosts may be,
In an English lane or meadow with wild flowers growing free.

In an English lane, where the primrose patches blow,
And the sweet spring rain hangs jewels high and low.

Mary Colborne-Veel, from 'New Zealand Verse', collected by Alexander & A E Currie, Walter Scott Publishing Co London 1906

For many years the dominant influences on New Zealand's musical heritage were British, Australian and American to a lesser extent. This does not mean there is no local tradition, far from it, but it obviously cannot and does not share the depth of the British Isles, USA or Australia. To understand this more clearly, we must take into account the time differences between the establishment of the countries, coupled with the fact that most people's awareness of folk music stems from their familiarity with recorded examples from the USA and British Isles. What is 'folk' in the USA is not necessarily 'folk' in New Zealand, although if we accept that 'folk' applies to the 'common people' we can expect a degree of similarity that will show New Zealand songs and ballads to have that certain quality which defines them as 'folk'.

A settlers' musical soirée.

Engraving from the 'New Zealand Graphic & Ladies Journal' v6, no37, 13 September 1890, ATL F624 1/4 MNZ

So far no New Zealander has attempted to record the unprinted old 'home-made' songs afloat in the bush and back-block communities in New Zealand — songs which though rough hewn as to rhyme and metre, sound well enough when chanted by strong lungs at a singsong. There are not nearly as many as in Australia certainly, but still the doggerel rhymester is not unknown in the New Zealand bush and on the little sailing coasters that ply from bay to market port and back again. The city man naturally never learns these songs, but the gumdiggers' camp and the bushfellers' shanty, the sawmill hands' and the flaxmill hands' camps, know them well enough, at any rate in the North Island.

I cannot speak from personal knowledge of the current shanties in the southern plains. I know this of the north, that some of the choruses bellowed around a camp fire or in the snug whare after kai, or out in a boat or canoe, date back at least fifty years. If they have no more value they have this, that they memorise more or less historic events of the troubled old days, which might otherwise be forgotten.

Thus wrote James Cowan in 1913 in his article on 'The Bush Poet', where he quoted several local songs. But despite making it clear that such songs did exist, Cowan made no attempt to collect the examples he must have heard in his travels, and his article was soon forgotten. Although Maori songs were assiduously collected, there were no efforts to record the old bush songs until the groundbreaking work of Rona Bailey, Bert Roth and Neil Colquhoun in the 1950s.

O I wish I was in Auckland town — Away O, aye O,
Where all the girls walked up and down — A long time ago!

Chorus It is a long time, a very long time — away O, aye O,
     A long time, a very long time — Oh a long time ago.

I wish to Gawd I'd never been born — Away O, aye O
To go wandering around Cape Horn — A hundred years ago.

'A Long Time Ago' was taken from James Cowan's article 'Sailor Memories — The Songs of the Sea' in the *Canterbury Times* of 12 June 1912. This is a local adaptation of a famous halyard shanty, which Cowan heard on a coastal trader in the Hauraki Gulf.

New Zealand folk music can be roughly divided into chronological steps from the early 1800s through to the present day. If there is a common thread linking the songs it is one of a work ethic as immigrants struggled to build the better society that had drawn them to this far-distant land. The earliest songs deal with the life of the sealers and whalers, who began visiting our shores towards the end of the 18th and the beginning of the 19th century. A number of these songs were collected in New Bedford from descendants of American whalers who had spent time off the coast of New Zealand in the 1820s and '30s. Obviously, they adapted shanties and songs to suit their environment, such as 'New Zealand Whales', a variant of a British song 'The Coast of Peru':

Come all of you whalemen who are cruising for sperm,
Come all of you seamen who have rounded Cape Horn,
For our captain has told us and he says out of hand,
There's a thousand whales off the coast of New Zealand.

'Twas early one morning just as the sun rose,
A voice from the masthead cried out "There she blows!"
Our captain cried "Where away and how does she lay?"
"Three points on our lee sir, scarce two miles away …"

"Then call up all lads and be of good cheer,
Get your lines in your rowboats and tackle falls clear."
We sailed off the west wind and came up apace,
The whaleboats were lowered and set on the chase.

We fought him alongside, harpoon we thrust in,
In just over an hour, he rolled out his fin.
The whale is cut-in boys, tried-out and stowed down,
He's worth more to us boys than five hundred pounds.

Our ship it is laden for home we will steer,
There's plenty of rum boys and plenty of beer.
We'll spend money freely for the pretty girls ashore,
And when it's all gone, we'll go whaling for more.

Whaling stations sprang up around the coast, and men signed on in Sydney before being taken to the shore station and provided with drink, clothing and tobacco. Many took Maori wives and in return for their housekeeping and support had to pledge support and allegiance to the interests of their wife's tribe.

A defining event in our history of settlement was the gold rush, bringing with it all the frenzied activity that comes with the discovery of gold. This period gave rise to the first truly home-made folk song, 'Bright Fine Gold', a good example of creative folk process at work — starting life as a miners' chorus, developing into a schoolyard skipping rhyme chanted to the well-known 'Hot Cross Buns', before picking up extra verses and a haunting tune, to become one of the finest songs to come out of our musical heritage. A full description of this is in Chapter 3.

Bright fine gold, bright fine gold,
Wangapeka, Tuapeka, bright fine gold.

Spend it in the winter or die of the cold,
Wangapeka, Tuapeka, bright fine gold.

I'm weary of Otago, I'm weary of the cold,
If my man strikes it rich, away we will go.

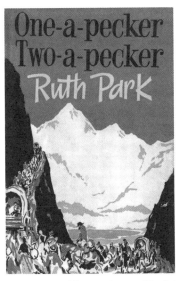

The names Wangapeka and Tuapeka were adapted as 'One a pecker, Two a pecker' in the skipping rhyme, before being adopted for the title of Ruth Park's novel set in the Otago goldfields of the 1860s.

Some fine songs have come out of the gold rush era — many from the pen of Charles Robert Thatcher, who made his living lampooning public figures and events. Others blossomed as a result of the gold decline in Otago coinciding with the news of discoveries on the West Coast. Overnight the miners began to head to the new El Dorado. Here's Thatcher's 'Cheer Boys Cheer':

Cheer boys cheer, a stunning goldfield's started,
Round upon the West Coast, there's golden ground for miles,
Good news for the diggers, so don't you be downhearted,
Take your passage now and go and make your piles.

The cry is now Rush Ho and away the diggers go,
Tramping to the westward, now they make their way
And when good news it comes down, we must hook it from this town,
To build another city for Thatcher at the Grey.

The country's first recession was on the heels of the golden boom as the early settlers and pioneers began to experience harsh times and economic downturn. Regardless of social standing and through no fault of their own, many found themselves out of work, tramping the roads searching for whatever job was available in what would become known as 'The Hungry Years'.

The winter ain't been hard as yet, though frost was pretty keen,
There's one thing I'll tell you mate, the country's getting mean.
The price of wool is looking up, the harvest ain't been bad,
But for them that's on the wallaby, there's little to be had.

Chorus And when skies are grey above us, it's getting hard to bear,
            The feeling that the country has of hunger in the air.

I mind the time when men was pinched and things was pretty blue,
For the mortgage burdened station and the struggling cockatoo.
But if work was hard of getting and a fellow had to tramp,
He was pretty sure of tucker and a decent place to camp …

from 'Hunger in the Air', adapted by Phil Garland from 'The Swaggers' by DM Wright

These hard times sent men into the swamps of Northland, digging for kauri gum, a true resin — solidified turpentine. There was no fortune to be made here, but it certainly provided a steady albeit lonely existence. The men spent the whole day 'hooking' and digging for gum, then singing and making music during the long evenings to help relieve the boredom of scraping the resinous substance clean.

> The end of the earth isn't far from here,
> And it's getting much darker year by year,
> The gum's getting smaller and deeper down,
> While never again will I see a town
> With pretty white houses all in a row,
> And women in aprons to and fro,
> And the bar at the pub down by the sea,
> Where a ship is waiting to carry me
> Back to the land from where I come,
> Where I was born, where I was young…

'The End of the Earth' ~ Anon

Hooking for gum was only the very beginning of the work. Diggers pushed a long metal spear into the ground to locate the gum, and experience helped them discern gum, rock or root by the feel of the spear. Storekeepers paid only a few pence for unclean gum; it had to be thoroughly scraped for its quality to be assessed. Joseph Smith of Dargaville, in a communication to Neil Colquhoun:

> One hundredweight of the gum takes about ten good hours scrapin'. That's all evenin's gone — scrapin'. We shared everything — family that is. Otherwise I don't know how 'twas to be done. But some men, as I recall lived on their own, worked on their own. All that scrapin' just by themselves — for the money — enough to live.

Music originating from the gumfields can be heard even today, played by those Bohemian musicians and their descendants who have been the cornerstone of the Puhoi Band, making music in the district since 1863.

Coal had taken over from gold on the West Coast and in this period the country's worst mining disaster occurred at the Brunner Mine on 21 March 1896. All 85 miners working below the ground perished and they are buried in a mass grave not far from the site, which is visible today. The tragedy gave rise to a song 'Down in the Brunner Mine'.

> They work in the heat and the coal black dust,
> Sticks to the skin like a burned pie-crust,
> We curse each day that the miner must,
> Go down in the Brunner mine …
>
> Down at the face of the Brunner Mine,
> Two hundred feet from the survey line,
> There's never a sign of sun or sky
> Down in the Brunner mine.

The miner's breath comes short and hot,
He's using all the breath he's got,
Whether it's good for his lungs or not,
Down in the Brunner mine.

A sound that'll creep through the miner's soul,
Is the shake and rattle and down she'll roll,
A hundred feet of rubble and coal,
Down in the Brunner mine.

A cave-in will give us a shut down day,
But that'll never make a miner gay,
For the trembling earth speaks judgement day,
Down in the Brunner mine.

Swaggers became a part of the landscape and this is an fertile period of growth in our folk heritage. This was due in no small way to the advent of Australian shearers, who worked at the high country station runs on a contract basis, exposing the locals to their songs and the poetry of Banjo Paterson and Henry Lawson. Both writers inspired the rhymesters and balladeers of the day, and Lawson's influence can still be seen today in the work of Naseby poet Ross McMillan.

The man most affected by all of this was David McKee Wright, who has been described as New Zealand's 'Outdoor Laureate'. His ballads capture the mood and sentiment of the times, and were taken up by farm labourer and swagger alike to be recited around campfires from one end of the country to the other.

There's a sound of many voices in the camp and on the track,
And letters coming up in shoals to stations at the back.
And every boat that crosses from the sunny other side,
Is bringing waves of shearers for the swelling of the tide.

Chorus For the shearing's coming round boys, the shearing's coming round,
And the stations of the mountains have begun to hear the sound.

This is but one of many fine songs emanating from a productive era.

For the first 40 or so years of the 20th century it appears that few New Zealanders felt the need to express themselves through ballad or song, perhaps due in some way to the onset of two world wars and their aftermath.

Certainly New Zealanders sang during the Great Depression, but mostly songs originating with the American experience. Records were becoming more readily available and the country had lost some of the isolation that fosters a unique oral music tradition.

Notwithstanding, a couple of fine balladeers surfaced at this time. George Meek, who was largely influenced by McKee Wright, began writing ballads because he was dissatisfied with the non-productive efforts of his fellow countrymen. One of his best is 'Wool Commandeer', written in 1940 about the government's massive stockpiling of wool for eventual use in the war effort.

> The commandeer is under way and blimey what a fuss,
> The blinking din and clatter sure would make a parson cuss,
> There's covies tearing up the floors and blokes in overalls.
> Slapdapping cans of whitewash on the rafters and the walls.
>
> *Chorus* For it's come from Haka Valley and it's come from Sunny Peak,
> It's come from up the river and down Waitaki Creek.
> It's come from the back of nowhere up the wild Mackenzie way,
> And a clip from Tipperary will get here any day.
>
> There's stackers swinging balehooks and barrows shifting wool,
> There's covies humping baskets, some half empty, some half full.
> There's classers squealing loudly for more bales of wool to class,
> And someone yelling "Where do you want this wool from Dansey's Pass?"
>
> There's wool on every siding and there's wool on every street,
> There's wool on every lorry and on every bus you meet.
> There's wool on every trailer and wool on every train,
> While the stock and station diggers have got it on the brain.
>
> There's wool in every corner and there's wool on every floor,
> There's wool dumped in the basement and jammed behind the door.
> There's wool in the old freezer and wool down at the dump,
> There's wool in the old dairy and still more bales to hump.

The other balladeer was Cecil Winter, who wrote as 'Riverina'. An expatriate Australian who took up residence in Southland, he regularly contributed to the *Bulletin* in Australia. He not only continued to write about his beloved Australian outback, but captured the essence of his adopted country as well. 'The Star Hotel' published in 1929 is powerful in its portrayal of rural workers, forced to camp out under the stars.

> The city streets are aglow tonight and the noise is harsh and loud,
> As hurrying on in the glaring light go the pleasure-seeking crowd,
> But there's one whose thoughts will drift again, where bushland breezes swell,
> As the pine trees whisper the old refrain —
> 'Come back to the Star Hotel.
>
> Here there is noise where the townsfolk tread, at the Star there is peace and cheer,
> A fire in the gums and a blanket spread and a quart pot standing near.
> The clink of the hobble chains in the trees and a softly sighed "All's well"
> From the leaves that stir in the cool night breeze, as the campers smoke and lie at ease,
> Out there at the Star Hotel.

There are men to meet from the runs up north with tales of the backblocks full,
And men from the south, who are making forth at the magic call of wool.
With the yarns of tallies that shearers know, or of sheds that proved a sell,
When the drought seemed a thing of long ago
and weeks of rain made the tall grass grow … Out there at the Star Hotel.

There are blokes who are going to lift a mob from the edge of the open plain,
And fellers on spec of a station job telling their tales again.
Swapping their yarns by a manuka blaze to the tune of the Maids Farewell,
Of silver cheques and bumper pays, giving a sigh for the other days,
In the glow of the Star Hotel.

By the deep lagoon they are camped tonight, far beyond the city's song,
On the quiet banks of the river and the big green pines among.
Hearing again the morepork's call, till the weird notes weave a spell,
As the hush grows deeper and stray stars fall, and the lure of the bush is over all
Who stay at the Star Hotel.

Although a definite Kiwi character is showing, a strong Australian influence remains. Kiwi vernacular of the day bore a close resemblance to a few Australian expressions, due no doubt to the shearers' influence and the proximity of the two countries.

The 1950s and '60s began with a flourish of activity, when vernacular songs and ballads appeared from the pens of Peter Cape, Joe Charles and Ross McMillan. Finally a real Kiwi character shines forth, overriding many of the previous outside influences. Cape's 'Taumarunui', 'Down the Hall on Saturday Night' and 'She'll Be Right' capture aspects of the Kiwi way of life and stand up to scrutiny today.

I'm an ordinary joker, getting old before my time
For my heart's in Taumarunui on the Main Trunk Line

Taumarunui, Taumarunui, Taumarunui on the Main Trunk Line.

You can get to Taumarunui going north or going south,
And you end up there at midnight and you've cinders in your mouth
You got cinders in your whiskers and a cinder in your eye
So you hop off to Refreshments for a cupper tea and pie.

Joe Charles was a poet with a firm sense of mission and a desire to record New Zealand's colourful folk-past in verse, while there were still old-timers with stories to tell. He wrote tall stories blended with genuine historical events, which find their strength in his love of the land and through his commitment to the oral history of ordinary people. His songs played every Sunday on the Radio ZB request session in the 1960s — gems like 'The Coleridge Run', 'The Phosphate Flyers', 'Mackenzie and his Dog' and 'Black Billy Tea':

Kick out your fire, boy, roll up your pack,
Don't forget your billy, boy, billy burnt and black.

Chorus Black billy tea, boy, black as it can be,
         Black billy tea, boy, that's the stuff for me.

Up on the snowline, chasing after deer,
I'd sooner have a cup o' tea, than all your blinking beer.
Down in a coal mine, driving in a drive,
Black billy tea, boy, keeps a man alive.

Drink her from a tin, man, drink her from a cup,
Fill her up again, man, turn the bottoms up.
Brew it in a billy, brew it in a pot,
Throw in a handful, pour it out hot.

Mouth-organ Jack, and John the Baptist too,
The old time swaggers, they knew how to brew.
Black billy tea, boy, black as Stockholm tar,
Black billy tea, boy, put us where we are.

Up in the bush, getting out a log,
Upset my outfit in a ruddy bog,
Took out my billy, made a cup o' tea;
Got the outfit out again, as easy as can be.

Used up all my ammo, lost my best dog,
With a Captain Cooker, bailed up in a log.
Hauled out my billy, brewed her up black!
Blocked up the log's end, and rolled the piggy back.

Although outside influences are discernible in Ross McMillan's poetry, his work captures the mood and feel of the New Zealand countryside, painting wonderful word pictures. To my mind no one does it better.

The city roar is in my ears, the glare is in my eyes,
Yet in my heart I long to see those sunny Central skies.
That stretch away and disappear behind the peaks of snow,
As I hear the magpies singing down a country road I know.

There are shearing sheds I shore in that are scattered by the way,
And I seem to hear the clatter of the cutters making play,
And the laughter of the shearers from the days of long ago,
When they called me 'Jim the Ringer' down a country road I know.

When the hard day's work was over and the sun was in the west,
And the vivid flash of evening stained that far off mountain's breast.
We'd share a smoke and bottle while we watched the shadows grow…
As they lengthened into darkness down a country road I know.

'Down a Country Road I Know' ~ Ross McMillan

II

LANDFALL NEW ZEALAND

The first hundred years

IN 1642 ABEL TASMAN BECAME THE FIRST known European to visit New Zealand, and his name graces many landmarks and Kiwi enterprises today. Captain James Cook, however, is the explorer we tend to remember best, stemming perhaps from his reputation as one of the greatest navigators in history. Born in Yorkshire in 1728, Cook learned the ropes as a merchantman and dropped rank to join the navy, where he rose to the top through his professionalism and ability. He made his name as a cool-headed, systematic and thorough explorer in North American waters, before being chosen to sail south to observe the transit of Venus from Tahiti. There was however a second agenda — the Admiralty wanted him to find and claim the great southern continent. Cook chose a Whitby coastal collier for his vessel and renamed her *Endeavour* before setting out on a remarkable voyage south.

> My name is Cook, I'm a sailor now, in Yorkshire I was born
> When I was a lad I would follow the plough and see that the sheep were shorn.
>
> I served some time as apprentice to a grocer and a tailor,
> But when I felt the tang of the sea, I knew I would be a sailor.
>
> Soon my King had honoured me and gave me my command,
> In the *Endeavour* I sailed south to search for an unknown land
>
> *'Song for Captain Cook' ~ Paul Metsers*

The story really begins in 1769, when surgeon's boy Nicholas Young sighted peaks through a haze covering Poverty Bay. Fortifications studded the clifftops and the mariners could see 'Indians' who appeared to be armed and threatening. On 9 October a party from the ship landed, only to be promptly challenged by Maori warriors. Through a misunderstanding an attack followed, during which a chief fell, shot through the heart. That subsequent massacres were prevented was undoubtedly due to the presence of Tupaia, a Tahitian friend of Cook's botanist Joseph Banks, who was able to converse haltingly with the Maori and convince them that the white men had come for peace, not war. Their first sighting of New Zealand is the subject of Janet Smith's Cook Bicentennial award-winning song 'Land Ahoy'.

> There's a long white cloud a-coming closer to us now,
> There's a long white cloud a-coming, it's land good land I know
>
> Land ahoy, land ahoy, it's land it's land good land I know
>
> It's many a night we've sailed across the southern sea,
> Our captain's name is James Cook, a sailor bold is he.

Captain Cook.

Cook set about mapping the coast of New Zealand before sailing on, but not before proving the country was a group of islands and not the elusive great southern continent he was keenly seeking. When he returned to England Cook reported on rich timber resources and the large numbers of seals and whales frequenting New Zealand coastal waters. Consequently sailing ships began visiting on a regular basis in the late 1700s, harvesting flax for rope making and kauri timber for masts. This continuous contact led to the establishment of a lucrative sealing and whaling trade, which would have a deep and lasting effect on the new southern land. In November 1791 some of George Vancouver's ships called into Cook's old anchorage at Pickersgill Cove in Dusky Sound, where they drank a toast to the memory of Captain Cook. But it was during these visits that the crews of such vessels began to appreciate the potential of the new country, and inevitably sailors began to desert ship in the hope of improving their lot. This was also the great era of sail, the time of the impressed (forcibly employed) sailor and the runaway-to-sea romantic Jack Tar, typified by the luckless able-bodied seaman John Smith, who was lost at sea. The song 'John Smith A.B.' is taken from the poem 'At Sea' written by DH Rogers.

> When the southern gale is blowing hard
> And the watch are all on the topsail yard.
> When five come down when six went up,
> There's one less to share the bite and sup.

Instead of the stone and carven verse,
This is his epitaph curt and terse,
John Smith AB, drowned in latitude fifty-three,
A heavy gale and a following sea.

Reports of the rich fur seal colonies in southern New Zealand excited entrepreneurs from New South Wales, for they had almost wiped out the seals of Bass Strait and were looking for fresh hunting grounds. The sealers and whalers who arrived on New Zealand shores became our earliest pioneers, playing an all-important role in helping make New Zealand known to Europe and America.

This is where the earliest of our songs originate, dealing with the hardships facing the sealing and whaling gangs working along the rugged coastline. Naturally these shanties reveal mainly British influences, such as 'Davy Lowston', a rewrite of the old British songs 'Sam Hall' and 'The Ballad of Captain Kidd'. It was first heard on the Sydney waterfront in 1814 as a broadside ballad, during the court case following the rescue of a sealing gang under the command of Lt David Lowrieston.

My name is Davy Lowston I did seal, I did seal,
My name is Davy Lowston I did seal.
Though my men and I were lost and our very lives did cost,
We did seal, we did seal, we did seal.

'Twas in eighteen hundred and nine we set sail, we set sail,
'Twas in eighteen hundred and nine we set sail.
Upon the sixteenth day of February,
For to sail, for to sail, for to sail.

We were set down at Open Bay, were set down, were set down,
We were set down at Open Bay, were set down.
We were left, we gallant men never more to sail again,
For to die, for to die, for to die.

Our captain John Bedar he set sail, he set sail,
Our captain for Port Jackson he set sail,
I'll return men without fail, but he foundered in a gale,
And went down, and went down, and went down.

We cured ten thousand skins for the fur, for the fur,
We cured ten thousand skins for the fur.
Brackish water, putrid seal, we did all of us fall ill,
For to die, for to die, for to die.

Come all ye lads who sail 'pon the sea, 'pon the sea,
Come all ye lads who sail 'pon the sea.
Though the schooner *Governor Bligh* took on those who did not die,
Never seal, never seal, never seal.

The *Sydney Gazette,* 23 December 1813, has this to say:

Yesterday, arrived from a sealing voyage, after a sixteen months absence, the colonial schooner, Governor Bligh, Mr Grono, master, with 14,000 seal skins and about 3 tons of sea-elephant oil. The vessel brings from the West Coast of New Zealand, a joyful gang of men, consisting of ten persons, left by the brig Active, Captain Bader, so long ago as the 16th February, 1809, in charge of Mr David Lowrieston.

The Active went from Port Jackson, December 11th. 1808, and having landed her people on an island about a mile and a half from the main of New Zealand, sailed again for this port, but doubtless perished by the way, and has never since been heard of. The men who were left on the island were reduced to the necessity of subsisting for nearly four years upon the seal, when in season and at other times upon a species of fern, parts of which they roasted or boiled, and other parts were obliged to eat undressed, owing to a nausea it imbibed from any culinary process. They were left upon the small island with a very scanty allowance of provisions and the Active was to come to Port Jackson for a further supply. They had a whale boat and their only edged implements consisted of an axe, an adze and a cooper's drawing knife. In a short time they procured 11,000 skins, part of which Mr Grono has brought up.

In the hope of finding upon the main some succour, which the small island did not afford, they went hither, but were nearly lost by the way, as some of the lower streaks of the boat were near falling out, owing as was imagined to the nails being of cast iron. On their safe arrival however, they found an old boat on a beach, which it subsequently appeared had been left there by Mr Grono on a former voyage. With the aid of this additional boat, when both repaired, they projected an excursion towards some of the more frequented sealing places and were on the point of setting out, when a tremendous hurricane in one night destroyed the boats and put an end to their hope of relief. The only nutritive the place afforded was a species of the fern root, resembling a yam when cut and possessing some of the properties of the vegetable. This could only be procured at a distance of six or seven miles from their hut, which was near the sea-side and had it been more plentiful, would have been a desirable substitute for better diet; but was unfortunately so sparingly scattered amongst other shrubs as to be found with difficulty; and they solemnly affirm that they have for a week at a time had neither this nor any other food whatever. With the assistance of a canoe made up of seal skins, a party visited their former island and found their stocks of skins much injured by the weather, but did all they could for their preservation. This was their only seal depot and out of the usual season they now and then found a solitary straggler, in some instances when they were so reduced by famine as to be scarcely capable of securing those that providence threw in their way. With their axe, adze and cooper's drawing knife they afterwards built a small boat, but with intense labour, as without saws they could only cut one plank out of each tree. The hoops upon their provision casks were beaten into nails and by the same patient and laborious process, they at length projected the building of a small vessel and had provided 80 half-inch boards for the purpose, all cut in the way above described. Truly a feat of great perseverance. The fortunate accident of

Mr Grono touching there has however preserved them from future suffering and peril, of which they have had full store, on that exposed and inhospitable shore.

There is a postscript to the story with news of the discovery of wreckage near Bluff Point in Southland in 1847. This account comes from *Shipwrecks – New Zealand Disasters 1795–1936* by Chas Ingram and Owen Wheatley:

> A report in a Nelson paper of September, 1847 stated that a little to the southward of Bluff Point (Southland) a sealing party found the hull of a brig, surrounded by bushes, with a small tree growing through a hole in her bottom, and lying about 200 yards above high water mark. They supposed it to be the wreck of the *Active*, a brig which left Sydney … for New Zealand and was never heard of again. The vessel, to judge from her position, was run ashore with all sail set, probably in the night, and her crew, it is likely, fell victims to the Natives.

The peak period of whaling in New Zealand waters was from 1792 until the late 1850s, after which time it had much less economic and social impact. The industry was of great importance to the world with whale oil in demand for use in lighting, cooking, tanning and lubrication, while whalebone strengthened chair seats and corsets as well as making fine buggy whips. The two kinds of whaling — ocean whaling and shore-whaling — would in time overlap. Ocean whaling had begun in the 1790s, with shore-whaling not getting under way until the 1820s to exploit the southern right whales that seasonally swam through Cook and Foveaux Straits. These whales often calved in New Zealand's east coast bays and being large, docile and slow, they were easy prey for the whaling industry.

The British were first on the local scene, with their interest paving the way for more permanent European settlement. Within twenty years the British had given place to an American dominance in technique and organisation, which brought large numbers of Americans to the New Zealand coast from 1830 onwards. It is therefore hardly surprising to find localised variants of their songs eventually being collected in the USA. 'The Bold and Saucy China' is an obvious reworking of the Scottish whaling song 'The Bonnie Ship the Diamond'.

> The *China* is a well-rigged ship, from New Bedford she is going,
> To where there's many a gale of wind and whale fish are blowing.
> When we do set sail m'boys, it's sou-sou-east we'll steer,
> Till we make the island of St Pauls and whale fish appear.
>
> > So be cheerful my lads, let your heart never fail,
> > While the bold and saucy *China* is cruising after whale.
>
> We'll set sail with the breeze, for the Isle of France we're bound,
> To leave again without delay for the southern whaling ground,
> Once the gale's cleared away, it's then we'll make full sail,
> With a fair wind for New Zealand, a-searching for the whale.

Five and thirty barrels, boys, is all we did stow down,
As we set sail gallantly for the southern whaling ground.
We left this cold and stormy place, first quarter of the moon,
And reached Otago's whaling ground before the first of June.

Soon hundreds of whale ships were visiting New Zealand and the crews of such vessels were sorely in need of rest and recreation. Kororareka (later named Russell) in the Bay of Islands was a favourite spot for American whalemen, providing everything they needed and more. William Colenso described it as being "notorious for containing a greater number of rogues than any other spot of equal size in the universe." The country's first grog-shop was opened on the foreshore by Ben Turner, a time-expired convict from Australia, who could easily have been the composer of the song 'Shore Cry' for it certainly displays an element of convict association.

I'm very very well I'm glad to tell, I fear no judge nor jailer,
I'm very very well I'm glad to tell, heed these lines from a whaler.

Oh what delight on a stormy night to sit beside a burning log,
A-swapping tales of wondrous whales and drink a glass of grog.

I'm very very well I'm bound to tell, now I've become a whaler,
I'm very very well I'm bound to tell, for that's the best trade for a sailor.

I'm very very well I'm pleased to tell, since landing at Cyprus Bay,
I'm very very well I'm pleased to tell, for it's here I'm bound to stay.

'Shore Cry' ~ Anon/extra verse by Phil Garland

The story of grog in the Bay of Islands is further covered in Chapter xiii. Shore-whaling gangs were commonly employed by the Sydney firm Weller Brothers, receiving an advance on their pay which some promptly spent. They were taken to the whaling station and provided with essential supplies such as drink, clothing, and tobacco. Those who wanted them were offered Maori 'wives', who were expected to feed them, mend their clothes and keep their home clean. The whaler was obliged to dress and treat his 'wife' well, to give part of his earnings to her family, and to support her tribe if required. This sometimes made things awkward for the whaler, having to deal with situations he would otherwise have preferred to avoid. Many a shore whaler couldn't wait to return to normal civilisation, as portrayed in the chorus of 'Soon May the Wellerman Come':

Soon may the Wellerman come,
And bring us sugar and tea and rum,
One day when the tonguin' is done,
We'll take our leave and go.

The trading conditions on these shore-whaling stations were rough and ready. Visits from the 'Wellerman' (Weller Brothers agent) were infrequent with the men being paid goods in lieu of wages, which were then marked against their account. Without ready money, they found it hard to obtain passage back to Sydney, or anywhere else for that matter, severely limiting their prospects of employment elsewhere. 'Come all ye Tonguers' is quite probably New Zealand's first true protest song.

> Come all ye tonguers and land lovin' lubbers,
> Here's a job cutting in and boiling down blubbers,
> A job for the youngster, the old or the ailing,
> The agent will take any man for shore-whaling
>
> I am paid in soap and sugar and rum,
> For cutting in whale and boiling down tongue,
> The agent's fee makes my blood so to boil,
> I'll push him in a hot pot of oil.
>
> Go hang the agent, the company too,
> They're making a fortune off me and you.
> No chance of a passage from out of this place
> And the price of living's a bloody disgrace!

A number of early whalers came ashore to stay and make lasting contributions to the new colony. They included Johnny Jones in Otago, Paddy Gilroy in Southland and Dicky Barrett in Wellington and Taranaki.

Born in Sydney in 1809, it was the whaling trade that brought Johnny Jones to Waikouaiti, north of Dunedin, where he established his principal whaling station and set up an agricultural settlement to keep his crews supplied. He brought immigrants from Australia to clear the land, construct buildings and harvest the crops. This whaling station would become the South Island's first permanent settlement. Jones was the most successful of New Zealand's bay whalers and an ambitious man, who continued to expand his whaling fleet and build an extensive empire, while acquiring real estate holdings throughout his lifetime.

Jones eventually owned sheep stations, farms and business properties in and around Dunedin, but his greatest legacy to New Zealand would be in the folklore that surrounded him. He is remembered as the two-fisted, dynamic founder of a South Island dynasty and a political autocrat used to having his own way. Although successful, wealthy and widely respected, Jones swaggered through Otago's early days and remained a brawler to the end. When he died in 1869, Dunedin came to a standstill for the day as a mark of respect for this optimistic whaler, land speculator, manipulative politician and benevolent despot. His obituary in the *Otago Daily Times* described him as "A large hearted man with the simple instincts of a child, who fought with adversity and was improved by prosperity like few others of his ilk before him."

Tom Kennard, the first Pakeha boy born in Otago, grew up near Jones's Moeraki and Waikouaiti whaling stations and got to know many of their colourful characters.

Asked by writer Herries Beattie if he could remember the local whalers' songs, Tommy recalled these verses, which he said were recited in a jocular manner:

Along the coast the *Magnet* came,
With Captain Bruce a man of fame,
But in his face there is no shame,
On the beautiful coast of New Zealand.

Mr Willsher sold to Bloody Jack,
Two hundred of flour tied up in a sack,
And a Maori carried it all on his back,
On the beautiful coast of New Zealand.

Waikouaiti and Molyneux,
Tautuku and Otago too,
If you do not want to be duped by a Jew,
Come to the beautiful coast of New Zealand.

Peter Shavatt has a shocking bad hat,
And old John Hughes has Maori shoes,
But for all that they are having some chat,
On the beautiful coast of New Zealand.

Whaler's Rhymes – Anon

Paddy Gilroy was one of New Zealand's most colourful whaling captains, idolised by his crew and a legend for his seamanship, courage and intimate knowledge of the southern coast. In a battered old whaling vessel called the *Chance* this inimitable Irish sea captain from County Mayo sailed the southern ocean with a crew of Yankee deserters, Maori friends and relatives and European sailors of dubious reputation, who could always find sanctuary among his crew.

The *Chance* was already a hundred years old before being owned by Paddy Gilroy in the 1860s & '70s, but she more than paid her way for her master. Eventually the time came for this dumpy, bewhiskered character to retire to Bluff. His faithful ship lay as a rotting hulk in Bluff Harbour for many years, until finally burning to the waterline in 1902, just a year before the demise of her master in 1903. Their story lives on in whaling legend and song:

He hunted the whale in days long gone by,
When skies were grey and the chase was nigh.
Excitement would grow with the strength of each gale,
The tang of the spray and the wind in his sail.

'There she blows!' was the lookout's cry,
Then on the crest of a wave the harpoons would fly,
He pitted his strength 'gainst the might of the whale,
There was never a chance Paddy Gilroy would fail.

Chorus   When the call of the sea beckoned no more,
          This old salt dropped anchor at his home ashore.
          With no challenge to meet, when the weather turned rough,
          He would spend his last days becalmed at the Bluff.

His best friends in life were his loyal crew,
Yankee deserters and bold Maori too.
They would follow their master wher'eer he would lead,
For no captain had more respect for the sea.

Though she ended her days, that once-faithful ship,
Beached as a hulk in Bluff Harbour she lay.
The *Chance* will forever continue to sail,
In old whaling legend, story and tale.

They laid him to rest where no shamrocks grow,
Far from the land he once knew as a boy.
A home near the sea, where tides ebb and flow,
Would become the last haven for Paddy Gilroy.

Becalmed at the Bluff – Maurice Skerrett & Phil Garland

No story about the Wellington settlement would be complete without mentioning Richard 'Dicky' Barrett, who came to New Zealand in 1828 as a trader before becoming a warrior, whaler, policeman, peacemaker and hotelier. When tribal war brought his trading to an end, he fought alongside Taranaki Maori against Waikato invaders in the early 1830s before marrying Rawinia, sister of Te Atiawa leader Te Wharepouri. He established a whaling station at Queen Charlotte Sound and was later employed by William Wakefield as a translator in land negotiations between Maori and the New Zealand Company. In return for services rendered to the Crown the company gave Barrett the rights to establish his own hotel, built on Lambton Quay in 1840 just below the present site of Parliament. Dicky was the epitome of a jolly whaler — he loved his ale and a good time, and Barrett's Hotel became the hub of Wellington's social life, hosting political gatherings and early settlement negotiations. Wakefield once remarked "A stranger was always welcome to share a meal, a drop of grog and a seat on the stool."

This vivid image of Barrett's appearance was painted by an unknown writer:

How can I make you acquainted for instance with Dicky Barrett, who looks as if he had approached the shape of a small calf whale from long residence among them. He has been in New Zealand 12 years — has been a whaler, has a cutter of his own and dozens of whale boats, is a great man among the natives, who adore him and is respected even by drunken whalers. He has befriended many a white man in his district and has got the largest heart of any man I know in New Zealand. His house is always full of castaway sailors and fat bellied Maoris, who are sniffing the grateful smell from his great iron pot.

After sustaining losses from his whaling business, Dicky relinquished the hotel in 1841 and returned to Taranaki, where he was on hand to welcome the first settlers off the *William Bryan* and help unload the vessel. Those settlers and subsequent arrivals relied on him to keep them safe from possible attack, with everyone appreciating his apparent control of an extremely nervous situation.

As with many of his ilk, Barrett may not have been above stretching the truth and using blackmail to achieve his ends. Although he had proved invaluable to Wakefield and the early settlers in Wellington and New Plymouth, his dubious land dealings coupled with his dodgy English/Maori translations began to anger more than a few, particularly Te Atiawa. Dicky's fall from grace was immediate as he lost all respect and mana — in a very short time he became known as 'Dirty Dick' to Maori and Pakeha alike. Te Atiawa turned their backs on him as they came to realise his broken promises had cost them dearly and contributed much towards their loss of land.

It had been a short life but a merry one for the whaling publican, when at 40 years of age, Barrett met his end off the Taranaki coast in 1847. His original hotel was later destroyed in the 1855 earthquake. When this account of his death appeared in the *Taranaki Herald* almost 100 years later, no one could vouch for the truth of it, for it sounded like one of his own tall stories:

> The whale was spouting blood in a vortex of spume when Dicky Barrett ran in to put the finishing lance into its 'life.' Suddenly the cry went up "There she's fluked — by Jove — she's done for Barrett." The great tail appeared to fall on the boat, which for the moment was lost to view in the churning cauldron worked up by the dying whale. Soon, however, Dicky Barrett was lifted from her bottom, insensible and carried ashore. He lay on the warm sand for some time above high water mark. Then he was carried and half walked between two strong supporters to Mr Richard Browns…

The Barrett name survived for almost 150 years in another building at the opposite end of Lambton Quay and still does so in parts of Wellington and New Plymouth.

> In the days of sail before I was born,
> My father sailed around Cape Horn.
> Wore my raincoat through a raging storm,
> With a whaler called Dicky Barrett.
>
> *Chorus* When the harpoon struck home and the line it ran out,
>   And the whale gave a flurry with its tail.
>   And we lost poor Dicky Barrett to a hundred barrel whale,
>   And no more he'll go rollin' on the sea, bonny lads,
>   No more he'll go rollin' on the sea.

I remember well that fateful day,
When the people lined up on the quay,
And Dicky Barrett was heard to say,
"There she blows — lay to your oars, boys!"

At a box made out of rimu wood,
New Plymouth round in mourning stood.
Asking why to die he should,
That brave whaler Dicky Barrett.

Barrett's Shanty — Grant Dawson

Meanwhile back in England, a couple of influential London actors, Edward Gibbon Wakefield and James Stephen, were setting themselves up as colonising entrepreneurs. Wakefield had begun to develop his theories on civilised colonisation in the 1820s and now proposed a scheme which would make emigration an attractive investment, especially to the 'cultured' classes. His idea was to create a settlement along the lines of an idyllic English farming community — one which would also make a tidy return for investors. Although Wakefield had merit as a thinker and promoter, time would prove his colonising ideas to be somewhat less than practical and show him up to be nothing short of an absolute menace.

An initial attempt at organised settlement had been made in 1826 by bringing a shipload of colonists to the Hauraki Gulf, but it ended in disarray. The original mission was to exploit the magnificent stands of rimu and kauri on the Coromandel Peninsula, cultivate native flax and establish the country's first permanent trading post. Frightened by the tattooed Maori inhabitants, the settlers ignored the peninsula and set up home on nearby Pakihi Island in the Gulf. Perceived problems with the Maori inhabitants didn't eventuate, but the seed of doubt had been sown and the immigrants hastily left New Zealand at the first available opportunity.

A New Zealand Association was formed in 1836 and converted into the New Zealand Company in 1838. Its manifesto stated that "men who could take a little money with them could make a fortune and that all workmen would receive high wages." Consequently thousands became interested in emigrating here. Many of our earliest settlers and pioneers were assisted in their emigration and resettlement by Wakefield's grandiose schemes. The company was responsible for the European settlement of Wellington, Nelson and New Plymouth and played a supporting role in the church settlements of Canterbury and Otago. After disputes and bitterness between the company and settlers in general, it was finally dissolved in 1858.

Wakefield's ambitions are best summed up in an advertisement of 1839, stating that the company's goal was:

> To transplant English society with its various gradations in due proportions, carrying out our laws, customs, associations, habits, manners, feelings — everything of England, in short, but the soil.

Five ships carrying over 800 people left England in September 1839 to establish the first New Zealand Company colony at Wellington. Five months earlier Colonel William Wakefield had sailed for New Zealand on the *Tory* to select a site for settlement. The *Cuba* carrying the company surveying staff followed soon after and landed at Wellington only a few weeks before the first immigrants arrived on the *Aurora*. The settlers must have been disappointed and disheartened for nothing was ready for them. They had to remain on board ship while shelter was prepared. A jetty was built on the Petone foreshore and the settlers started their new lives housed in tents or huts built by the Maori. Within three months the settlement had grown to over 1000 people with still more on the way — 200 houses were built in the first four months. By the end of the first year there were some 2500 inhabitants, and the housing shortage provided everyone with employment constructing huts and whares to house their families. Roads were a priority and soon afforded delightful rides through the forest and bush, although parts were still quite rough and rutted. When Charlotte Godley landed in 1850, she was surprised to find that Wellington exceeded all her expectations:

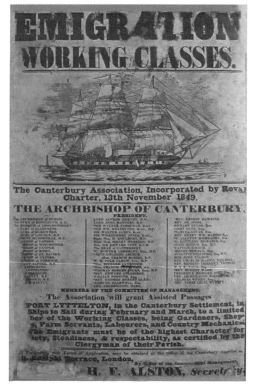

> It really is uncommonly pretty and with very good comfortable houses, although certainly no fine buildings, but they are generally built with a gable onto the street, which looks very picturesque and there is an almost continuous row along the beach for about two miles, something like the bit of Hastings which joins the old on to the new town, with a patch at each end of level ground; one is getting very full of houses with barracks, a new church, a meeting house etc … and the other, which is at the west end, where we live is used for cricket, flying kites, soldiers exercising ….

Charlotte found the weather delightful except for the gales: "I never saw such weather as we have had today — the water is coming in at our doors and windows and at two or three soft places in the roof, and the wind everywhere….the whole house shakes with it and we shiver for fires cannot warm us…"

She continues: "You never see anyone who does not look comfortably off."

That Wellington was looking so settled and pretty certainly belied the first confrontation between Wakefield and his surveyor-general, Captain William

Mein Smith. When Smith first arrived and saw the bush-clad hills of Wellington, he thought it would be too difficult to survey a suitable site for the town there and decided to plan the new town on the Petone foreshore. When Wakefield and Smith met on the beach, Wakefield demanded an immediate change of site, but when Captain Smith refused to change his plans their relationship never recovered. Eventually flooding from the Hutt River caused him to rethink the situation and move to Thorndon to continue his survey work there.

Within a few months he had surveyed some 1100 sections and his new city plan was laid out on a large table in Barrett's Hotel. It allowed for considerable green reserve land and was quite forward-thinking in its entirety, but Wakefield constantly criticised his best efforts, which eventually led to disillusioned settlers leaving for Australia.

Wakefield replaced Smith with Samuel Brees, but Smith decided to stay in the country, setting up as a private surveyor in Wellington. He was asked to explore and survey the major harbours of the South Island in 1842 and subsequently sailed into Lyttelton, named Whakaraupo by Ngai Tahu. He became the first white man to set foot on the island of Otamahua, renaming it Quail Island because of the native quail (koreke) that ran freely on its shores.

> Otamahua is my name and I've stood here for years,
> Watched the coming of the Maori and early pioneers.
> I was christened Quail Island when the Europeans came,
> Their footsteps changing history to leave a mark of shame.
>
> *Chorus* I am a living link with the days of future past,
>   The jewel of Whakaraupo on a sea of broken glass.
>
> The brothers Ward took passage aboard the *Charlotte Jane*,
> Built a little homestead but drowning caused their plans to change.
> My cliffs were scarred when sailors started mining rock for ballast,
> Hard labour building new stone walls that still are standing fast.
>
> *from The Jewel of Whakaraupo by Phil Garland*

While returning from points south Smith's cutter, the *Brothers,* sank during a squall in Akaroa Harbour and all his instruments, maps and sketches were lost. My brother and I still recall being hugely impressed when told by our mother how our illustrious ancestor and the crew had rowed all the way back to Wellington in an open whaler — certainly no mean feat even in those frontier days.

> We reached the Middle Island in eighteen forty-two,
> To search for land to southward that Captain Bruce well knew
>
> *Chorus* Oh, blow the *Brothers* down, boys, haul the hook away.
>   The wind is in the south-east, and we must leave the bay.

The old New Zealand Comp'ny failed to buy the land.
Around the shores of Tara, their schemes they weren't so grand.

Captain Smith shipped with us to chart the coves and shores,
All down to Ruapuke, where at last we stowed our oars.

A sou'west gale blew boldly and raised the seas too high,
So we close-reefed down the mainsail, as Squally Bay passed by.

We ran in to Akaroa and scraped past Timu head,
The wind dropped off to nothing, then a squall towards us sped.

Our ship capsized beneath us and sank there like a stone,
A mast-length down we lost her with everything we own.

The Frenchmen couldn't raise her from the muddy-bottomed bay,
Nor the *Guide* with all her tackle, where the hapless *Brothers* lay.

She's down there somewhere broken and there's nothing left to see,
But there's tears for the children the sailors could not free.

Chorus Oh, blow the *Brothers* down, boys, haul the hook away.
   The wind is in the south-east, and we must leave the bay.

'Blow the Brothers Down', Coll Cameron

In 1845 William Mein Smith and family moved to Huangarua in the Wairarapa, where he went into partnership with Samuel Revans and helped establish our wool and beef industry. He returned to survey work for the New Zealand Company after Wakefield's death in 1848. In the 1850s he laid out Masterton and Carterton (where my mother Ruth Tully was born) and surveyed the boundaries for Greytown. Mein Smith's daughter Fanny married John Tully and they became my mother's grandparents, which helps explain the illustrious ancestor relationship previously mentioned. His wonderful landscape paintings are another of Mein Smith's contributions to New Zealand.

The time has come for leaving,
As an emigrant I'll be bound
I'll bid farewell to those I love
And dear old London town.

Chorus Her eyes they shone like diamonds,
   I couldn't let go of her hand,
   For soon we'll be sailing o'er the main
   To far-off New Zealand

I know not when I'll see you,
As I wish you a fond adieu,
I'm bound away to New Zealand
To see my contract through.

I shipped aboard the *Arrow*,
All in the month of May.
Soon we'll be landing on the beach,
In beautiful Wakatu Bay.

Now when my time is over.
I'll set up in Nelson town,
I'll send back home for my true love,
And then we will settle down.

Black Velvet Band variant — anon

The New Zealand Company settlement of Nelson got off to an inauspicious start particularly when the brig *Lloyds* arrived on 15 February 1842. She had undergone a prolonged and harrowing voyage and the women and children on board had many sad tales to tell, with 65 children having been lost along the way. Fortunately later arrivals aboard the *Thomas Harrison* had kinder stories to relate, while their first impressions would soon be at odds with the realities ashore. Passenger Mary Ann Hodgkinson described her arrival:

> Then one day we were wildly excited — land appeared and a snowy mountain reared its lovely head above a haze of blue. Captain Smith said we were nearly there and we knelt on the deck and thanked God. We sailed down a silver coast and gazed with wonder at the high land covered with a magnificent forest.

The *Nelson Examiner* of 29 October 1842 wrote:

> The *Thomas Harrison* arrived on Tuesday morning, and came direct into the Haven in beautiful style. She was greeted with cheers by those on shore, which were heartily replied to by the newly-arrived. She has been so long looked for, that a feeling of distrust of her ever arriving had begun to prevail, which was the cause of her hearty reception …

The long voyage was over and a new life was about to begin. The following year the new settlement was stunned by the clash between settlers and Maori at Wairau near Blenheim, but the shared loss and feeling of common danger helped bring sections of the community closer together. Hunger soon became widespread as many new settlers found their pre-purchased land hadn't even been surveyed and unbelievably some sections were almost impossible to reach. A few settlers died with broken hearts, dispirited by the difficulties of ekeing out a living for their families. Children went hungry to bed night after night, seldom experiencing a decent meal. To feed their starving children, despairing settlers dug up the very seed potatoes they'd planted. Alfred Saunders had this to say in the Christchurch *Press* 11 April 1898:

> It will always be difficult for future generations to understand why all three of the New Zealand Company's settlements were planned with so little caution, so little

wisdom and so little good faith, that the early settlers of Wellington, New Plymouth and Nelson were all exposed, one after the other, not only to the most painful losses and privations, but to a very real danger of starving to death.

By the end of May 1842, some 1700 people were crammed into Nelson, because not one acre of country land had yet been made available. Not until August was suburban land finally open for selection and yet another season passed before fern land was ready for sowing and swamp lands drained. The Wakefield system of colonisation was blamed for all the inadequacies and delays — as one settler wrote: "It was all unfulfilled promises, shuffling procrastination and hopeless executive incapacity."

Fortunately for both purchasers and labourers alike, the situation began to improve after the appointment of William Fox as resident agent. It was noted later that the withdrawal of company assistance would prove beneficial in the long run. Families were forced to support themselves, more land was cultivated and because of the shared hardships, much of the bitterness between land purchasers and labourers began to disappear. By 1848, many of the differences over land titles had been settled as negotiations between the New Zealand Company, William Fox and the purchasers resulted in a redistribution of land. The settlement was over the worst of its troubles as people moved into the surrounding countryside to begin establishing more permanent homes. Harry Moffat, who later became harbourmaster for Port Motueka, made his first visit to Nelson as a lad in 1857 and commented in his autobiography that the town appeared well laid out and looked a good place in which to live.

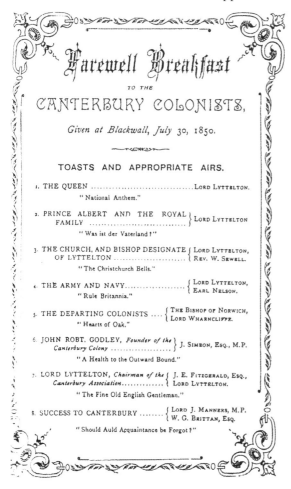

Part of the company's premise appears to have been that any poor farm or city labourer who accepted free or assisted passage would not complain of the conditions in steerage or having to work for low wages upon arrival. However the

Colonists dancing on the *Randolph* to the Coldstream Guards band,
before departure to found the settlement of Canterbury, 1850.
Illustrated London News

newly formed Canterbury Association was quick to point out that they could offer better conditions aboard their vessels, with superior food and accommodation. Shipboard diaries would soon tell a different story.

The association's first ship, the *Lady Nugent* under Captain Joseph Thomas, braved mountainous seas in the Tasman before arriving safely at Port Chalmers in 1849 and Port Cooper (Lyttelton) in 1850. This almost forgotten ship carried John Robert Godley, founding father of the Canterbury settlement, along with his family and hundreds of workmen, who were to build the Bridle Path in readiness for settlers, and lay the foundations of a new town. Some of these details and more are mentioned in my song 'Shores of Lyttelton'. An excerpt:

> Did you see those ships sailing far across the sea,
> Far across the sea, far across the sea,
> Did you see those ships sailing far across the sea,
> To the shores of Lyttelton?
>
> The *Lady Nugent* carried workers by the score …
> To the shores of Lyttelton.
>
> They cleared the land to build the Bridle Path …
> On the shores at Lyttelton.
>
> The First Four ships arrived later in the year …
> At the shores of Lyttelton.

The pilgrims landed on the shores of Lyttleton …
Just in time for Christmas Day.

The pilgrims clambered up the Bridle Path …
To view the Promised Land.

They built new lives on the Canterbury Plains …
Where their dreams were not in vain.

Dreams of creating another England were launched with the departure of the first four ships from Plymouth, southward bound to the new colony. Ships had hearty send-offs with bands playing and flags flying as migrants ate dinners of roast beef and plum pudding, washed down by beer — all calculated to ease the pain of parting and promote the virtues of emigration.

Come all of you assembled here and listen to my song,
I'll have you pay attention, since I'll not detain you long.
The cost of living's very high, of that you well do know,
So we're taking passage on a ship, to New Zealand we will go.

'Twill be next Sunday morning, from Portsmouth we'll set sail,
All with our wives and families, we'll pray for pleasant gales,
Our ship she is well loaded for Port Lyttelton we're bound,
Where good fortune is awaiting us and cheerful hearts abound…

from 'Southward Bound' – Phil Garland

The sadness of parting was matched only by the warmth of greeting. The arrival of each ship was an important event and people flocked to the jetty to meet the fresh arrivals. Each new family with its stories, news and songs brought relief to the isolation so keenly felt by the colony. One such arrival at Lyttelton is described in *Light and Shadows of Colonial Life* by Sarah Amelia Courage:

It was the 24th of March when we arrived at Lyttelton Heads in the evening. The night was clear and bright and we could see the Port Hills, which are high and seemed to us imposing and would be called mountains back home. There were no houses to be seen, for the township was not visible from where the vessel lay at anchor — that was a treat reserved for the morrow.

Edward Ward arrived optimistically at Lyttelton on the *Charlotte Jane* in 1850:

The land we passed was most beautifully situated — high and wooded, with glades of grass running up through the forest here and there. We were all enchanted as fresh beauties broke upon our view every moment. As we rounded to, we shot past a little point of land and the town of Lyttelton burst upon our view like a little village, but nothing more than a little village in snugness, neatness and pretty situation.

Charles Martin used to sing protest and parody in the bar of the White Hart Hotel in central Christchurch, and his 'Young Man Out from England' was popular with the patrons in 1862 — his hero is Bill Larkins, a Lancashire lad who feels unfairly taken advantage of on arrival by settled members of the Canterbury establishment.

> I'm a young man just from England, from Lancashire I came,
> I'm a free and easy sort of chap, Bill Larkins is my name.
> Now I know my way about a bit, with both eyes I can see,
> Although I'm just from England, you don't put over me.
>
> I landed safe at Lyttelton when up comes Mr Hay,
> Says he, "M'lad, come clear my bush just round at Pigeon Bay.
> I'll pay you by the hundred foot" "How much?" "Ten bob," says he,
> Says I, "I'm fresh from England but you don't top sawyer me!"
>
> My luggage went by the Sumner road addressed 'B.L., White Hart'
> I saw it tightly corded down on John Smith's two-horse cart.
> And when in Christchurch I arrived, "I'll take ten bob," says he,
> Says I "I'm green from England, but here's half-a-crown for thee."
>
> * * * * * * * * * *

We felt we were in a new world, yet a very short time sufficed to show us that people and things generally were much more homelike than we had anticipated, in fact we were agreeably surprised to find everybody and everything so civilised.

Sarah Amelia Courage *Lights & Shadows of Colonial Life*

We started from Lyttelton about three o'clock and almost immediately began to ascend the Zigzag. It was a tremendous pull for the poor horses, who, however never flinched and at length we reached the top — it was worth all the bad road to look down on Lyttelton, which seemed much more imposing and important as we rose above it…

We were soon rattling along the Sumner Road by the seashore and in half an hour we reached Sumner itself, where we stopped for a few moments to change horses. It began to rain hard and the rest of the journey, some seven or eight miles was disagreeable enough and when we reached Christchurch, we drove at once to a sort of boarding house, where we had engaged apartments and thought of nothing but supper and bed!

from *Station Life in New Zealand* by Lady Barker

The first verse of my song 'Age of Grace' sets the scene for new arrivals in the St Albans suburb of early Christchurch and acknowledges what they have achieved.

> When the early settlers landed on Port Cooper's shore,
> And clambered up the Bridle Path to see what lay in store.
> They looked down on tussock grassland, where flax and cabbage tree,
> Would give way to build St Albans on the plains of Canterbury.

Upon arrival at Lyttelton, the pilgrims had to struggle up the steep Bridle Path to the summit of the enclosing Port Hills to view the new land. According to family legend my great-grandmother was carried over the Bridle Path astride a white bullock in 1854. From this superb vantage point they looked across the vast expanse of plains extending to the distant rolling foothills and the rugged snow-capped mountain barrier behind. That their dreams were not in vain is evidenced by the rapid population growth Canterbury then experienced, with shiploads of colonists arriving at a steady rate. They would be supplemented by settlers from elsewhere in New Zealand, along with Australian graziers known as 'shagroons', who came seeking suitable land for sheep. Pastoralism and agriculture became the backbone of the new economy, as the province rose to prosperity on the sheep's back. It wasn't all hard grind: formal or informal dances and other entertainments, which enabled people to meet and relax together, became popular. Country people would travel long distances to such affairs in bullock drays, on horseback, or even by walking, sometimes for many miles through the cold and wet. "But what a time we all have!" the settlers said.

Christchurch soon became the hub of Canterbury, consolidating links between port, town and country. Its key role was enhanced in 1867 with the opening of a rail tunnel through the Port Hills to the sheltered deep-water port of Lyttelton. However, the discovery of gold in West Canterbury in the 1860s fostered a hectic diversion, heralding a large influx of manpower from around the globe, further boosting organised settlement — but that's another story and one we'll cover in a later chapter.

The story of the Waipu settlement begins with the Reverend Norman McLeod, who grew up in the Scottish Highlands during the Clearances. After his religious conversion, he sought to reform the established church by tearing their conformist beliefs to shreds whilst evangelising moral purity. His illegal preaching gained much support and led to his becoming a charismatic leader — brave, tough, moralistic, cruel, bigoted and chauvinistic. As his reputation grew, so did his following.

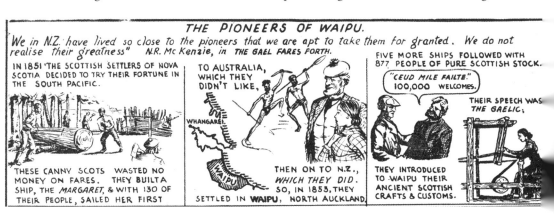

THE PIONEERS OF WAIPU.

"We in N.Z. have lived so close to the pioneers that we are apt to take them for granted. We do not realise their greatness" N.R. McKenzie, in THE GAEL FARES FORTH.

IN 1851 THE SCOTTISH SETTLERS OF NOVA SCOTIA DECIDED TO TRY THEIR FORTUNE IN THE SOUTH PACIFIC.

THESE CANNY SCOTS WASTED NO MONEY ON FARES. THEY BUILT A SHIP, THE MARGARET, & WITH 130 OF THEIR PEOPLE, SAILED HER FIRST

TO AUSTRALIA, WHICH THEY DIDN'T LIKE,

WHANGAREI.

WAIPU

THEN ON TO N.Z., WHICH THEY DID. SO, IN 1853, THEY SETTLED IN WAIPU, NORTH AUCKLAND.

FIVE MORE SHIPS FOLLOWED WITH 877 PEOPLE OF PURE SCOTTISH STOCK.

"CEUD MILE FAILTE." 100,000 WELCOMES.

THEIR SPEECH WAS THE GAELIC;

THEY INTRODUCED TO WAIPU THEIR ANCIENT SCOTTISH CRAFTS & CUSTOMS.

Accompanied by his wife and family he sailed for Canada in 1817, searching for the religious freedom he craved. He landed in the Nova Scotia town of Pictou but

was so disgusted by its vices that he sailed on to St Anne's Bay to build his own religious community, which survived for 33 years. By 1840, McLeod had become a tyrant and master of all he surveyed. Prospective families sailed from Scotland to join his Nova Scotian congregation, but many began to find his fanatical Puritanism and moralistic fervour too strict for their liking and rifts appeared. He banned all singing and dancing in the home, while his special wrath was reserved for women, who he constantly railed against, charging them with constantly and deliberately dressing in such manner as to tempt the carnal pleasures. His obsession with sex and his fanatical denial of it would eventually split his community asunder.

Meanwhile Norman McLeod's son Donald had gone on to Australia, from where he began sending newspapers home in 1848 describing the abundant opportunities that appeared to exist there and in New Zealand. The time seemed ripe for McLeod senior to leave and he sailed for Australia with 136 dedicated followers, but it was not the haven he was expecting. Gold fever, crime and dysentery ambushed the flock and he lost his three youngest sons to typhoid. Norman then wrote to Governor George Grey in New Zealand, who encouraged the Gael and his flock to migrate across the Tasman. Although now 72 years old, McLeod sailed on to New Zealand in 1853, landing at Waipu to establish a Gaelic-speaking community 100 miles north of Auckland. By 1860, another 800 loyal parishioners had followed him from Nova Scotia to start their lives anew.

It has been suggested that McLeod had mellowed somewhat by the time he reached New Zealand's shores, but his fanatical zeal and moral leadership certainly hadn't lessened.

Above: Norman McLeod, from the cover of *Lion of Scotland*, by Neil Robinson.
Left: The Waipu story, from Ross Gore's *It Happened in New Zealand*.

Despite inspiring dogged belief and devotion, the Gael would remain unloved by many, including his own family. Although he had succeeded in preaching the denial of human love and caring relationships, McLeod's legacy is that of a colonial founder and strong leader, who for all his faults was a great teacher, and this is reflected in the number of his descendants who became successful scholars, writers and teachers around the world.

Willow Macky tells the story of the Waipu settlers in her song:

When the landlords pressed their claim in Scotland long ago,
The crofters lost their little farms and bitter was their woe,
And the Reverend Norman McLeod, he lifted up his head,
"With the help of God, we'll find a ship and I'll lead you forth," he said.

Chorus And the Gael fared forth, where he never fared before,
         Across the wide and stormy sea, to seek a kinder shore.

So in Nova Scotia's land they lived for 30 years,
And hard their toil in stubborn soil through winters long and drear.
Then one day a letter came from a kinsman far away,
Who had sailed for fair Australia and had never rued the day.

Then they looked at the leaden skies and the snowdrifts on the ground,
And they longed to go to Australia, where the sun shone all year round,
And the Reverend Norman McLeod, he raised his aged head,
"If your sons will build and man the ships, I'll lead you forth," he said.

So in ships that numbered six, in faith they sailed away,
And braved again the raging main through many a wintry day,
Over thirteen thousand miles for as far as they could rove,
Till they came to fair New Zealand and the bonny Waipu Cove.

Chorus And the Gael fared forth, where he never fared before,
         Across the wide and stormy seas and he found a kinder shore.

As more and more settlements were established, families began to move inland, colonising rural outposts and creating regional towns so that all of New Zealand's major centres had been founded by the late 1860s. A new nation had been born in one of the loneliest corners on Earth and wasted little time in making its presence felt around the world.

'Musical bouquet no. 397' – The Emigrant Polka, arranged on airs from
'The Emigrant's Progress' by Henry Russell, 1857.

III

BRIGHT FINE GOLD

Otago's gold rushes

THE PERIOD OF HISTORY THAT BEGAN when Gabriel Read discovered gold in Otago in 1861 has spawned some of our first truly indigenous Pakeha songs.

Although traces of gold were discovered by whalers at Coromandel in 1842 and then by survey parties in Nelson a few years later, there was no sign of any significant quantities. It was not until the 1850s, with settlers leaving for the gold rushes overseas that Auckland offered a reward for the discovery of payable quantities near the town. The reward was claimed by Charles Ring of Coromandel in September 1852, but after a three month rush the goldfield petered out. It wasn't until the cessation of the Maori wars that miners felt safe once more to prospect for gold around Thames in 1867, leaving their rusted and aging relics on display as reminders throughout the area today.

The atmosphere is captured by Dave Jordan with his song 'The Hills of Coromandel':

The trees grow ancient green and tall as they have always done there,
And press together over all, to shield the earth from sun there.
The seedlings spread, young trees grow old, old ones fall and fall to mould,
Till bush returns to hills once clear and man it seems was never here,
But the apple trees still bloom each year in the hills of Coromandel.

It was the gold that brought the men, when thousands here did rally,
Their secret shattered shafts remain abandoned in the valley.
The roads they fashioned in the clay are overgrown or washed away,
With fences built by settlers hand, all gone restoring broken lands,
And a rusted gateway lonely stands in the hills of Coromandel.

No more the taverns where they stood, no more the thousand people,
And timber church is gone for good with ruined rotted steeple.
It's years now since the miner came, to work the gold, exhaust his claim,
Then leave the place for other gain than that he'd found, but just the same
The toppled tombstones bear their names in the hills of Coromandel.

Those days of gold are past and gone with the men who took their chances,
The bush is slowly marching on in a silence no-one answers.
Now birds call loud to empty air, there's no-one comes, there's nothing there,
But a gate that's opened to nowhere and the names on sandstone, faint but clear
And the apple trees that bloom each year in the hills of Coromandel.

In 1856, payable gold was discovered in the Aorere River Valley near Collingwood in Nelson, and another small rush was under way in Golden Bay. This scenic spot had been named Murderer's Bay by Abel Tasman after losing four crewmen to Maori in 1642, but after gold was found it was renamed in 1857. The new rush declined almost as rapidly as it began, with miners drifting away once the river bed had been worked out. Although gold was known to exist throughout the South Island, the countryside was vastly different from the land formations in California and Victoria, where most of the prospectors came from, and there was little enthusiasm for following things through until the arrival of Gabriel Read. In 1856, Charles Ligar, surveyor general of New Zealand discovered a few specks of gold just below Tuturau on the Mataura River. A gold rush followed with forty miners descending on the area, but the field declined. It soon became common knowledge around Southland that there weren't sufficient quantities of gold at Tuturau to warrant any sort of claim. However, the news of Ligar's discovery proved to be the catalyst that attracted Gabriel Read to New Zealand.

Gabriel Read

Sam Perkins, an ex-whalerman and spinner of tall tales, concocted a rush at the Mataura in 1862 for reasons known only to himself. He somehow duped five hundred miners from Gabriel's Gully to follow him and his mate to new diggings at Tuturau. Whether he had men ready to jump the abandoned claims at Gabriel's or just had a pecuniary interest in the cart his mate was using to carry the miners' gear, we may never really know. The miners grew restless, suspicious of Sam's elusive answers to their queries about the new goldfield. Finally he confessed on the banks of the Mataura River that there was no gold! The angry mob decided to lynch Perkins on the spot, but they were dissuaded from dispensing such rough justice by the arrival of the local runholder, who convinced them to tie Sam to the cart, shave off his hair and beard before administering a severe horse-whipping and sending him on his way. That part of the river near Tuturau is known as 'Sam's Grief' to this day.

The folk are going mad outright, the yellow fever's at its height,
And nothing's heard both day and night but gold at the Mataura.

Chorus We'll leave the womenfolk behind, out of sight and out of mind,
We're off to Tuturau to find gold at the Mataura.

To a man we've heard Sam's call, a fortune's waiting for us all,
High hopes will surely have a fall when we're at the Mataura.

from 'At the Mataura' ~ Anon/Phil Garland

Gabriel Read was the son of a wealthy Tasmanian landowner and is generally credited with having discovered gold near Tuapeka in Central Otago in 1861. As a young man he had worked on the Californian goldfields, before having minor success on returning to the Victorian fields in Australia. After his arrival in New Zealand he prospected around Central Otago with little to show for his labours, until meeting 'Black Peter', a Hindu from Bombay who had already effectively fossicked the area. Peter indicated to Read where gold might be found and he soon struck paydirt, describing his find as "shining like the stars of Orion on a cold frosty night." This discovery culminated in the first gold rush worthy of the name, to what would become known as 'Gabriel's Gully.' Having claimed the government reward for his discovery, Read continued prospecting further afield before returning to Tasmania, where he later died in an asylum near Hobart in 1894.

Gabriel's Gully was the cradle of the New Zealand goldfields, giving birth to a fevered immigration and even richer discoveries, which continued to amaze for many years to follow. Miners flocked to New Zealand from around the world via California and Australia, bringing with them a whole new order of society.

Black Peter

It was in the eighteen-sixties, when word began to spread,
Gabriel Read had found a gully, where gold shone in the river bed.

Gold became the catchcry, 'cross this wild and rugged land,
Luring thousands to Otago, keen to join the digger band.

Chorus Some came from California and some from Melbourne town,
     A few would make their fortune, while some would surely drown.

They flocked to Tuapeka, pick and shovel in their hand,
Ill prepared to face the winter as they panned the river-sand.

Many came but few got lucky, as they braved the bitter cold,
For they opened up the country, in their fevered search for gold …

from 'Gabriel's Gold' ~ Phil Garland

The mention of 'drowning' in the chorus is a strong reference to what became known as the New Zealand death, with more people dying in that manner than any other in our early history.

It was common knowledge among gold miners, that when they died, they automatically went to Heaven. Logically speaking there came a time when Heaven was chocker-block full of gold miners creating 'merry hell.' St Peter became concerned with the overcrowding and asked one grizzled old-timer if he would start a rumour that gold had been discovered in Hell.

Away went the old-timer and within half-an-hour there was an exodus of gold miners through the Pearly Gates in a downwards direction. St Peter watched the unruly mob pass by until he noticed the same grizzled old-timer in the midst of it all. "What are you doing?" he shouted to the old bloke. "It's only a rumour!"

"Ah well, you never know," replied the old fellow. "There just might be some truth in it after all."

The novelist Ruth Park received a grant from the New Zealand government in the 1950s to assist her research for a novel based on the Otago gold rush of 1863, and this book was published as *One-a-pecker, Two-a-pecker* in 1957. Incredibly it would set the wheels in motion for tracing the 'birth' of what has generally been considered the first authentic New Zealand folk song to come out of the Otago gold rush. The following lines appear in her book — "that other Otago song sung by a young digger" and described thus: "It is a sad song and the young digger made it sound sadder, for he was far from home and not more than a lad. We joined in the chorus, singing soft and low…."

One-a-pecker, two-a-pecker, bright fine gold,
Spend it in the summer and you die in the cold,
It cannot light a lantern, nor ever ease a pain,
And yet we go on searching, tho' we search in vain.

One a pecker, two-a-pecker, send me home,
To my sweetheart waiting far across the foam.
I'm weary of Otago, I'm weary of the snow,
But let me make one lucky strike, before I go.

One-a-pecker, two-a-pecker, years go by,
All the gold I'll ever find is in the sky.
Some are sons of fortune, but I have come to see,
There's riches in the river but they're not for me.

Someone in their wisdom must have thought they had discovered a genuine folk song and a good one at that (which it most certainly is) for in very short time it had appeared on record and in print as follows:

Bright fine gold, bright fine gold,
One-a-pecker, two-a-pecker, bright fine gold.

Spend it in the winter or die in the cold,
One-a-pecker, two-a-pecker, bright fine gold.

Some are sons of fortune and my man came to see,
But the riches in the river are not for such as he.

> I'm weary of Otago, I'm weary of the snow,
> Let my man strike it rich and then we'll go…

The folk process had certainly been at work, for lines had been altered to suit the gender of the singer. When the Song Spinners first recorded it back in the early 1960s **Lorna McLeod** sang the song. For the next few years it was introduced by many singers as a traditional New Zealand song from the Otago goldfields. A couple of years later I chanced upon a book *The West Coast Gold Rushes* by Philip Ross May, who mentions the song and interestingly states that the verse "Gold, gold, fine bright gold — Wangapeka, Tuapeka, bright red gold" is frequently misquoted as "One-a-pecker, Tuapeka", further stating that "Crosbie Ward may have been the author of the original. Research led me to discover that Crosbie Ward in his capacity as editor of the *Lyttelton Times* in the early 1860s did indeed publish this verse, while musing that: "Mothers may soon be singing their babies to sleep with the following words…"

When gold was discovered at the Wangapeka Valley in Nelson province in 1861, some three hundred miners pegged claims, but no sooner had this field settled down than news of the rush to Gabriel's Gully in the Tuapeka district of Otago filtered through. A large migration south gave rise to the Crosbie Ward verse, where 'red' probably referred to the gold bearing quartz at Wangapeka, which had a reddish tinge to it.

Subsequent research by Frank Fyfe and me uncovered many versions of the song. Folk process played a strong part in the changes, with a variant of this chorus being sung as a lullaby in the 1890s and well into the 1930s. It was probably during this time that the chorus, with its wide currency, became a schoolyard skipping rhyme chanted to the tune of 'Hot Cross Buns'. We have traced this rhyme to various schools from Auckland down to Southland, documenting former pupils who could remember singing it in the school playground up to the 1950s.

Frank Fyfe contacted Ruth Park in Australia, who told him that she only had the chorus to go by when she started and wrote two of the verses for the song herself, while her husband Darcy Niland wrote the other. The song as it stands today is a good example of creative folk process at work, adapting and gathering extra verses from various people — Park, Niland, Neil Colquhoun and others — to give us an outstandingly evocative song.

The following lyrics 'Looking for the Yeller' were collected from Betty Manufui by members of the Auckland branch of New Zealand Folklore Society.

> Hey boys, look around but you won't find Johnny,
> He'll not be coming in here as he did of old.
> Hey boys, say, where's our old mate Johnny,
> He's gone to Gabriel's Gully to look for gold.

Johnny's gone, he's looking for the yeller,
He's got that fatal fever in his head.
All he sees before his eyes are those little lumps of yeller,
So have a drink for Johnny, 'cos he might as well be dead …

When I was field collecting in Otago in 1969, Syd Stevens in Alexandra presented me with the next piece of verse, which expresses the sentiments of an impending gold rush extremely well. I have used it as a spoken introduction to 'Bright Fine Gold' ever since.

A flash in the pan, a glint of gold,
A shift of sand, a story told.
A rumour that swells and grows and grows,
A strike! A strike! A fabulous strike!
Where is it? Where is it? Nobody knows,
Excepting perhaps it's probably down
At Hamiltons, Styx or Hartley town.
Or maybe it's Hyde or Skippers or Blacks,
But meanwhile ten thousand men are out on the track,
Searching, searching, searching,
A flash in the pan has bid us stray,
Over the hills and far away.

The gold rushes spread rapidly throughout Central Otago, moving from Tuapeka to the Dunstan (near Cromwell on the Clutha River) and onwards to the Arrow, Bendigo and Cardrona fields, before the fever lost its impetus in 1863–64.

There beside the Arrow River, I saw the years roll back,
Saw the first of Arrow's miners tramp the old time river track,
Saw the gold rush in the glory of the days of long ago,
'Neath the backdrop of the mountains in the brilliant summer's glow.

Saw that band of miners toiling, saw the comradeship and strife,
That made old Arrow's history, made the story of its life.
Saw the troopers riding escort as the gold coach clattered nigh,
Wealth of Arrow proudly guarding, as they did in days gone by.

from 'Wheels of Arrow' ~ Tod Symons

Life on the Otago goldfields was extremely hard, especially in winter. New Zealand's worst snowstorm on record took place in July 1863, with blizzard conditions atop the Old Man Range. Hundreds of miners perished up there and folklore has it that the only survivors were those who cut open their horses, gutted them and crawled inside the carcasses to keep warm. Once the thaw came, hundreds more perished as the rivers and streams flooded and carried their bodies out to sea. This terrible event is commemorated by a stone cairn near Gorge Creek and in an evocative ballad 'The Tents of Chamounix' by Tod Symons.

Where the Gorge Creek flows, where the tea-tree grows,
Near the highway where all can see,
There's a cairn of stone that stands alone,
Where once stood Chamounix.
'Tis simple and plain but it tells of pain
And death, by that quiet stream,
Where it marks the end that fate can send,
The end of a miner's dream…

Paul Metsers also mentions the big storm in his 'Farewell to the Gold':

Shotover River your gold it is waning,
It's weeks since the colour I've seen,
But it's no use just sitting and Lady Luck blaming,
I'll pack up and make the break clean.

Chorus Farewell to the gold that never I found,
Farewell to the nuggets that somewhere abound.
For it's only when dreaming that I see you gleaming,
Down in the dark deep underground.

We sluiced and we cradled for day after day,
With hardly enough to get by,
When a terrible flood swept poor Jimmy away,
During six stormy days in July…

The Otago goldfields began to lose their lustre in late 1864 as the Depression set in and disillusioned diggers made arrangements to leave the country. On cue, however, came news of fresh rushes in West Canterbury and an exodus swiftly followed.

When I came and took up my claim, well Bill Muggins was my name,
Although I'm a young man and able, here I'm stuck a-rocking the cradle.

Chorus But I'm a wake up, I will break up, I'm never more going to roam.
I've panned in my dug-out, with never a nugget,
I'm packing my things to go home.

I've hunted Otago for gold, in the wind and the rain and the cold.
And I've holed up all winter under the snow, all along the winding Molyneux,
And that is where you need to have holed.

In those shanties where you spin, away all your hard earned tin.
Nancy's smiles are quite beguiling, that's why Nancy's always smiling.
Landlord says he's not taking you in.

'Packing my Things' - Anon

Gold mining continued to make its mark throughout Otago, using dredging and stamper batteries well into the 1890s. The signs can be seen over a hundred

Cairn at Gorge Creek commemorating men who lost their lives on the Old Man Range, Central Otago, in the blizzard of 1863.

years later, with history and tourism fast becoming the new gold in Otago. In 1984 the Department of Conservation opened the Otago Goldfields Park, preserving twenty-four varied sites from further deterioration and making them available to visitors. Television New Zealand, in conjunction with the Department of Conservation, produced a publicity film about the park and its importance in the overall scheme of things, which necessitated filming at different times of the year. I took part in this film as an actor and musician, and during stints between filming I was able to research and compose a couple of songs, both of which — 'Hillsides of Bendigo' and 'Kawarau Gold' — were filmed on location and included on the soundtrack. Here's verses from the latter:

> We'll sing of Moonlight and Molyneux, Shotover River so cold,
> Of Skippers and rugged Cromwell Gorge, of Clyde and Kawarau gold,
> Of Clyde and Kawarau gold.
>
> The diggers came from near at hand and far across the sea,
> In search of gold and wealth untold, chasing the miner's dream,
> Chasing the miner's dream…
>
> The years have washed their claims away, there's nought but just a trace,
> All else is past and gone it seems save some tailing and a water race,
> Save some tailings and a water race.
>
> Seasons come and seasons go, the years have taken their toll,
> Where heaps of rubble and stone remain, only sheep and rabbits will go,
> Only sheep and rabbits will go.
>
> Tinkers, Drybread and Bendigo, Macetown and Blackstone Hill,
> They are no more, wealth beyond recall, but their memory is living still,
> Their memory is living still.

Rona Bailey came across 'The Lonely Digger' in her southern travels in the 1950s, the song of an old miner reminiscing about the time he spent searching for gold.

> I'm heartsick and tired of struggle and strife,
> As my thoughts drift back to the twilight of life.
> Those grand days, the brave days of not long ago,
> When we hurled the old banjos for weeks to and fro.

It's the music that haunts me wherever I go,
It's the barracking laughter of the diggers you know,
Against luck on the gold we didn't play a lone hand,
But we studied the butcher and grocer the grand.

So the ones who won't give the diggers a show,
Are not to be mentioned down here you know.

Alexandra poet Tod Symons tells it as it really is, especially for anyone who has ever spent time goldmining and believes that they still know a place. It's entitled 'A Prospecting Man' and dedicated to his old mate Syd Stevens.

Let me go where the wanderlust wills me,
Let me tramp with a shovel and pan.
Where I fossicked for gold as a young bloke,
For at heart I'm a prospecting man.

Once you have searched for that metal,
Once you've seen bright gold gleam in the pan,
As you loused over gully and creek bed,
You're forever a prospecting man.

Now my family need me no longer,
They've grown up and all gone away,
They've kids of their own, kids like they were,
And I'm nearing the end of my day.

For you never just know when you're digging,
You never just know what you'll get,
Why I might strike it rich! Start a gold rush,
For there's gold in those Central hills yet.

In those mountains I knew as a young bloke,
Every bluff, every gully and track,
I get a strange kind of feeling,
That somehow they'd know I was back.

So I'd like to go out just this last time,
To see what an old bloke can do,
Just to wander around and try places,
And my needs are simple and few.

Some tools and a pack full of tucker,
A billy, a pot and a pan,
Then I'll go where the wanderlust wills me,
For at heart I'm a prospecting man.

The last word goes to Henry Scott, who wrote these verses in a letter back in 1873, while looking back on his years searching for gold in Central Otago. He obviously enjoyed the life, despite not 'making his pile'. It would seem that he felt camaraderie was the real bounty to be found on the diggings — a philosophy that I've found not uncommon for the time. The text for this song comes courtesy of John A Lee:

I might have been rich had I wanted the gold,
Instead of the friendships I've made,
I might have had fame had I wanted renown,
Instead of the hours I've played.
Now I'm standing today on the far edge of life,
And I'm just looking backward to see,
What I've done with the days and the years that were mine,
And all that has happened to me.

I haven't built much of a fortune to leave,
To those who shall carry my name,
And nothing I've done will entitle me here,
To a place on the tablets of fame.
But I've loved the great skies and their spaces of blue,
I've lived with the birds and the trees,
I've turned down the splendour of silver and gold,
To share in such pleasures as these.

I've given my time to the making of friends,
Together we've worked and we've played,
And I wouldn't recall the glad hours spent with them,
For the money that might have been made.
I chose to be known to be loved by the few,
And was deaf to the plaudits of men,
And I'd make the same choice should the chance come to me,
To live my life over again.

I've lived amongst friends and I've shared in their joys,
Known sorrow with all of its tears.
I've harvested much from my acres of life,
Though some say I've squandered my years.
But much that is fine has been mine to enjoy,
And I hope that I've lived to my best,
I have no regrets as I'm nearing the end,
For the gold that I might have possessed.

'No Regrets' ~ Henry Scott

Sheet music cover, circa 1868. The nom de plume Y.T. Mata is a is a play on 'Waitemata'. Lithograph, hand-coloured.

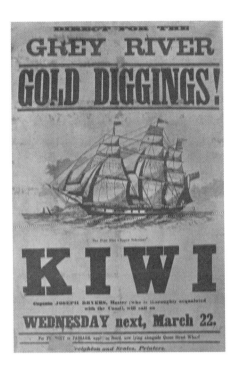

IV

THE GOLDEN WEST

West Coast gold rushes

THE WEST CANTERBURY GOLDFIELDS, as they were originally known, are a typical rags-to-riches story of a lonely, desolate and unwanted wilderness rocketing to fame and fortune virtually overnight. Until the eve of its gold rush, the West Coast had failed to attract European settlers, despite early reports of gold traces in its rivers. This apparent lack of interest was due to the area's situation and isolation — from snowline to seashore it was clad in almost impenetrable rainforest and native bush. Overland routes were long and rugged, the rivers were treacherous and the climate offered little encouragement.

Fewer than a hundred Maori lived on the Coast, along with a few hardy explorers and a handful of miners who had gained a precarious foothold in the Buller district in 1861. Prospects for colonisation were poor until 1864, when news of payable gold was broken to the world. In January that year two Maori men discovered coarse gold near the Taramakau River while searching for greenstone — pounamu.

Their chief travelled to Westport to get tools to split the stone and mentioned the gold they had seen to two Pakeha friends. Excitedly the friends journeyed to the Taramakau, soon striking good gold. Adhering to the unwritten code of the early diggers, they returned to Westport to spread the news and round up a few of their mates. The West Coast gold rush was under way.

> Off to the diggings, we're leaving today,
> From all walks of life we come,
> There's new chums and old, chasing after the gold,
> Who'll soon be humping the drum.
>
> Off to the diggings, we're joining the rush,
> To search for the golden ground,
> Come heed the call, there's plenty for all,
> With riches still to be found.
>
> Off to the diggings, we're leaving in droves,
> To see what we can find,
> Taking a chance with no backward glance,
> For the life we're leaving behind …

from 'Off to the Diggings' - Phil Garland

A short time later Albert Hunt found gold at Greenstone Creek, and after informing the authorities in Christchurch returned to the area at the forefront of a new gold rush. The creek supported only three hundred men, however, and towards the end of 1864, with all the good ground taken and pegged out, new arrivals had no choice but to move on in search of new ground. By the end of the year the rush had become a virtual stampede — from Greenstone it spread to the Totara River just south of Hokitika, laying the foundations of what would become the capital of Westland. From here the rush spread onwards to the Taipo and Kapitea Creek, then south again to the Totara River. Hundreds of excited diggers poured into the Coast by land and sea, with the human tide sweeping up the Waimea to Goldsborough and Stafford, then back to Saltwater Creek, German Gully, Maori Gully and Kaniere. This constant movement is aptly summed up in the phrase: "One day it was here, another day it was there!"

> Farewell to the Greenstone diggings, where the winters are hungry and cold,
> And the frost it clings to your whiskers, when the last drop of whisky's been sold.
>
> Farewell to the Totara Valley, where nuggets are still in the ground,
> We've dug till our hands are all blistered, and never a one have we found …
>
> There's few of us made any fortunes, to relieve all the anguish and tears,
> But if friendship and comrades are valued, then we've riches to last us for years.

from 'The Last Drop of Whisky' - Harold Lowe/Sue Allan/Phil Garland

Each new day saw somebody shoulder their swag and head for the hills of some new place or other. Big-name prospectors like Fox and Moonlight were out scouring the countryside for bigger and better fields — any whisper of their success was enough to empty the diggings overnight.

Born in Scotland, George Fairweather Moonlight came to New Zealand via the Californian and Australian gold rushes. He left his mark on the New Zealand landscape, naming mountain ranges, rivers, streams and towns in his travels throughout Otago and Westland. In the spirit of folklore, legends abound as to how he got his name, usually drawing from his propensity for travelling at night. Most notably, however, his integrity was never under question, and the respect accorded his reputation was perhaps his finest memorial.

George arrived in New Zealand in 1861 accompanied by his cousin Tom Moonlight and close friend Jack Tarrant, who would share his life and ultimately meet a similar fate. After finding good gold in Otago, Moonlight left to prospect the Nelson, Buller and Westland diggings, not so much for the gold he might find, but more for his love of adventure. His richest strike was in the Paparoa Ranges. The stream that bears his name to this day, Moonlight Creek, became famous for the size of its nuggets, and the surrounding area was worked well into the 1940s. That district is now called Atarau (the Maori word for moonlight).

After marrying in 1865, George Moonlight built an accommodation house in the nearby Maruia Valley, a store on the Glenroy River and another at Hampden (later renamed Murchison). From Hampden he forayed into the countryside, where he named a number of creeks after rivers he'd known in America. The Shenandoah, Rappahannock and Minnehaha are reminders of his legacy. After his wife died in 1882 and the creditors moved in, Moonlight sold off everything, setting out to recoup his fortune by fossicking once again. It was not to be; he disappeared while on a prospecting trip in the Station Creek area of the Maruia in 1884. After much searching his body was discovered by his old mate Jack Tarrant, down a gully in the heart of beech forest. George Moonlight was buried with his wife in the Nelson cemetery, closing the final chapter on a remarkable life.

'Twas in a valley near Moke Creek,
Large nuggets lay in store,
The romance of that golden dream,
Captured him for ever more.

Gold fever held him in its grip,
Starvation lay in store,
After battling flooding rivers,
He vowed to return once more.

Chorus   Travelling at night and resting by day,
         A wanderlust caused him to stray.
         When darkness fell he'd be on his way,
         Tramping the Moonlight Trail.

At Hokitika George would land,
In the year of sixty-five,
At a place that's known as Atarau,
He made his greatest find …

The news is out, Moonlight is lost,
Near where the Shenandoah stands.
A mate Jack Tarrant found his remains,
Beneath some ferny strands.

His legend lives throughout the land,
Where prospecting deeds abound.
George Moonlight is remembered still,
For the diggings that he found.

from 'The Moonlight Trail'- Phil Garland

After success at Greenstone Creek, Albert Hunt continued to prospect throughout the ranges, with his movements being constantly monitored by the diggers, something he found embarrassing. In March 1866 he returned from a trip to Bruce Bay south of Hokitika, but before he could even lodge a claim for an area round the 'Waitemati' (Black River) a great crowd of diggers headed south, without knowing exactly where they were going. On his return to the district, Hunt was met by five hundred angry men, who demanded that he should lead them to the new ground, threatening to attack him unless he did so. When he replied that he had never led anyone to believe gold was to be found in great quantities, they refused to believe him and took him into custody, believing they might persuade him further in the morning. Somehow he slipped away in the night and made off into the bush. He was never seen again on the Coast, but surfaced later as the probable discoverer of the Shotover Lode at Thames.

For there's gold in the mountains, there's gold in the valleys,
There's gold in the rivers that run to the sea.
Where fortunes are waiting for those who can claim them,
But only misfortune was waiting for me.

I left Christchurch town one fine summer's morning,
Tramped over the mountains to Blackball I came.
Then on to the diggings where they seemed easy pickings,
So it's there I decided to stake my own claim.

When I met her in Charleston, she gave me her favours,
And like a fool I thought I'd make her my wife,
But now to my sorrow and sad lamentation,
She's turned out the curse and plague of my life …

from 'Rocking the Cradle' ~ Phil Garland

New fields appeared thick and fast — Blackball Creek, Moonlight Creek, Red Jacks, No Town, Arnold River, Donaghue's Creek, Bruce Bay, Hunt's Beach, Charleston, Brighton, Addisons Flat, Canoe Creek and Mokihinui. Gold seemed to be everywhere. Even when the main rushes petered out there was still more to come, with the as yet undiscovered reefs of Inangahua, Lyell and the big Kumara gold rush of 1876. The West Coast gold rushes had brought a vigorous, lively population of 30,000 people to an area that had been expected to remain an inhospitable wilderness forever.

A range of devices were used to obtain the gold. The ubiquitous gold pan was always in use, but mainly to find traces and colour before getting on with the real business of mining it properly. The three main devices were the cradle, the long-tom and the sluice box, which proved to be most effective. This was a long, riffled, open-topped box, several of which could be laid in 'strings' or coupled together to prolong the washing process. Once likely dirt had been shovelled into a hopper it was carried down the box by a steady stream of water, with the gold filtering through a sieve to be finally caught by the riffles. The more sophisticated stamper batteries soon came into their own, whereas sluicing and dredging proved to be among the most effective methods — but were particularly destructive of the countryside.

Music and dancing were popular on the goldfields, with orchestras and dancing girls imported at great expense. Any hotel worthy of the name provided entertainment. Merrymaking abounded, with drinking, dancing and the inevitable fights leading to uproarious nights, as often as not with the Inimitable Thatcher at the helm.

Men dressed in style for important concerts, plays, balls and all manner of public functions. Businessmen in natty Victorian suits with top or bun hats mixed with diggers in high crowned hats, bright shirts, neckerchiefs, white moleskin trousers and high boots, finished off by a broad, coloured sash around the waist. Even the nights were colourful with the hotels' big kerosene lamps glowing on the crowded streets, the bellman parading up and down proclaiming the latest news and items of interest. Gamblers wagered their gold in the casinos, horses fidgeted at the hitching rails, coaches, buggies and horse trams rattled in and out of the darkness. The bustling scene was completed by ladies strolling in their crinolines alongside the men in their colourful finery, as described in 'Shanties by the Way'. This song began life as a poem 'The Public by the Way', written in Australia by EJ Overbury. It found its way to New Zealand and underwent considerable transformation by the miners, evolving into a song that became as typical of Hokitika as 'Oh Susanna' was of the California gold rush of 1849.

It's in a first rate business section,
Where four bush roads cross and meet,
It stands in a quiet and neat direction,
To rest the weary travellers' feet.

Kerosene lamps are shining brightly,
Cards and lo the billiard balls,
Men and maids are dancing lightly,
To the music inside those walls.

Rows of bottles standing upright,
Labelled with bright blue and gold,
Beer so cold it needs no icing,
From the cellar's drear dark hold …

from 'Shanties by the Way' – Anon

By the time Charles Thatcher arrived in Hokitika it was one of the busiest towns in New Zealand, and certainly one of the most exciting and colourful. Early impressions describe it as "the most rising place on Earth" at the height of its boom days. It exploded into existence from a 'stick and calico' tent and flax-hut village into a town of over a hundred pubs and six thousand people in less than two years. Life and entertainment on the goldfields revolved around the stores and hotels, where the prosperity of a new community was measured by the number of stores and shanties that sprang up in the camp or town. Diggers were such a transient bunch, and store-owners and hotel-keepers were often of a similar character.

Where the gold goes, there goes I!

Buildings were insubstantial — frequently just a 10 × 12 tent would be sufficient to acquire a licence to sell spirits, whenever a new camp was founded. In the more permanent towns elaborate hotels were built, with many bearing ornate wooden frontages that hid canvas or corrugated iron frames behind. Some of these hotels didn't stay in business long, being sold off cheaply with the gradual decline of mining camps and boom towns, while a host of others were simply abandoned to the ravages of time and nature.

On Mulligan's Flat in '65, stood the store of Scarcity Sam,
Who earned his name from the motley crowd that clamoured for rice and jam,
And most of the things a digger needs when toiling with bar and pick,
When men go mad with the lust for gold and the chance to get rich quick.

Now Scarcity Sam was a wily bird and spoke with an oily tongue,
He would laugh the loudest of everyone whenever a joke was sprung.

So, when Carraway Bob from Pegleg Creek came in for a case of meat,
He backed and filled in his jovial style and shuffled on clumsy feet.

So he weighed Bob up with his crafty eyes and said, "Well, Bob, my lad
I've almost run out of meat this week, there's not a case to be had,
But I'll give you a couple of tins, perhaps to keep you on the job,
But as everything now is in short supply, the price has gone up a bob.

Bob threw the tins in an onion bag, then bolted without a stop,
To give advice to the boys in camp, "You'd better get in for your chop
Old Scarcity Sam has run out of grub, but I've got two tins of meat,
You'd better make tracks for the store at once or you won't get a thing to eat."

In '69 the field went bung and the diggers all moved on, broke,
But Scarcity Sam had a wad so big it would make an old hippo choke.
And when he was asked how he made his pile, he just blinked a bleary eye
And said "If you want to get rich like me, pretend there's a short supply."

'Scarcity Sam' – Denis Hogan

The diggers' main amusements were found at the shanties and often, because there were few women in those early days, men had to dance with one another, as recorded by George Preshaw in *Banking Under Difficulties or Life on the Goldfields*. A full description is in Chapter x, 'Clear the Board'.

Among the many combination hotel/dancehalls in Hokitika stood the notorious Casino de Venise, which held an irresistible attraction for hundreds of diggers, mainly because of the dance girls who added colour and gaiety to the nightlife of the place. These girls received a percentage of what their partners spent, keeping them in demand at the different hotels, which offered all kinds of inducements to increase their patronage. Most of the girls came from Australia, with some enticed from homes in Sydney and Melbourne by offers of good jobs, only to find on reaching Hokitika the true purpose of their employment.

The arrival of a new batch of dance girls was an event of great interest and each landing attracted a large crowd of men. The new women were eagerly sought after marriage by well-to-do diggers and townsmen alike. In fear of what the future held, many accepted proposals, while others flouted their contracts and sought and found domestic or bar duties. The less fortunate were trapped and forced into leading a night life until they were able to break away from their associations. Money came easily, with the hotels, dancing halls and theatres being the only source of amusement. Expensive presents to pretty barmaids or dance girls lightened the purses of hundreds of carefree, prosperous diggers and local businessmen.

There once was miner by name Davy Gray,
Who rode into town with the pile that he'd made,
The bank was the first place he headed straight'way,
To cash in his fortune for sport and for play …

To the pub for a drink, Davy quick made his way,
With a smile on his face and a gleam in his eye.
As he entered Kitty tossed him a beckoning glance,
So he quickly walked over and asked her to dance.

She accepted with pleasure and tipped him the wink,
Soon Davy was ordering drink after drink.
Before the night ended he'd slipped to the floor,
While Kitty emptied his pockets and fled through the door.

Next morning he woke feeling crook in the head,
The landlord was standing right next to the bed.
'Tis a fortune you owe me for last night's display,
And I'll be calling the sergeant unless you can pay.

Davy searched though his pockets then let a groan,
That lassie had left him not one single coin,
The landlord as promised sent for the law,
Who arrested and dragged Davy out through the door.

from Ross Gore's
*It Happened in
New Zealand.*

Now all you young fellows take a warning by me,
If you cash in your pile don't go out on the spree.
Or else you'll regret it and lose all your pay,
To end up in gaol just like old Davy Gray.

from the 'Ballad of Davy Gray' ~ Phil Garland

Eventually central government moved to forbid the employment of females to dance or act as escorts on licensed premises.

News of fresh finds in the Grey Valley caused a stampede as diggers rushed northwards from Hokitika, travelling to Maori and Red Jack's gullies. In the twinkling of an eye the sea beach became a congested highway of diggers, drays and packhorses all heading from Hokitika to the Grey. The exodus was keenly felt in the town and the business community suffered accordingly. With harsh prospects now facing them, it was time to move on, with Thatcher having his say yet again:

The cry is now 'Rush Ho' and away the diggers go,
Tramping to the northward now they make their way.
And when good news it comes down, we must hook it from this town,
To build another city for Thatcher at the Grey.

from 'Cheer Boys Cheer' ~ Charles Thatcher

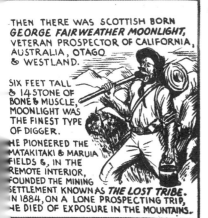

THEN THERE WAS SCOTTISH BORN *GEORGE FAIRWEATHER MOONLIGHT,* VETERAN PROSPECTOR OF CALIFORNIA, AUSTRALIA, OTAGO & WESTLAND.

SIX FEET TALL & 14 STONE OF BONE & MUSCLE, MOONLIGHT WAS THE FINEST TYPE OF DIGGER. HE PIONEERED THE MATAKITAKI & MARUIA FIELDS &, IN THE REMOTE INTERIOR, FOUNDED THE MINING SETTLEMENT KNOWN AS *THE LOST TRIBE.* IN 1884, ON A LONE PROSPECTING TRIP, HE DIED OF EXPOSURE IN THE MOUNTAINS.

PRESHAW WOULD OFTEN TRAVEL MILES ALONE, AT NIGHT, THROUGH DANGEROUS COUNTRY, CARRYING 3 OR 4 HUNDRED OZ. OF GOLD.

ONCE WHEN HE LOST 35 OZ. OF DUST, THE BIG HEARTED CITIZENS OF THE COAST CLUBBED TOGETHER TO MAKE UP THE £140 SHORTAGE.

BUT THE BANK INSISTED ON *STANDING THE LOSS.* THOSE WERE THE DAYS WHEN MEN WERE *MEN* & BANKERS WERE *HUMAN.*

ROSS GORE.

The year 1866 saw the area between Westport and Greymouth attracting plenty of attention, as new fields opened up at Nine Mile Beach, Blackball, Addisons, Brighton, Charleston, Canoe Creek and Barrytown. Here it is my intention to concentrate primarily on Charleston, which generated considerable interest through song and reminiscences.

At the height of its popularity Charleston boasted twenty stores, three churches, three breweries, three banks, a casino and over two hundred houses, with a population of one thousand and a further three thousand living close by in the diggings surrounding the town. Throughout Charleston's 'golden' existence Constant Bay was a regular port of call for a direct sea link with Australia via Melbourne. Today Charleston is a shadow of its former glory, with just one hotel, a few houses and holiday homes and an old cemetery.

The golden rush to Greenstone has seen the last of me,
I've joined the rush towards the north to dig the rich Pakihi,
To dig the rich Pakihi m'boys, to Charleston I have come,
To see if I could learn the way to beat the Charleston Drum, m'boys,
To beat the Charleston Drum.

I stepped ashore at Constant Bay and there to my amaze,
A township in the wilderness met my astonished gaze.
A sight of eighty pubs or more was like to strike me dumb,
But diggers are a thirsty mob who beat the Charleston Drum, m'boys,
Who beat the Charleston Drum …

from 'The Charleston Drum' ~ Alwyn Owen

Gold at Charleston was originally found on the terraces directly behind the town and in the pakihi (swampy flat) area, which was quite rich as diggings go. An early strike was at Dirty Mary's Creek. This name, a corruption of Mary's dirty creek, is said to have arisen from a complaint lodged by an accommodation house proprietor, Mary Boyle, when her creek was fouled with mud and slush from the mine workings. More Charleston gold was found in the black sand of old beaches, mostly now high above sea level. The iron sands had hardened into cement, which had to be crushed to a powder, giving rise to the stamping batteries that now came into their own. A stamping battery consisted of one or more heavy iron stampers or heads lifted by a camshaft, which let them fall on the solid mass or quartz, in which gold was also found. The powdered residue was mixed with water and passed over a riffle box or a set of gold tables to extract the gold. The noise of the batteries was enough to wake the dead:

I stood there on the beach m'boys and heard a fearful sound,
That rolled like thunder round the hills and echoed through the town.
I asked a digger what was the noise that seemed to throb and hum,
Why that's the centre battery, we call the Charleston Drum, m'boys,
We call the Charleston Drum.

From Charleston through to Addisons you'll hear the drummers play,
A hundred stamper batteries are working night and day.
In Candlelight and Kynnesley there's gold for all who come,
To set up a camp and boxing to beat the Charleston Drum, m'boys,
To beat the Charleston Drum.

I joined a band of diggers, who worked some likely ground,
And nigh five miles of flume we built to bring the water down.
It ran into a raging flood from here to kingdom come,
For water-wheels are thirsty things that beat the Charleston Drum, m'boys,
That beat the Charleston Drum.

from 'The Charleston Drum' ~ Alwyn Owen

The focal point of the town was the huge European Hotel, a notorious palace of pleasure featuring a large, well-patronised ballroom. The town lasted longer than many other boom towns mainly because of its hotel and the accessibility of Constant Bay. At the height of Charleston's popularity it was actually considered a promotion for Bank of New Zealand employees to be transferred there from Wellington.

The multi-storeyed European Hotel was one of the largest edifices in the Southern hemisphere and outlasted everything in the town — one hundred years before the licence lapsed it had already become an important halfway house between Westport and Greymouth. The building finally succumbed to the ravages of climate, nature and disrepair in the 1960s. The town is commemorated in Peter Cape's evocative poem, 'The Stable Lad', which I set to music:

> When Cobb & Co ran coaches from the Buller to the Grey
> I went for a livery stable lad in a halt up Westport way
> I gave my heart to a red-haired girl and left it where she lay
> By the rolling Westland highway from the Buller to the Grey
>
> I've neatsfoot on my fingers and I've lampblack on my face
> And I've saddlesoaped the harness and I've hung each piece in place
> But my heart's not in the stable, it's in Charleston far away
> Where Cobb & Co goes rolling by from Buller to the Grey
>
> There's a red-haired girl in Charleston and she's dancing in the bar
> But I know she's not like other girls who dance where Coasters are
> I can't forget her eyes and all the things they seem to say
> That day I rode with Cobb & Co to Buller from the Grey
>
> There's a schooner down from Murchison, I hear it in the gorge
> I'll have to blow the bellows now and redden up the forge
> I'm going to strike that iron so hard, she'll hear it far away
> In the roaring European, that the road runs by to Grey
>
> One day I'll be a teamster with the ribbons in my fist
> And I'll drive a Cobb & Co express through rain and snow and mist
> Drive four-in-hand to Charleston, and no matter what they say
> I'll take my dear up on the box and marry her in Grey!
>
> They've a graveyard down in Charleston, and the moss trails from the tree
> And the Westerlies come moaning in from off the Tasman Sea
> There they laid my red-haired sweetheart in a pit of yellow clay
> As Cobb & Co went rolling by from Buller to the Grey

Local West Coast historian Les Wright dispelled my notions about the accuracy of Peter's song when he told me that the road from Westport to Greymouth was not fully completed until 1929. Apparently the coach could only travel as far as Charleston — if it wanted to go through to Greymouth, it had to come through

The European Hotel, built in 1867 at Charleston on the West Coast.
Photographer unidentified, Alexander Turnbull Library F11550 ¹/₂

the Buller gorge and take the inland route. Les loves the song regardless and I'm more than happy to go along with Peter's poetic licence.

Gold rushes are notorious for attracting men of all kinds and scruples and the West Coast was no exception. Four men in particular, Kelly, Burgess, Levy and Sullivan (all ex-Australian convicts) formed themselves into a gang of bushrangers for the express purpose of robbing miners returning from the diggings. This proved to be a most successful exercise on more than one occasion, until they were finally apprehended at Nelson in 1866 — see the story of the Maungatapu Murderers in Chapter VII, 'Crooks and Nannies'.

Gold, and the lust for it, turned the West Coast into a settled district in less than three years. The gold is still there — witness the gold dredge on the Taramakau and the occasional 'hatter' working in the dense bush.

They had come in their thousands, heeding the call — English, Irish, Scots, Americans, French, Swiss, Germans, Australians, Maori and Chinese — as cosmopolitan a crew as you'd find anywhere. The diggers themselves, the publicans, ferrymen, rogues and vagabonds, dancing girls, sea captains, troopers, roadmakers, coach drivers and many more, were probably the most skilled body of immigrants New Zealand had ever seen. When the gold waned in the 1870s (aside from the last great rush at Kumara in 1876) the golden decade was all but over and many left our shores, chasing that elusive pot of gold elsewhere. Others, however, stayed on to help settle the region and thus Westland was born. Few areas have had such a wild, short-lived and riotous beginning, but a stable district grew, achieving separate political recognition and inheriting a sense of history that would be the envy of many for years to come.

> It's just as you say I'm off once more,
> The Palmer River that's my way.
> I landed here in sixty-four,
> That's ten years struggle along the Grey.
>
> Ten long years since I landed here,
> In a trackless land of wet and cold.
> Some of our lives were pretty severe,
> But who lacks hardship, looking for gold.
>
> Latterly gold has been hard to find,
> I've enough to carry me, none to spend,
> Going away and leaving behind,
> Not one deserving the name of friend.
>
> Now the ground was pretty near duffering out,
> When Bill, my mate, he says to me,
> "There's gold at the Palmer, beyond all doubt,
> So here's for sailing over the sea."

There's the whistle, a drink before we part,
A step to the corner, I hear you say.
My last on the Coast with all my heart,
Mine's brandy straight then I'm away.

Here's a long farewell to the old West Coast,
With a heart prepared for whatever I find.
"Success to the Palmer", is that your toast?
Mine's — "Here's to the land I'm leaving behind."

'The Digger's Farewell'/'Farewell to the Grey' ~ Anon

Charles Thatcher

V

THE INIMITABLE THATCHER

Goldfields balladeer

> Oh, the golden land of Otago,
> There's plenty of gold, so I've been told,
> In the golden land of Otago.

THIS WAS THE SENTIMENT OF SHIPLOADS OF DIGGERS as they arrived at Dunedin in early 1862. Fresh from the Victorian goldfields, they came in their thousands to boost the already bursting town to overflowing.

The muddy streets were soon crowded with diggers, dressed in red Crimean shirts and white moleskins, intermingling with soldiers of the 70th regiment in their bright red uniforms, and policemen clothed in blue, all adding to the vibrancy of the scene. A motley collection of clerks, sailors, wharfies, and customhouse officers joined the teeming multitude, excited by the prospect of easy money. The discovery of gold in Central Otago had caused Dunedin to become a bustling metropolis almost overnight, with Manse Street playing host to shops and cafés, barbers and jewellers, all busily plying their trade. As evening fell the criers would announce the entertainment at theatres and hotels.

These would be the sights greeting goldfields entertainer Charles Robert Thatcher upon his arrival at Dunedin in February 1862. The 'Inimitable' Thatcher had already built a reputation for his improvisational burlesque and seemingly inexhaustible repertoire of topical songs in Australia and he wasted no time in establishing himself at Dunedin's Theatre Royal.

Thatcher was born in Bristol in 1831, the son of a natural history collector, growing up in Brighton when his family moved there shortly after his birth. He left home at sixteen, seeking work as a flautist in London theatre orchestras during the rise of music hall entertainment which incorporated singing, dancing, comedy, acrobatics and novelty acts. There he was exposed to all the variety London had to offer, including the street broadside hawkers and unsparing satirists, who poked fun at all classes and creeds without fear or favour. Topicality was profit and ballads were often written, printed and sung within the space of an hour. Thatcher came to know London's theatre world well and music hall showed him how to divert his fellows from their everyday cares, setting him up with a profession that would offer fame, fortune and the adventure of a lifetime.

When news of the Victorian gold rush filtered through to London, the prospect of easy money tempted the young Thatcher, so he set sail for Australia. It was 1853 but Thatcher's luck was out, for no claim yielded him any satisfaction. He needed money and set about returning to his profession as a musician, drawing on his London experience. Bendigo's night life was in need of decent entertainment, so Thatcher established himself in the Royal Victorian Theatre. A keen observer of life, he wrote topical songs set to popular tunes and presented them with great success. His songs about life on the goldfields became a major attraction and as his fame grew he was able to appear as an independent and favourite performer at gold rush entertainments throughout Victoria. His songs have come to be regarded as oral history of the times — songs of the people, speaking in the popular voice. The language was the racy speech of the diggers, spiced with words and expressions coined by Thatcher himself. Students of Australian and New Zealand slang would find a rich vein permeating his ballads. His satirical jingles made him a champion of the gold boom as he was dubbed "comic poet of the people."

When Thatcher arrived in Dunedin he became aware of the state of local roads, treacherous morasses of clay in wet weather and generally unlit. The newspaper had already dubbed the place Mud-Edin, so Thatcher attacked the town board:

> The streets here in Dunedin are now a sea of mud,
> This place is very much the same as 'twas before the flood.
> Everything's so primitive, improvement is ignored,
> By that provincial guilded sham — the old town board.
> Just twig them all together and you'll very quickly see,
> It's a nice conglomeration of the old identity,
> And though our filthy highways are much to be deplored,
> You'll get no reparation for the old town board.
>
> Today I had some business, so I walked about the town,
> And it was a blondin' feat to keep myself from going down.
> For many a pedestrian through slipping down was floored,
> And they vented implications at the old town board.

A female too I twigged who was going up the hill,
She slipped so many times there's no doubt she's climbing still,
Upon her latter end no less than three times she was floored,
And she wept and hinted something at Dunedin's town board.

He also performed a song in a similar vein entitled 'Why don't you mend the roads?'

If Thatcher ever coined a phrase it was the 'Old Identity', which became a catchword applied by Victorian immigrants to the more conservative and old-fashioned local settlers. In return the new gold seekers were nicknamed the 'New Iniquity'. Naturally he capitalised on the popularity of this tag at every opportunity, inserting it into many songs, which would ensure their ongoing success. The 'Old Identity' became so popular that local scribe Alex Bathgate later recorded:

When the rush to Hokitika was in full swing, I travelled to Port Chalmers on the 'Golden Age' which was crowded from stem to stern with diggers on their way to the West Coast. An old man with a violin and a woman harpist, who also sang, were on board and after a tune or two, someone called out — "Give the Old Identity." The woman sang Thatcher's song which was greeted with uproarious applause and when the hat was passed round … half-crowns and shillings were showered into it.

After performing in Dunedin for a few months Thatcher decided to visit the goldfields before taking himself off to Christchurch, where his fame had gone before him, so much so that on arrival he was able to increase his fees to three and five shillings. The state of the Bridle Path over the hill into the Heathcote valley immediately gave him material for a new local song 'Over the Hill'.

The Christchurch *Press* duly acknowledged Thatcher's safe arrival and suggested that his entertainments "will be a great addition to the stock of public amusements and we have no doubt that he will meet with a hearty reception and find the people of Canterbury as ready to appreciate his wit and humour as their neighbours in Otago."

Thatcher appeared in the Christchurch Town Hall, a wooden building on High

Street erected in 1857 but destroyed by earthquake in 1869. The hall was used by the provincial government and a covered verandah over the porch held regular sessions of the Supreme Court, but at night the building functioned as the town's entertainment centre. Thatcher's attention was drawn to the comic juxtaposition of courthouse by day and amusement hall by night:

> By day with great solemnity,
> Delinquents here they're bringing,
> But at night how laughable the change —
> With songs this hall is ringing.
>
> But Thatcher on the stage you'll see,
> Presiding 'stead of Gresson [a prominent local judge]
> Not armed with terrors of the law,
> But reading folks a lesson.
>
> Man's laughter is a charge of which
> You're sure to be acquitted.

The Inimitable proved none too popular with the 'Canterbury swells' because according to the *Press* "he cultivates the habit of irreverence to authority."

The *Lyttelton Times* also had a few words to say, noting with disgust that it had "heard men every way worthy of the respect of their fellows, made the subject of coarse and silly jokes and saw them exposed by a practised hand as food for the laughter of fools!"

When the need arose, however, Thatcher could be serious as well. He gave a concert in aid of Lancashire cotton workers thrown out of work as a result of the American Civil War, appealing to the audience thus:

> To save a suffering people from starvation,
> How sad their lot, how fearful their distress,
> By others plunged in grief and wretchedness,
> Willing to toil their sustenance to provide,
> But finding honest toil to them denied.

Wellington was Thatcher's next port of call, and shortly after his arrival he was observed strolling through the streets with notebook in hand, glancing curiously at signboards and passers by. His audience was not disappointed as he delighted all and sundry in his usual telling fashion. The itinerant satirist was on his way, but not before describing Wellington as "the dullest town without exception in New Zealand."

Continuing northwards, Thatcher made a brief visit to Auckland, where his 'locals' were received as always with rapturous applause. Coromandel had been proclaimed a goldfield in June 1862 and came in for his attention as he sang of its attractions in 'The Rush to Coromandel':

Look at the specimens and say what man can be a doubter,
That this goldfield will turn out a regular out-and-outer.
The richest reefs of Bendigo they say can't hold a candle,
Unto the claims of Driving Creek down there at Coromandel.

Although the Coromandel rush was short-lived, its heyday had created prosperity, as many rich pockets were discovered in the vicinity.

Thatcher's arrival in Napier at Christmas 1862 occasioned comment from the Hawkes Bay *Herald*: "The arrival of Mr Thatcher … was quite an event in this dull town of ours … his reputation having gone before him through the medium of the Colonial Press." The *Herald* noted that a rich treat was in store for the people of Napier. Thatcher was into his stride, presenting nightly concerts in the council chamber, where large audiences roared with laughter at his witty allusions to local individuals and events.

The southern goldfields were beckoning, so Thatcher set sail once again towards the El Dorado that was now Central Otago. With the rush at the Dunstan, new fields were opening up and one of the first to be visited by Thatcher was Arrowtown, where he became briefly involved with the notorious Bully Hayes by performing at the opening of his establishment, the Prince of Wales hotel. Across the road stood the Provincial, run by the well-known Buckingham family, and competition for patronage was keen.

Prince of Wales Hotel & Theatre.

Vocal and Instrumental Music every Evening by talented artistes.
W. H. HAYES, Proprietor.

W. H. H. has great pleasure in informing the public that the inimitable Thatcher and Madame Vitelli will shortly make their first appearance in this township, at The " Prince of Wales Hotel".

Harry Redfern had helped discover Arthur's Point on the Shotover River and built the first theatre in Queenstown, the Theatre Royal, with an immense concert room with rough boards for reserved seats and bare ground to stand on for the shilling audience. Here Thatcher began his popular season in March 1863. The Queenstown diggings offered every variety of incident and character to inspire his ballads and ditties. He took it all in as he beheld the great changes the discovery of gold had brought to the hitherto untouched landscape with his song 'Olden Days of Lake Wakatipu':

Gold's a wonderful thing, what a change it can make,
Who'd have thought we should ever have come to this lake.
Like magic there springs up a populous town,
And hundreds to get gold are here settling down.

Oh! How it must knock off his perch, Mister Rees,
To see such a township and buildings like these,
When a few months ago he was here all alone,
And the fact of goldfields near the lake was unknown.

His attention turned to notorious and eccentric scallywags such as Cockatoo Jack and One-Eyed Jimmy, the legendary loafer of the lake, before starting his famous lampooning of the 'Southland Gold Escort'. It was the custom to transport the gold from Queenstown to Dunedin under armed escort, but a group of Southland merchants, envious of Otago's prosperity, decided they wanted a share of the gold. They appointed an agent, Edward Jackson, providing him with a large safe and eight-man escort, and sent him off to Queenstown. The new agent was ignored by virtually everyone on the diggings, where he became a laughing stock, especially when the safe made the long journey to Invercargill under escort, carrying only a few ounces of gold. This was the ideal subject for Thatcher and he lost no time in composing the following ditty. The 'Old Identity' in this case refers to the group of Southland merchants:

The Southland folk are stirring, but they're a deal too slow,
In cutting out Otago they find it is no go.
In vain they send an agent, but slewed he's sure to be,
The diggers all fight shy of the Old Identity.

A large striped tent's erected, a safe stands on the floor,
For fear someone may take it, a trap stands near the door.
But no one lodges gold there in that iron sanctuary,
The agent of the safe smells of the Old Identity.

Invercargill sends an escort of eight men, but I'm told
Sergeant Morton in his pocket could carry all the gold,
And not be incommoded and this escort soon they'll see,
Is a luxury too expensive for the Old Identity.

Now the agent's slowly pining, death will be his doom,
In the safe they can inter him, 'twill make a spacious tomb.
Inscribed upon the big safe at the funeral they'll see,
Sacred to the memory of the Old Identity.

Edward Jackson took exception to this, but remained reasonably calm, despite becoming the ongoing victim of many practical jokes. Thatcher once told him he had discovered an enormous nugget, too large to fit into the safe. When Jackson excitedly asked to see it he was taken to the shores of Lake Wakatipu, where Thatcher pointed out the wreckage of a vessel named the *Nugget*. As if this wasn't enough, Thatcher alleged in another song that the safe was used only for storing potatoes and called Jackson nothing but a potato merchant. This was the last straw — Jackson bailed Thatcher up in the streets of Dunedin and demanded a public apology. Thatcher was a big man (over six feet tall and weighing over sixteen stone) and extremely able with his fists, to which many a heckling digger could attest, so he made ready to settle the dispute on the spot. At this juncture a constable intervened and a court case resulted, ending with Thatcher being fined twenty shillings and costs for insulting language and threatening behaviour. Some 200 people attended the proceedings and afterwards adjourned *en masse* to the Theatre Royal, where Thatcher treated them to a brand new song about the case and Mr Jackson, recouping his fine many times over.

Thatcher returned to Queenstown, where he ran his own pub for a short time before announcing his departure to Australia, sailing for Melbourne in mid-1863. He would not be away for long. Christmas that year found him back in New Zealand for a second tour of duty, travelling throughout the country before finally arriving back in Dunedin in early 1864. His appearances at the Union Hotel in Stafford Street once again gained him tremendous popularity.

He stayed here until 1865, when news about the discovery of gold on the West Coast arrived. The rushes were on once again and Thatcher lost no time in joining the exodus from Otago. 'Cheer boys cheer', he wrote:

> Cheer boys cheer, a stunning goldfield's started,
> Round upon the West Coast there's golden ground for miles.
> Good news for the diggers, so don't you be down-hearted,
> Take your passage now and go and make your pile.
>
> Lots of your mates such letters now are writing,
> Telling you to come and declaring it will pay,
> And in flattering terms you fellows are inviting
> To pitch into the gullies and make your ounce a day.

Men were leaving Otago in droves heading for the new diggings at Okitiki (as it was known) and a seething mass of humanity was gearing up to follow, as Thatcher captured in 'The Rush to Okitiki':

> The diggers are coming down each day,
> And at night to us a visit they pay,
> And then they all get under way,
> And start for Okitiki.
>
> Each old tub, you know
> Is advertised to go,
> I fancy they'll be a month or so,
> In reaching Okitiki.
>
> Six bailiffs here so I've heard say,
> Were watching on the wharf today,
> To see no debtors went away,
> On the sly to Okitiki.
>
> And we'll get rid, oh what a treat,
> Of the girls who live in Walker Street,
> They'll leave that classical retreat,
> For the diggings of Okitiki.

And that nice French gal,
Along with her pal,
Will find it beneficial,
To go to Okitiki.
A nice cigar shop they'll begin,
And return and tell us with a grin,
We've made bon grand lot of tin,
At the diggings of Okitiki.

Thatcher followed his own advice and left for the new diggings in May 1865, travelling on the *Wakool*, an unseaworthy steamer which broke in two just off Okitiki, fortunately without loss of life. The passengers had to wade ashore minus their luggage, something that annoyed Thatcher no end but provided a couple of excellent songs for his opening concert at the Corinthian Hall.

The West Coast puts folks in a fright
It slews them when they first catch sight
Of the sand.

Awful terrified they are,
When the steamer bumps the bar,
On the sand.

Chorus Hurrah for Hokitika
Oh-hi-oh
They look very blue and they're all wet through
When they land at Hokitika

It puts the new chum in despair,
It costs a deal for living there,
On the sand.

In every blessed thing you eat,
No matter whether bread or meat,
You've the sand.

Chorus Farewell to Hokitika
Oh-hi-oh
Now is it not a charming spot,
Farewell to Hokitika.

'Experiences of Hokitika'

By the time Thatcher arrived, Hokitika was one of the busiest towns in the country, if not the most vivid, vigorous and colourful. The 'Inimitable' lost no time including his arrival experiences into three songs entitled 'Experience of Hokitika', each one sung to a different air.

To the West, to the West where the diggers repair,
There's no flies about it, the gold is all there.
And chaps who've been digging a very short while,
Walk into the bank and dispose of their pile.

Where the rain falls in torrents and leaves such a flood,
And you sleep on the ground and your mattress is mud.
When a fresh in the river may come down some day,
And very near sweep Hokitika away.

To the West, to the West, where the ships run ashore,
Of wrecks we have witnessed two dozen or more.
Where bushrangers are many, as you've been told,
And simple bank clerks are deprived of their gold.

Where beef's eighteen pence and where diggers devour
Rusty bacon and bread made of vile damaged flour.
How pleasant in Nelson to get a nice rest,
'stead of knocking it out in the land of the West.

The Corinthian, or Thatcher's Gall as it became known, was a large building of galvanised iron without floorboards or seating, A stage stood at one end, while bars occupied each corner of the room. Two bellmen tramped the streets advertising Thatcher's concerts by shouting "Roll up! Roll up! A new local from the Inimitable". Admission was one shilling and all drinks (hard or soft) cost the same. For three months Thatcher performed in Hokitika to packed houses, causing a Christchurch newspaper to sneer at everything he did and what they called "a noisy, dirty, drinking, smoking, cursing crowd", going on to slate the Corinthian Hall as "an immense stall for horses or asses." Thatcher replied thus:

The awful correspondent of the *Canterbury Times*,
It seems has got an awful down on Thatcher's vulgar rhymes.
He gave this hall a rare rub up and the audience he vowed,
Was a regular noisy, dirty, drinking, smoking, cursing crowd.

My word I've got a character, by jingo so have you,
A pretty mob I'm singing to, if what he says is true,
According to this scribbling cove I really should be proud,
To sing to a noisy, dirty, drinking, smoking, cursing crowd.

According to a story recounted by Bert Roth in a 1950s *Joy* magazine, it seems that when Thatcher decided to leave the West Coast and visit Wellington once again, the reception afforded him while visiting Parliament House clearly demonstrated what could happen to a successful satirist.

On arriving in Wellington, Thatcher paid an early visit to the House of Represent-atives and betook himself to the reporters gallery as the spot most suitable for taking notes. Admission to this gallery can only properly be claimed by gentlemen attached to the press and for which an order must be obtained from the clerk of the house. This rule we are told is not very rigorously observed.

No sooner was Thatcher seen pencil in hand among the reporters than members became fidgety. Soon he was waited upon by an officer with an enquiry of the name of the paper for which Mr Thatcher was acting as reporter. The 'Inimitable', in no way taken aback, answered promptly "The *Hokitika Bouncer.*" After sufficient time had elapsed to carry the name of this newly established West Coast journal to the speaker, the officer returned and informed Thatcher that he must leave the reporters' gallery, unless he could produce the formal identification which alone could entitle him to remain there. Thatcher accordingly retired and the next evening entertained his audience with 'Thatcher in Parliament':

I'm filled with grief and great discontent
I've lost my seat in this great Parliament.
I went up to take notes the other night,
And hon'rable members got in such a fright.
Went to the speaker pointing out the danger,
As well as pointing out th' obnoxious stranger,
And over-ruled by what they said, mor-o,
Reluctantly sent up word I must go.

After briefly visiting the Wairarapa in October 1865, Thatcher's troupe disbanded and he bade us farewell, returning to Australia with his wife, but revisiting New Zealand three or four years later.

For several years he toured throughout Australia with a painted panorama of 'Life on the Gold-Fields', each picture of which he illustrated with song and anecdote. When he returned to New Zealand he brought this exhibit with him for his third and final tour.

In 1867 a goldfield had been proclaimed at Thames and thousands of diggers from Otago and the West Coast rushed to the Coromandel Peninsula. As usual whenever a new goldfield was discovered, the 'Inimitable' Thatcher would appear on the scene. On his previous visits to New Zealand Thatcher had usually appeared in hotels or attached halls, but on his arrival in Auckland he opened at the Prince of Wales Theatre in June 1869 with 'Beautiful Auckland' among his repertoire:

Oh the would be swells of Auckland, with their trousers cut so tight,
A short flash coat and curly hair, in which the girls delight.
A paper collar, price one penny, a black bell-topper tile,
And whiskers clipped carefully, in the Lord Dundreary style.

Chorus Auckland town of shams and swells,
Drains and mud and horrid smells,
Oft I sigh and sigh in vain,
When I tread thy dirty streets again.

After two months in Auckland Thatcher set off to the current goldfield. His farewell stunt to Auckland was an attempt to ride a horse up Queen Street. A huge crowd turned out to watch the performance, which apparently ended in dismal failure.

When Thatcher arrived on the Thames goldfields he appeared at the Theatre Royal (yet another giant galvanised structure) in Grahamstown, where the usual motley crowd was in attendance, augmented by a large number of Maori, who always comprised a good proportion of Thames audiences. The Maori–Pakeha wars were almost over, but Te Kooti was still at large and fighting a rearguard action, so Thatcher obliged his listeners once again:

> A panic's been raging up in town,
> News from the Waikato has just come down.
> That Te Kooti a warrior of renown,
> Is going to do the settlers brown.
>
> This is the chief that Whitmore said
> Was on the battlefield left for dead.
> We said bravo when the news we read,
> It appears he's alive and kicking instead.
>
> At Papakura a few days ago,
> The Militia were called out, you must know,
> But though they were summoned, they seemed very slow,
> In appearing themselves in the ranks to show.
>
> Papakura's a place of martial renown,
> Two militiamen at last came down,
> One's a shoemaker called Mr Brown,
> And the other's a butcher that lives in the town.
>
> Such a sight the captain in charge did stun,
> Says the butcher "Round with my tray I've had to run,
> And as soon as this little job I've done,
> I'll clean myself up and come down with my gun."
>
> "If Te Kooti should come to Grahamstown,
> The diggers here, I bet a crown,
> Would very quickly do him brown,
> They'd show him a reef and let him down."

Thatcher moved from the Theatre Royal to the American Theatre, a hall attached to Butt's Hotel on the corner of Pollen and Grey streets. All his concerts at Thames had been profitable, for the miners loved their entertainment and were ready and able to pay for it. The main difference in mining gold here was that it wasn't washed from the river beds as elsewhere in the country, but mined from the hills, which Thatcher referred to in his final song before leaving Thames:

As you come down in the steamer with surprise your mind it fills
To see a lot of holes bored all about here in the hills.
It looks just like a rabbit warren as you're coming down,
And you'll see the digger's whares perched high above the town.
It's a fearful climb to get up, but it's easy tumbling down,
When they come here for their tucker to the stores at Grahamstown…

We have a small post office and a lady going there,
One day got jammed between a couple of diggers I declare.
She couldn't extricate herself all through her crinoline,
She struggled all in vain, I'm told it was a funny scene,
At last she cut the strings and let the blessed steel hoops down,
And left the crinoline behind in the passage at Grahamstown.

Thatcher now began a leisurely tour of New Zealand. His reception varied, but whatever he did made news throughout the country; even the smallest incident was reported at length. In Hokitika, for example, he tried his hand at pigeon shooting, defeating the local champions by killing ten out of eleven birds. This feat, it was reported throughout the country, had never before been equalled. Thatcher bade the West Coast goodbye with 'I've Packed My Traps':

It's time for me to leave this place, I must say with regret,
It's been a good claim to me and it isn't worked out yet.
It's paid me more than a pennyweight, a pennyweight a tub,
I think I've knocked out of it, a little something more than grub.

Chorus So from this arena, I will now retire,
        And leave other entertainers here, who'll for your smiles aspire.

Now I know my claim it has been jumped and I feel sad at heart,
And so to fossick somewhere else, I fear I must depart.
So it's time for me to pack my traps, I must say with regret,
It's been a good claim to me and it isn't worked out yet.

Upon returning to Dunedin he adopted a novel method of advertising by posting up faked testimonials from respected citizens as follows:

From a member of the Provincial Council.
Sir,
Having herd of your sevear remarks on my grammatikal inkompetency, I have been indeavouring to remove these obstruktions that stand in the way of my future advansement.
You will see by this note that I am greatly improved to what I was and hope soon to be a Precedent of the board of Edukation and inspector of Skools. Hoping you will be able to give a more favorable akount of me in your future lokals.
I remain, Sir, your obediently

AJB-N-S

Dunedin citizens had no trouble guessing the identity of the alleged letter writer as A J Burns, founder of the Mosgiel Woollen Company. Burns had recently offered to assume the duties of Immigration Agent for Otago, which caused the *Otago Daily Time*s to comment:

> From a candidate for such an office as the one in question, the least that can be expected is a capacity to write English. As specimens of bad spelling, bad grammar and execrably bad taste, the letters penned by Mr Burns could hardly be surpassed by a swagman.

April 1870 saw Thatcher in Oamaru and Timaru, giving his final concert at Temuka before departing once more for Australia. He was not heard of again until 1871 from Paris, where he said he was not likely to return to the colonies, but was going to start in business in London's West End. He became an importer of curios, a job which he did well. He died in 1878 aged 47 after contracting cholera in Shanghai, having gone there in search of further curios.

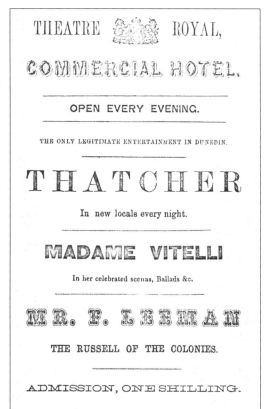

Thatcher's songs remained popular with the diggers, bullock drivers, swagmen and workers long after his departure from these shores. He expressed people's aspirations for a better life in a new country in a language they could easily understand through songs that have since guaranteed him immortality, while the brightly coloured 'Songsters' and 'Vocalists' he published have become collector's items.

At home aristocracy seems all the go,
On the diggings we're all on the level you know.
The poor man out here ain't oppressed by the rich,
But dressed in blue shirts, you can't tell which is which.

And this is the country with rich golden soil,
To reward any man's industrious toil.
There's no masters here to oppress a poor devil,
But out in New Zealand we're all on a level.

Thatcher's various Songsters and Minstrels can be found and viewed at the Auckland Public Library; Auckland Institute and Museum; Hocken Library, Dunedin; Otago Early Settlers Association; Canterbury Public Library; Alexander Turnbull Library, Wellington; National Library of Australia, Canberra; Mitchell Library, Sydney; and the New Zealand Folklore Society (Christchurch branch — photocopies in my possession).

A further collection of Thatcher's New Zealand ballads is held as part of the Bernard Hall collection in the State Library of Victoria.

VI

SWAGS TO RICHES

The swaggers

Now the tent poles are rotting, the camp fires are dead,
And the possums may gambol in the trees overhead.
I am humping my bluey across this fair land,
Where the prints of my boots sink deep in the sand,
I am out on the wallaby, humping my drum,
As I come down the tracks where the sundowners come.

Though the way of the swagman is mostly uphill,
There are joys to be found on the wallaby still.
When the day has gone by with its tramp or its toil,
And your campfire you light and your billy you boil,
There is comfort and peace in the bowl of your clay,
Or the yarn of a mate, who is tramping that way.

But beware of the town, there is poison for years,
In the pleasure you find in the depths of long beers,
For the bushman gets bushed in the streets of a town,
Where he loses his friends, when his cheque is knocked down.
He is right till his pockets are empty and then …
He can hump his old bluey up country again.

from 'On the Wallaby', Henry Lawson

The Romance of the Swag

The swag is usually composed of a tent 'fly' or strip of calico (a cover for the swag and a shelter in bad weather — in New Zealand it is oil cloth or waterproof twill) a couple of blankets, blue by custom and preference, as that colour shows the dirt less than any other (hence the term 'bluey' for swag) and the core is composed of spare clothing and personal effects. To make or 'roll up' your swag lay the fly or strip of calico on the ground, blueys on top of it across one end, with eighteen inches or so to spare, lay your trousers, shirt etc… folded, light boots tied together by the laces, toe to heel, books, bundle of old letters, portraits or whatever little knick-knacks you care to have or carry, bag of needles, thread, pen and ink, spare patches for your pants, bootlaces etc … lay or arrange the pile so that it will roll evenly with the swag (some pack the lot in an old pillowslip or canvas bag) take a fold over of blanket and calico the whole length on each side, so as to reduce the width of the swag, to say, three feet, throw the spare end with an inward fold over the little pile of belongings and then roll the whole to the other end, using your knees and judgment to make the swag tight, compact and artistic. When within eighteen inches of the loose end, take an inward fold in that and bring it up against the body of the swag. There is a strong suggestion of a 'roley-poley' in a rag about the business, only the ends of a swag are folded in, in rings and not tied. Fasten the swag with three or four straps, according to judgment and the supply of straps. To the top strap, for the swag is carried (and eased down in shanty bars and against verandah posts when not on the track) in a more or less vertical position — to the top strap and lowest or lowest but one, fasten the ends of the shoulder strap (usually a towel is preferred as being softer to the shoulder) your coat being carried outside the swag at the back, under the straps. To the top strap fasten the string of the nose bag, a calico bag about the size of a pillowslip, containing the tea, sugar and flour bags, bread, meat, baking powder, salt etc … and brought, when the swag is carried from the left shoulder, over the right onto the chest and so balancing the swag behind.

But a swagman can throw a heavy swag in a nearly vertical position against his spine, slung from one shoulder only and without any balance, and carry it as easily as you might wear your overcoat. Some bushmen arrange their belongings so neatly and conveniently with swag straps in a sort of harness, that they can roll up the swag in about a minute and unbuckle it and throw it out as easily as a roll of wall-paper and there's the bed ready on the ground with the wardrobe for a pillow. The swag is always used for a seat on the track; it is a soft seat, so trousers last a long time and with the dust being mostly soft and silky on the long tracks.

Travelling with the swag is variously and picturesquely described as 'humping bluey', 'walking Matilda', 'humping Matilda', 'humping your drum', 'being on the wallaby'. 'jabbing trotters', and 'tea and sugar burglaring' but most travelling shearers now call themselves trav'lers and say simply 'on the track' or 'carrying swag…'

from 'The Romance of the Swag' by Henry Lawson

'AUSTRALASIA' MAY HAVE BEEN AN UNACCEPTABLE CONCEPT to New Zealand politicians back in 1901, but to the miners, shearers and itinerants who carried their swags along the roads of both countries it was already a reality. The New Zealand author and Labour politician John A Lee walked with swaggers in the early 1900s, and remembered that with low fares and the seasonal drift of workers, both countries seemed very close. They may have been three and half days travel apart, but in most people's eyes 'Australasia' was a perfect description.

Swaggers became part of the heart and atmosphere of early Australia and New Zealand, with some assuming almost legendary status on both sides of the Tasman. These men made up a huge itinerant workforce, helping to provide labour that burgeoning rural economies needed. They made an important contribution to rural and farming heritage, which has benefited greatly from the recording of their exploits, yarns and home-grown verse.

Our pioneers were often, of necessity, loners at the frontiers of settlement. From the earliest days, thousands of immigrants walked in search of a living, be it gold mining, bush-felling, shearing, droving, harvesting, or any job on offer. Many adapted easily to a new way of life, but some could never adapt — those with a restless streak who became permanent wanderers. They would be joined later when the economic depression of the 1880s and '90s forced men onto the roads in search of work. Most found the courage to start again, but when times had settled down once more a large number of men, now used to carrying a swag, refused to put down roots, having acquired a wandering habit, for better or worse.

Early immigrants were frequently housed in barracks until work was found for them, but another way to find work was to shoulder a swag and tramp across country to one of the great station runs, or join the fevered search for gold. The country needed hard workers at this time, and swaggers often fitted the bill. Many sheep runs and wheat stations had huts where these seasonal labourers could receive shelter and food. Itinerants worked as shearers, harvesters, ploughmen or rouseabouts, taking whatever work was at hand, then walking from station to station until work became available again. When no swaggers' hut existed, the men of the road camped under the stars, sometimes in large numbers. There was no social welfare in those days, so a man had to survive as best he could or simply perish.

Legends of the road: Russian Jack, Comrade Shellback, Shiner Slattery, Barney Whiterats, Jack May, and John the Baptist.

He's staying tonight at a boarding house,
That's known as the Starlight Hotel,
Where most of the guests are travellers,
Stuck halfway 'twixt Heaven and Hell.

He's trudging the roads looking for work,
But chances keep passing him by.
No roof overhead to protect him,
Save a million stars in the sky.

A camp fire glow puts the men at ease,
There's great stories and yarns to tell,
Everyone's made to feel at home,
In the lounge of the Starlight Hotel.

You'll find a warm welcome every night,
If you book into the Starlight Hotel,
And join the travellers taking their rest,
Stuck halfway 'twixt Heaven and Hell.

The Starlight Hotel – from an anonymous informant in Geraldine, South Canterbury.

Men regularly came to New Zealand from Australia for the shearing and harvesting, walking long distances to find work. If none was available, time on the road didn't matter too much because a man could cross most of the South Island in a fortnight or so. They erected calico tents and makeshift whares on Otago or Canterbury plantations and were always ready to work when the season or boss was ready. Once settled around the fire, out would come the fiddles and concertinas as they sang or played their favourite tunes and airs, often yarning, reminiscing or reciting the wealth of backblocks poetry and verse that was so close to their hearts. When the job was done they moved on to the next one.

Old-timers used the reserve at Waipawa as a camping ground, beside the Tukituki River, which was a piece of ground overgrown with basket willow and frequently covered with water. One Sunday morning my mate and I having been turned out of a shepherd's hut and chased off a station run, made our way towards Waipawa and the reserve, where we felt sure there would be a large gathering of men. There were over a hundred or so camped amid the willows … Campfires were burning and the odours of cooking food permeated the still atmosphere. Since we had no food, the aroma was quite maddening to say the least. Nearby a very tough looking swagger was frying sausages in a pan made from the cut-off bottom of a kerosene tin. I had a treasured half-crown saved for some final emergency, but the sausages were beyond resistance, so I went up to the man and offered him the money for some of the sausages. I hoped that he would only charge me a few pence and return me some change. However he stood and looked at me for a long time, ignored my money and handed me a loaf of bread and a number of sausages, wanting no thanks for his kindness. We enjoyed a meal as few have been enjoyed in a lifetime.

As evening drew near, everyone in the reserve started to move towards our benefactor's tent, gathering around in a circle. We followed along unaware of what was about to happen. Presently out of his tent crawled our benefactor and all general conversation ended. Our benefactor held a concertina in his hand and as we all grew silent, he began to play — he held that swagger audience entranced and spellbound. Music I could not identify and old ballads I knew full well and loved and the music pleased everyone there present. As the twilight grew towards darkness, he played lively music. He played and played without speaking a syllable with shouts of applause welling up from the assembled swaggers. Amid the lengthening rounds of applause, he retired to his tent, but despite the continuing applause he refused to play again. He was a true artist and he knew when to stop. The assembled multitude quietly retired to their tents or shelters and we lay on our backs underneath the willows and gazed up at the stars.

from John A Lee's 'Roughnecks, Rolling Stones & Rouseabouts'

Once more you'll find me on the track,
And through the mountains steering,
With swag and billy on m' back,
I'm heading for the shearing.

Chorus Pass the billy round boys, let's all have a steamer,
     While I play you all some tunes upon my concertina.

At night I pick the driest camp,
And build a three-logged fire.
For when a man is on the tramp,
What more could he desire.

The sky above is clear tonight,
The stars are shining brightly.
It's time to play a song or two,
While you're sitting quietly.

from 'Concertina Joe' ~ Anon/Phil Garland

Men travelling on the road got to know one another throughout New Zealand and Australia. Yarns and stories were carried with the swag and became common property, while characters became public personalities. Tall stories, pioneer rhymes and verses were readily accepted by all, so the legends of swaggers and their deeds could not help but take root in the world of those men upon the track.

Did you ever see a fellow who is down upon his luck,
All the worldly goods he has wrapped up in a sack.
Hasn't got a stiver, not a solitary bob,
Trudging round the country, just looking for a job.

His clothes are torn and tattered as they hang upon his back.
He's everybody's rouseabout, the man upon the track.
He's weary and careworn just longing for a meal,
With a sort of empty stomach that you shouldn't want to feel.

He's begging for his breakfast, his dinner and his tea,
He earns a little money then goes out on the spree,
Sleeping in the open, underneath a stack,
Anything is good enough for the man upon the track.

from 'The Man upon the Track' ~ Arch McNicol

Many men who later rose to prominence in New Zealand and Australia, once carried a swag with these blokes and never lost their community of interest in later life. At that time the gap between swagger and respectability wasn't immense — a bad season or foreclosed mortgage easily saw to that. Many leading citizens of yesteryear have settled back, while reminiscing with pipe and glass, to say: "When I carried the swag…"

There developed a camaraderie of the road, where men helped their fellow travellers regardless of their past or background. Allowances were made for human failings — "We're all in this together, let's make the best of our situation that we possibly can."

For we are brothers of the road and we've had troubles in our life,
We got sold out for the mortgage and we couldn't keep a wife,
We were footloose and moving when that first old rooster crowed,
We were up and packed and moving down that long and friendly road.

from 'A Meeting, or Long and Friendly Road' by 'Taiwai'

Station owners encouraged the swaggers to move freely up and down the country following the seasonal work, by building swaggers' huts and providing food and firewood. This also prevented fences from being used as firewood and gardens from being raided. Among the army of swaggers tramping the country's roads during the recession were remittance men (emigrants supported or assisted by payments of money from home) whose very existence helped perpetuate the swagman's notoriety. Swaggers sweated and worked, loafed and drank, sang and yarned and came from all walks of life, but the 'Hungry Years' were a time when everyone knew and respected physical achievement and that respect was clearly written into our pioneer verse and song. The sentiments and atmosphere of those times is captured by backblocks balladeer David McKee Wright:

The winter ain't been hard as yet, though frosts are pretty keen,
There's one thing I'll tell you mate, the country's getting mean.
The price of wool is looking up, the harvest ain't been bad,
But for them that's on the wallaby, there's little to be had.

Chorus And when skies are grey above us, it's getting hard to bear,
        The feeling that the country has of hunger in the air.

I mind the time when men was pinched and things were pretty blue,
For the mortgage-burdened station and the struggling cockatoo.
But if work was hard of getting and a fellow had to tramp,
He was pretty sure of tucker and a decent place to camp.

It isn't falling wages that makes a fellow sick,
We had our turn of fairish times, there ain't no cause to kick.
And drink that's cursed the most of us, helped pay the country's way,
There's thousands tramping on the roads that do no work today.

A rabbiter or digger cove will stand a bloke a feed,
The poor man helps the poorer best in any time of need.
But cockatoos with decent homes and firesides warm and bright,
Will send a starving fellow man to sleep outside at night.

Well there ain't much use in talking, I'd best hump my bluey on,
There'll be good men and meanish men when we're all dead and gone.
I'd be happy as a skylark if I dropped across a job.
And as for saving money, well it's hard to earn a bob.

from 'Hunger in the Air', adapted by Phil Garland from 'The Swaggers' by David McKee Wright

A passage 'Round the Fire', from John A Lee's *Shining with the Shiner*:

There were a dozen white calico tents under the Canterbury pines. The pines were on an edge of flat land, which dipped down seven or eight feet to a stream of clear water. When heavy rain fell, or when warm spring winds thawed the snow on the foothills, the stream swelled to a dirty torrent. On the sheltered edge of the plantation was a fire from which, on that clear day, a pillar of smoke could be seen for miles around. Not far away a tree had been blown flat by a violent storm and when the camp congregated, someone produced an axe and the tree was chopped into mighty logs. The men were fit and waiting for work and no one minded adding to the wood pile. Other men had taken branches and gone around knocking cones off other pines so that, if the fire was generous, the fuel seemed likely to last out the emergency.

Shearers, shed hands, gathered for the shearing. The sheep station was half-a-mile away and the boss, although a good employer, liked to keep the big assembly of unemployed from invading his station cook-house until hiring day. One or two from the road he could feed, three, four, but when a large number gathered they were like locusts and their present period of idleness could corrupt all his efforts at future discipline. So he caused permanent tent frames to be rigged in the pines and lent the men an axe and allowed them to work for their wood. And all camped in the pines near the bed of the stream ready to pick up swag and be at the job call on shearing day. Each lucky one would get a start and when the shearing was finished, gather his cheque and move at once to the next station or descend upon a pub and wash the beer out of the first cheque before a second one was earned.

The stations staggered their commencing dates and across the years the itinerants came to know and were on the spot for each date and if steady, went from shearing board to shearing board and if not steady, from job to drinking bout to job from drinking bout. Some never touched liquor, but earned the few pounds which would allow an independent start. Some remained sober for the shearing season, although the cheque was still swallowed in a blaze of alcoholic glory.

Men who were not swaggers would ride to the station for the call on commencing morning too. But the work would no more be theirs than the possession of the men on the road. Shearers were not selected for respectability of sobriety, for morals or for Bible reading, but for the ability to shear better than the men who were not selected, when the pressure was on and the sheep were being crowded in. What did it matter to the station owner if the best shearer was the mightiest drinker and if he was penniless the week after, shorn faster even than the sheep, for the publican was something of a shearer too but never tempered the wind afterward. What did it matter to the station owner. He wanted a congregation of men to shear, not a congregation upon which to unload a temperance lecture or a prayer.

The sheep had been lambed heavily and would be good fettle. Yes the prospects were bright. There had been little snow on the hills, the feed was abundant, wool was up a penny. Canterbury would shear a record number of sheep so the shearer had a feeling of prosperity too. The winter had been kind to man and beast and the spring was in harmony. The shearers gathered. Some had landed from Australia at Bluff to roll their swags and walk a couple of hundred miles across country. They knew the date. They could make it in those days of long distances and no rural telephones. Some came from other seasonal jobs to be on the spot on starting day and some had been penniless and out all winter on the tramp.

There were a dozen calico tents on the Wednesday night and two dozen on the Thursday and all would strike camp sometime after midnight on Sunday to be at the station by the rise of Monday's sun.

Some never went near hotels and some never passed a hotel while money was to spend. Some spent the years of their lives cursing the day they had first seen liquor but were victims still. And in this camp there was a sharing of fortune. The station boss rode over to see the men as they gathered, joy in his heart at the fertility of the ewes and the lack of mortality of the season. Calico camp was gathering.

The characters and personalities were legendary: Barney Whiterats, so named for carrying performing white mice; Joe Fleming, the poet of the road; John the Baptist; Concertina Joe; Dirty Dick; Crowing Jimmy; the Highland Chief; the Honorable John Bourke O'Brien, one of the great remittance men, and last but not least Ned Slattery, alias The Shiner. Many of these loners and wanderers spent a lifetime tramping New Zealand roads, only to end their days collapsing and dying beside the tracks they had come to know and love so well.

Jock McKenzie, the Highland Chief, was one such person, renowned for hard work and a capacity for hard liquor. As a rabbiter, fencer and shearer his exploits were famed from Blenheim to Bluff. Once, after busting a cheque in Oamaru, he was on the verge of the DTs around 5 o'clock in the evening, but at nine next morning he was up the Waitaki at Otematata Station, ready for the shearing roll call. Despite being drunk at five, he had walked fifty miles through the night with his swag. He sheared all day and his tally wasn't bettered by anyone, and his boast that he could outwork and outwalk any man in the country was always believed. He died by the side of the road he loved so well and was finally buried there, so that his spirit could hear the footfall of other pedestrians 'padding the hoof'.

Crawling into the scrub, bush or tussock or falling into a ditch along the road to die was a common fate of many of that itinerant brigade.

> *Chorus* Gone are those years of humping the swag,
>   Living the life of a rover.
>   And the good times I spent on the wallaby track,
>   While I travelled this country all over.
>
> Tonight when I viewed the old station gate,
> My past came flooding back.
> How once proud and tall I answered the call,
> To follow the wallaby track.
>
> Those restless years have taken their toll,
> My body is aching full sore,
> Age now weighs heavy upon these old bones,
> I'll not travel these roads any more.
>
> I travelled this way chasing a dream,
> It must be years ago now.
> But how this country has altered it seems,
> With miles of it under the plough.
>
> I've always been blessed with a laugh and song,
> Whenever I greeted a mate.
> But the sights that I've seen and the places I've been,
> I'll treasure whatever my fate…
>
> I'll always remember the blokes I once knew,
> The ones that I'd still call 'mate.'
> Jock McKenzie, the Shiner and old Ginger Jack,
> We last met at the old station gate.
>
> There were campfires I've set 'neath clear starry skies,
> For warmth in frost and snow.
> From old mining camps to new shearing sheds,
> I've watched this young country grow…
>
> *'The Old Station Gate'* ~ *Phil Garland*

No 'pedestrian' entertainer was better known throughout the South Island than Barney Winters, nicknamed Barney Whiterats. As well as carrying his troupe of performing mice, he would set up a screen and throw shadowgraphs of birds and animals onto it — a once popular form of entertainment. Before he grew too old and weak he even carried a magic lantern and a Punch'n'Judy show. Children excitedly waited for his visits to both home and school, while shearers and farm workers also welcomed his woolshed visits. Barney finally collapsed by the side of the road in the 1890s, before ending his days in an old folks home in Timaru just a few days later.

Barney Winters

> They say I am a drifter knocking aimlessly about,
> Haunting towns and cities and the stations further out,
> You'll meet me on the bush tracks by the campfire's warm glow,
> As a roving star keeps leading where'er I have to go.

> *Chorus*   But I'm drifting, always drifting, as the ocean sand is shifting,
> Tramping forever on my way.
> I'm searching, always searching, for a dream that's slowly fading,
> Tramping forever and a day.

> *from 'The Homeless Drifter' ~ CH Winter/Phil Garland*

Joe Fleming was called the 'Poet of the Road' and was a well-recognised character throughout Otago and Canterbury. His beat ranged from Oamaru to Rakaia and back inland to the mountains. He always wintered over in Geraldine, but with the onset of spring would set off in search of work. He had a regular round and rhymed his itinerary so people would know his whereabouts. Over the years John A Lee picked up a few versions of Joe's itinerary. One of these, *Path of a Walking Man* (see the new edition of *Songs of a Young Country* by Neil Colquhoun), has a different chorus and varies considerably from the one he published in his book *Roughnecks, Rolling Stones & Rouseabouts.*

> Farewell to you old Geraldine, I am now upon the track,
> I'm travelling down that long & weary road, with a swag all on my back.

> I'm heading towards Temuka town, and if work I cannot find,
> I'll make my way on towards Washdyke, leave Temuka far behind.

> I'll call in next to old Timaru and round there take a look,
> But if no farmer should want me there, I'll drop on down to the Hook.

> I'll push ahead then to Oamaru, Ngapara and Duntroon,
> Where farmers often work late at night by the pale light of the moon.

When harvest days are over and corn is in the sack,
I'll shoulder bluey once again and by the rattler I'll be going back.

from 'Farewell to Geraldine' ~ Joe Fleming. The Hook is a locality in South Canterbury;
a bluey is the swagger's sack, i.e. the swag, and the rattler is the train.

Other swaggers also learned his rhymes and songs, repeating them on many an occasion. Anyone who offered him a meal, work or bed would usually find a rhyme of praise left by Joe on the hut door. One of his efforts was contained in a letter to John A Lee:

Wherever you dwell may content be your lot,
May friendship like joy encircle your cot,
Shed health on your dwelling, your pleasures increase,
May your honest endeavour be crowned with success,
May you ever be happy, never witness distress,
Under your roof may the blessings descend,
In the wish of all others, the wish of a friend.

Joe's reputation for verse had spread far and wide throughout Canterbury and Otago, though he vented his feelings against farmers who didn't afford him the welcome he felt he was entitled to. Farmers were careful not to offend lest they acquired a reputation for meanness as a result of his verse. Joe had a 'good lurk' before he was finally found a frozen corpse beside the Christchurch–Dunedin railway line, close to the road where he had tramped and rhymed his itinerant lifetime. Joe had rhymed his own obituary, found on a dirty piece of paper neatly folded inside his pocket.

Poor old Joe Fleming had a habit,
He never burrowed like a rabbit
Across the country far and wide,
He walked until one night he died.

John the Baptist was yet another who made a name for himself among the back-country stations of Canterbury. He became a regular visitor, refusing to work for a wage as he travelled along the foot of the Southern Alps. He was reputed to know all the river fords better than any man around and got his name because he was a swagger-evangelist. His forte was preaching sermons, usually just as everybody knocked off for a meal break. In those times religion was widespread and his preaching helped him to eke out a living. His arrival on a station would break the routine of back-country life, and he was always made welcome. He loved children, who flocked to him as he played the harmonica and danced around to the music he made. Blessed with a flowing white beard, he maintained it was nature's way of camouflaging him like the animals. "Shaving is a fool's game — never mind my whiskers, I'll play you a tune!" John finally collapsed near Ashburton, while journeying south to Timaru. A passing farmer returned him to Christchurch, where he died a few days later in 1947.

Kick out your fire boys, roll up your pack,
Don't forget your billy boys, billy burnt and black.
Black billy tea boys, black as it can be,
Black billy tea, that's the stuff for me.

Drink it from a tin, drink it from a cup,
Fill her up again and turn the bottoms up.
Brew it in a billy and brew it in a pot,
Throw in a handful and pour it out hot.

Mouth-organ Jack and John the Baptist too,
The old-time swaggers they knew how to brew.
Black billy tea boys, black as Stockholm tar,
Black billy tea put us where we are.

from 'Black Billy Tea' ~ Joe Charles

The Honourable John Bourke O'Brien is the classic example of a remittance man becoming a notorious but tolerated scallywag throughout the country. Always flamboyantly dressed in a top hat and frock coat, he played the character of an honourable gentleman to the full, gaining as much credence as possible from the merest suggestion of English gentility. He would announce in a stentorian voice to the world that he was the Honourable John Bourke O'Brien, almost daring anyone to challenge his supposed aristocracy. Stories of his exploits abound, due in no small measure to John A Lee's confusion in attributing the same feats to two markedly similar characters — The Honourable Mackay in *Shining with the Shiner* and The Honourable John Bourke O'Brien in *Roughnecks, Rolling Stones & Rouseabouts*. This identity mix-up has contributed to the legend, as stories attributed to both characters featured in the news ascribed to one or the other. Folklore has O'Brien frequently stripping off to bathe unashamedly in town water troughs, keeping a lookout for any approaching constabulary. He even had a standard introduction, which he used to good effect in many bars and court rooms, where he announced himself to all and sundry as follows:

My name is The Honourable John Bourke O'Brien. The sky is my roof and the open paddock my private bedroom.

He may have languished in gaol on a few too many occasions, but most of his life was spent outdoors under the open sky. When asked by one magistrate where he had slept the previous night, he replied: "In the Starlight Boarding House under the canopy of heaven, and I had a real cuckoo alarm on the branch of a tree to wake me in the morning. I was a guest of honour and I did not have to pay the landlord."

He had a glass eye, which he used to great effect in pubs. His special trick was to lean over someone's glass, allowing his eye to fall into their drink. He would then apologise profusely and retrieve the eye before drying it off and inserting it back in its socket. Naturally horrified, folk didn't want to finish their drink, so O'Brien would polish it off. This trick gained him free drinks from one end of the country to the other.

Once he managed to delay a train from its scheduled departure time by phoning the station master and telling him to hold the train, because the Honourable John Bourke O'Brien was on his way, but would be a few minutes late. The train was duly held up and everyone waited to see the VIP arrive. Eventually a battered old swagman in top hat and frock coat duly arrived, dropped his swag on the platform and informed the station master that he could let the train go now that the Honourable John Bourke O'Brien was aboard.

Like many of his swagger contemporaries, O'Brien was adored by children, who followed him in droves whenever he arrived in town. He would dance around and play games with them, and when asked why he was so popular with kids, he replied "When I am with children, I behave like a child." O'Brien was a natural entertainer and something of a rhymester, reportedly leaving the following farewell verse at the office of the *Temuka Leader* in acknowledgement of local hospitality:

Oh Temuka, sweet Temuka, You I never can forget,
I came to you with nothing, I'm leaving you in debt.

It seems he made an inauspicious exit from life after finding his way into a bottle store, where he lay down beside a barrel and turned the tap on to a trickle. He was found the following morning, lying in a pool of beer. Like his old mate, The Shiner, this flamboyant character also managed to generate a couple of press obituaries.

Peggy Hamilton, in her book *Wild Irishman,* remembers that in the 1920s swaggers were still passing through the Mackenzie Country, tramping the long dusty shingle roads from station to station. They seldom wanted work but were always given a hot meal, a shakedown for the night, breakfast and food to take with them. They usually arrived on their own, but would leave together in the morning. Her favourite was Freddy Ambrose (often confused with John the Baptist) a small, frail-looking man, who liked his solitude and walked alone, carrying a swag almost as big as himself. In the distance all one could see was an enormous swag with a little pair of legs twinkling at high speed underneath. Freddy also carried a gramophone, records and his well-used but treasured accordion.

Another interesting character was Crowing Jimmy, so-named for his 'engaging' habit of arriving at a station or farmhouse kitchen door, where he would flap his arms and crow like a rooster until food came his way.

If there was ever a king of the swaggers, it had to be Ned Slattery, universally known as the Shiner. A professional tramp around Otago and Canterbury in the late 19th and early 20th centuries, he spent fifty-plus years on the road, seldom if ever stooping to the level of working for a living. Few of his kind became national heroes meriting full media attention, but the Shiner did just that.

Edmund (or Edmond/Edward/Ned) Slattery was born in County Clare, Ireland in 1840, emigrating to Australia as a young man and spending time on the goldfields before coming to New Zealand in 1869. People were pouring into the new colony at this time and he began walking the tracks and roads of Otago and Canterbury like many others, looking for work. Just over six feet tall, he was strong, broad-shouldered, and had a restless streak — and being of Irish origin, a quick and ready wit with an entertaining fund of stories, coupled with an uncanny ability to get on with practically everyone he met. His keen sense of humour would serve him well in the years he spent on the road.

He wore a straw boater tied to the lapel of his coat with a bootlace, while around his neck was a clean celluloid collar and a dark tie showing serious signs of weathering. He wore these until the hat grew dark brown and greasy with sweat, the collar turned yellow and the tie green. They were the stock and trade of his eccentricity.

The Shiner.
ATL 2050133F

Most swagmen were ashamed to be on the road looking for work, but the Shiner glorified the profession and constantly crowed about how he dodged work, feeling shame only when someone offered him a poor handout or a job. He became a specialist in the art of not working for a living — John A Lee described him as 'the champion of anti-sweat'. The Shiner reserved his trickery only for those he thought deserved it, especially publicans.

> Now some folk drink tea, but water's less risky
> And with others it's sherry or beer makes 'em frisky.
> But give me the Irish in Jameson's whiskey,
> The warmest and best stomach liner.
> And many's the infamous trick I've conceived,
> And many's the barman that's gladly believed 'em,
> So of many free whiskey's I've often relieved 'em,
> Hooray for the swag and the Shiner.

One hot day as I tramped with me mate Gypsy Lee,
He points down at the road, "A dead sparrow" says he.
"It's a skylark" says I, "and a free drink for me,
If you follow the plan of the Shiner."
So at the next pub, I says "You wait outside,
But stay by the door with your ears open wide,
And at the right moment you come straight inside,
But you don't know the swag or the Shiner."

So at the next shanty I swear it's a lark,
"It's a sparrow" the barman is heard to remark.
Says I, "I'm so sharp I can tell in the dark,
The difference 'twixt magpies and mynahs"
"I'll wager a whisky all round then," says he,
"That the next man comes in here a sparrow will see"
So in comes old Gyp, "It's a skylark," says he,
"Free drinks for meself and the Shiner."

from 'Hooray for the Swag and the Shiner' ~ Paul Metsers

Despite his vagrancy he was never in strife with the law, and was as regular a churchgoer as his itinerary allowed. His favourite pastime was the Irish jig, which went some way towards making him a most likeable character, if not perhaps a wholly admirable one. In the Shiner's younger days he was a familiar figure at the Old Caledonian sports meetings held in Oamaru in the New Year period. Always competing in the Irish jig competition, he became known for his spectacular double shuffles and back-skips, with people coming from miles around to see him dance. His appearance was always greeted with cheers, while people who got to know him well became angry when he wasn't placed among the winners. His dress (three straw hats on his head and a red handkerchief round his neck) could scarcely have been correct attire for such an occasion, especially among so many earnest competitors who were at great pains to suitably clad themselves. Common sense prevailed and the organisers introduced a special category, which the Shiner won every year he competed. When John A Lee was 15 or 16, he says in *Roughnecks, Rolling Stones & Rouseabouts,* he saw him dancing at the Oamaru Caledonian Society:

> Each New Year's Day he came to dance in the Irish jig competition. While Caledonian sports were a Scottish festival, with piping and dancing etc… there was always an Irish jig and a hornpipe, the latter eminently suitable, since most of the population had come to New Zealand from Britain in wind-driven vessels. The Shiner put his swag in the corner of the ring, the music started up and he danced. His clothes were scrupulously clean and as scrupulously ragged.
>
> He could foot it with the best. He never won the competition, but he attracted most attention. The hat would go round and the coins would jingle and he would climb down in his tired dignity to pocket the tribute.

I wrote 'The Good Old Way' in honour of the Shiner:

> Who was that last New Year's Day,
> Dancing a jig in the good old way,
> With his old straw hat and walking cane,
> Will we ever see his like again.
>
> That was the king of anti-sweat,
> Once seen you never could forget.
> From Ireland and Australia came,
> What a charming rascal he became.
>
> He sailed here to Maoriland,
> And quickly joined the swagger band.
> The Shiner lived up to his name,
> Avoiding work was one big game.
>
> His reputation spread afar,
> Through each and every public bar.
> Oh what tricks he used to play,
> In those shanties by the way.
>
> There he stands so proud and tall,
> No whisky ever too large or small.
> He had no need of ready cash,
> His exploits always made a splash.
>
> Beneath the Southern Cross he roamed,
> Always on the road alone.
> Fifty years upon the track,
> He never once laid down his swag.
>
> To Oamaru he came each year,
> Dancing jigs he held so dear.
> People came from miles around,
> To see his feet float o'er the ground.
>
> Before his final race was won,
> The legend had long since begun,
> Spinning yarns both long and tall,
> How the Shiner entertained us all.
>
> Now this story is complete,
> No more we'll see his dancing feet.
> Never again on a New Year's Day,
> Will he dance in the good old way.

Because of his aversion to any form of labour, the Shiner learned to loaf in prosperous times and survive when the world turned harsh. In the days when pioneering New

Zealand toiled and prospered there was ample room for a tolerated layabout and plenty of laughter for the comic deadbeat.

The Shiner arrived at the McCarthy family farm near Oamaru looking for a friendly meal and bed as he was accustomed to do. The old man was away visiting Dunedin and Denis Junior didn't make Ned feel welcome at all. Instead of offering friendly hospitality as his father would have done, he was determined to make the Shiner earn his keep.

Ned wondered what the world was coming to, when he was expected to work for wages like a common labourer, but he found himself having to agree to some hard work.

Denis was determined to take the 'shine' out of the Shiner and informed him there was a well that needed cleaning out and deepening.

"We'll feed you for three days if the job takes that long and we'll pay you thirty bob once it's completed — ten shillings more than I'd give anyone else because you're a friend of father's."

Denis fed him well and gave him decent straw in the stable, but that was as far as he intended to go — he felt it was time someone stood up to the Shiner, something he could boast about later. In the morning Ned was given a spade, a shovel and a pack then taken to the site of the collapsed well. No one had even contemplated repairing it until Denis decided to take the Shiner down. "The water's not far down, the earth will be soft because it's been dug before" said Denis as he left Ned to it.

The Shiner glared at his departing form and commenced working furiously with the spade.

Ned could work when he wanted to, but had no real desire to do so. However he worked hard throughout the day until his head couldn't be seen above the surface.

Denis was impressed, he offered him a tot and fed him well that evening. The Shiner was too exhausted to eat or sleep well — tossing and turning throughout the night. Early next morning he was at it again, until the untimbered sides suddenly collapsed and the well caved in. When lunchtime came and the Shiner didn't arrive, Mrs Denis expressed concern to her husband that maybe the work had killed the old man.

After she told Denis he'd be in trouble with his father should anything happen to Ned, Denis decided to check on him. As they drew closer to the well they noticed there was no sign of activity. The Shiner's folded coat lay nearby — the spade handle was sticking up amid the collapsed earth and his boater lay on top. He immediately thought that the Shiner was buried beneath it all. He jumped into the pit clawing with his hands and reached for the shovel. Denis asked his wife to fetch help and tell them that the Shiner had been buried alive in a collapsed well. Help quickly arrived once the news got around and soon there were up to a dozen people digging frantically in an attempt to save the Shiner's life. As they dug, someone commented; "Who on earth would give an old man like that a well to dig?"

They continued digging all day, thinking he must be right at the bottom. As evening approached, the lanterns were lit and the women couldn't stop weeping.

Meanwhile the Shiner had been sleeping in the nearby plantation as he'd had enough of well digging. He'd woken once and noticed the spades and shovels hard at work, so settled back to sleep. Finally, in the late twilight, one of the women collapsed into the well crying out that she'd seen the Shiner's ghost approaching.

Everyone started laughing hysterically, but they were relieved to see him looking so well, despite being covered in pine needles. Denis wanted to flatten him with the spade, but enthusiastically shook his hand because he was alive! The Shiner got his pay, a decent meal of steak and onions, some extra tobacco and a few more glasses of whisky. He ended up dancing a jig and sang an Irish song to round off the celebrations.

Although young Denis had been humiliated, he saw the funny side of it all until his father returned home to make him "fill in the damned big hole that nobody wants."

The Shiner had become the clown of the road and of the Irish in particular. Everywhere he went he took advantage of his own notoriety — priests fed him, nuns befriended him — police knew him well and even went out of their way to help him. Ordinary folk accepted him for what he was, coming to recognize him as a loveable rascal, with most being able to laugh at and with him.

Ned always enjoyed the company of women, and any young single girl who proved herself a good cook would invariably receive an offer of marriage from him. If anyone was rash enough to take him seriously and accept (which did happen on more than a few occasions) he would extricate himself gracefully and looking suitably innocent, tell the luckless female "Ah, it wasn't you I asked, it must have been another one!"

Looking to slake his thirst, the Shiner carried a crockery demi-john into a pub and asked for it to be filled with draught whisky. The publican dutifully obliged and once it had been filled, Ned remarked airily "Just charge that to my account my good man" and made to leave the bar.

"Oh no you don't, Shiner!" exclaimed the publican, grabbing the container back and emptying its contents with a triumphant flourish back into the whisky barrel, from whence it came. "I've been had too often by you. Be off with you!"

"You're a hard man," grumbled the Shiner, departing crestfallen to the nearest clump of bushes, where he joyously broke open the demi-john and squeezed some very satisfying drams of whisky from a sponge he'd placed inside earlier in the day.

Most of the tricks played by the Shiner have gone down in history to be recounted time and time again by those purporting to be present when the exploit occurred. It has never ceased to amaze me the number of older informants, who have told me they were present when Ned pulled off one or more of his legendary tricks. Remarkably, these often seemed to happen in many different places at the same time, demonstrating that folklore has that wonderful ability to strike a responsive chord with people, despite frequently stretching the boundaries of truthfulness.

Here's how I've heard one such story:

A thirsty Shiner wandered into the town of McRaes, where the two publicans were deadly rivals. He visited Paddy Griffen's pub first and ordered a whisky.

The publican said, "How are you going to pay?"

Ned Slattery replied, "I haven't any money. I've only got stamps."

"Have you got enough stamps?"

"I've got plenty of stamps."

Paddy said, "Have you got enough for a whisky?"

"I've got plenty. Enough for a barrel of whisky!"

The publican handed over a bottle and a glass, which the Shiner downed and licked his lips.

"What about the stamps?" said the publican.

"Right," said the Shiner, "Watch and count, while I stamp my foot."

He stamped noisily on the floor and counted out loud — "One, two, three, four, five, six."

The publican glared and muttered "Postage stamps and crooked nonsense" while the customers laughed. Paddy Griffen's anger abated as he saw the funny side. He realised he'd been had and offered the Shiner another drink.

"The bill is paid; if you go on stamping you'll knock my shanty down. That's a really good trick, when did you think that one up?"

"Just as I was coming down the road," he replied.

"Well, I'll tell you what — if you can pull that trick on Mick Scanlan, I'll give you a meal and a bed for the night as well as all you can drink for the night."

The customers in the bar rushed down to Mick Scanlan's. The Shiner duly arrived and walked into the bar. Scanlan was on his guard, having been taken for a ride by Ned Slattery before.

"What do you want?" he asked, "and none of your tricks."

"I want a drink," Ned replied.

from Ross Gore's *It Happened in New Zealand*

123

"You already owe me for plenty, let's see the colour of your money."

"I haven't got any money, but I've got plenty of stamps."

"Never been used before?" asked Scanlan.

"Of course not, they're unused stamps," said the Shiner. Scanlan replied that stamps were quite acceptable, because the miners often used them.

"I'll have a whisky," said the Shiner.

"Right-o, that will be six penny stamps, Shiner!"

"Who said penny stamps? I just said stamps, didn't I, mates?" he said to the assembled audience, who all grinned in agreement.

Ned began stamping — "One, two, three, four, five, six — say when!"

"What do you think you're doing?" asked Scanlan, as he stepped out from behind the bar rolling up his sleeves.

"I'm stamping" continued the Shiner — "seven, eight, nine, ten…."

Mick Scanlan's face was black as thunder as he advanced on the Shiner.

"Can't you take a joke?" Ned asked.

"I'll give you a joke!" roared Scanlan.

Whereupon the Shiner said, "I'll bet that Paddy Griffen would be able to take a joke!"

Realising that he'd been the butt of a very good joke, Mick Scanlan softened his demeanour and asked "Do you reckon you could put one over Paddy Griffen up the road?"

"I do indeed," said the Shiner.

"Well," said Scanlan, "if you could pull a trick like that over Paddy Griffen, I'll give you a bottle of whisky for your trouble."

So the crowd made their way back down the road in readiness for the fun and entertainment. Once again the Shiner walked back to McRaes with Scanlan following close behind. Scanlan stood outside the door as the Shiner entered the bar.

"What'll you have?" asked Paddy Griffen.

124

"I'd like a drink!" said Ned.

"Sure, and what would you like to drink? We're honoured to serve you, Ned, and it's on the house!"

The Shiner downed yet another whisky, then said "I'd like to buy the boys a drink."

"Certainly," said Paddy Griffen. Mick Scanlan slipped quietly into the bar to observe the proceedings.

"What about some money?" said Griffen.

"I haven't got any money, but I'll pay you in stamps."

Paddy said "I don't normally take stamps, but I'll make an exception for you Shiner!"

The Shiner stamped his foot and counted — "One, two, three, four…" and carried on to twenty.

"Is that enough?" he asked.

"You've paid too much, Shiner, here's your change," said Paddy Griffen and stamped half a dozen times.

"You're a real gentleman, Paddy Griffen," said the Shiner.

Mick Scanlan appreciated the joke and handed over the promised bottle of whisky, before retreating to his establishment down the street. The Shiner left town the next day still drunk as a lord, having obtained a meal, a bed, a bottle of whisky and countless drinks on the house. All in all a pretty good day's work!

After more than fifty years of endless tramping, with the last twenty-five spent on a beat from Ashburton to Gore, he reluctantly allowed himself to be placed in a Caversham nursing home, where he passed away at age eighty-seven in 1927. The *Oamaru Mail* paid tribute to "a Knight of the Road", bemoaning his loss, while the *Otago Witness* published an obituary complete with photo, under which were the words:

The Passing of the Shiner

Edmond Slattery, better known as 'The Shiner' the nomad of Otago and Canterbury, whose death was recently reported at the age of 87 years.

The following lines were discovered on the wall of an Otago shearing shed, allegedly written by the Shiner, possibly in a more enlightened moment:

Don't blame the wealthy squatter if your luck it should be out,
Don't blame the struggling cockatoo, for he knows what he's about.
Don't blame colonial government if your children lack for bread,
But blame the wayside shanty for the reckless life you've led.

The story was now complete.

These four lines should be always be recited rather than sung, but Frank Fyfe in his wisdom thought he would sing them, and wrote two further verses to complete his song:

I came out here to Maoriland me fortune for to make,
Giving up my native hearth for what shelter I could take.
Hard luck has always dogged me through wind and rain and snow,
Followed by old Jameson's wherever I may go.

Travelling through Otago I tramped the whole year round,
Although I worked at many things, me fortune was never found.
At working for another man, I could but only try,
Until the shanty calls to me — "I'm coming sir, says I."

The swaggers' world has long since faded into myth and legend. Few New Zealanders can remember the days before unemployment benefits, when men tramped the roads seeking work. Swaggers were free of the restraints placed upon the more civilised forms of existence, as their lives became unending migrations and shiftless wanderings, totally pointless to society at large. Men lived for the present with scant regard for tomorrow. Out here all men were equal, and this manifested itself in a true camaraderie of the road.

Swagmen's hut on the Hokitika Road
— a wood engraving from the
Illustrated New Zealand Herald 1875.
Making New Zealand collection, ATL F644 1/4 MNZ

VII

CROOKS AND NANNIES

Early rogues & scoundrels

NEW ZEALAND HAS HAD ITS SHARE of crooks and scoundrels in its frontier history, and more than a few have made a lasting impact on oral history, folklore and balladry. Seven such villains appear in this chapter: Bully Hayes, the four Maungatapu murderers, Minnie Dean and Stanley Graham. Their legacy will not be forgotten or overlooked as long as our poets and rhymesters can wield a pen.

Bully Hayes

Come all ye bold and tarry sailors — blow boys blow,
Here's a four year trip on a southern trader — blow me bully boys blow.

With our quarters manned and the rigging ready — blow boys blow,
Let's heave away and keep her steady — blow me bully boys blow.

What do you think we've got for cargo — blow boys blow,
Why 'black sheep' that have run the embargo — blow me bully boys blow.

Who do you think is the captain of her — blow boys blow,
Why Bully Hayes that pirate skipper — blow me bully boys blow.

from 'Blow Boys Blow'- Anon

Few buccaneers in history could match exploits with Captain William Henry Hayes, the Prince of Rogues who pirated his way around the Pacific for a quarter of a century. An American, born in Ohio, he began his nefarious career early in life. After stealing money from his own father, he left home to become a sailor and married young, deserting his wife for another woman after being accused of horse-stealing. He made his way to the South Pacific, after selling a stolen ship for a handsome profit in Singapore. This heralded his graduation from petty thief to notorious buccaneer.

In the years that followed, this scoundrel would become known as 'Bully' Hayes, visiting every Pacific port or island, while conducting his criminal deeds. He is thought to have committed just about every crime known to the civilised world, but curiously enough was never charged with murder. His long record of piracy, slave-trading, bigamy, rape, kidnapping, extortion, fraud and embezzlement clearly established him as the Prince of Rogues.

Bully Hayes was a big, powerful man, handsome and well-mannered should the occasion demand it. Well over six feet tall, he had flowing, dark, shoulder-length hair. He was a clever navigator, an astute financier before becoming a blackbirder, and was renowned as a cheat and a swindler who frequently visited New Zealand ports during his years in the South Pacific. He sailed into Port Chalmers in September 1862 aboard the *Cincinatti*, a battered hulk which promptly ran aground in the harbour. On shore, and seeing the opportunity for quick money, he joined up with the talented Buckingham family troupe of entertainers who were about to leave on a tour of the Central Otago goldfields.

In January 1863 the group played to full houses in Dunstan before arriving in Fox's, later named Arrowtown. There the Buckinghams opened up a hotel and business boomed, so Hayes decided to open his own hotel and gather profits from the thirsty diggers. Using his roguish charm he persuaded miners to erect a sod building measuring 60 by 30 feet, with a calico roof. This rough-hewn grog shop, which became known as the Prince of Wales Hotel and Theatre, featured the Inimitable Thatcher and wife 'Madame Vitelli' as the prime entertainment.

The picture is captured in 'Wheels of Arrow' by Tod Symons of Alexandra:

While beside the Arrow River I saw the years roll back,
Saw the first of Arrow's miners tramp the old time river track.
Saw that gold rush in the glory of the days of long ago,
'Neath the backdrop of the mountains in the brilliant summer's glow.

I forgot the crowds that gathered and the burning heat of day,
As I watched the past unfolding in a great and living play.
Men and horses, packers, miners, churning wagon wheels that rolled,
Up the river track to Arrow in that fevered search for gold.

Saw the good-time girls arriving at the Prince of Wales pub,
A pole and canvas shanty midst the boulders and the scrub,
Saw the miners making merry, giving gold for doubtful grog,
To Bully Hayes, the slaver, that one time gay sea-dog.

Hayes' name and reputation were soon feared throughout the Arrow, after many a gold-seeker called at the Prince of Wales with pockets bulging, to be plied with liquor and never seen again. The new venture was going well and money poured into this den of iniquity, while across the way the Buckinghams also had a roaring trade. One of their daughters, Rosie, a fine singer and an attractive and talented young lady, was the main drawcard. Bully Hayes disliked this threat to his trade and set about enticing Rosie from her family and promptly married her, whereupon open hostilities commenced.

Somehow a rumour began that Hayes was minus an ear, which was why he wore his hair long. It was suspected that he had been caught cheating at cards during the California gold rush, and in retribution, the miners had cut off one of his ears. The Buckingham family offered £5 to any barber in Arrowtown who would cut off Hayes' hair, and finally one plucky barber took his opportunity, revealing to all and sundry — one missing ear! Whereupon Hayes wrecked the barber shop, blustered and threatened to shoot everyone on sight, and had to wear a bandage round his head for some time thereafter. His humiliation didn't end there, as the Buckinghams weren't slow to capitalise and swiftly presented a comedy entitled *The Barbarous Barber or The Lather and the Shave* which proved popular and ran for several months. Hayes threatened libel action, but from that moment on he was no longer taken seriously in the Arrow.

WILLIAM HENRY HAYES

has great pleasure in informing the public that

THE INIMITABLE THATCHER

and

MADAME VITELLI

will shortly make their first appearance in this township at the

PRINCE OF WALES HOTEL

Poets seem to find romance at every turn in Arrow's golden days, and FWG Miller of Invercargill proves no exception with this verse:

I muse upon the golden days, the sixties of renown,
As in the sun I sit and bask in tranquil Arrowtown.
Oh let me live again once more those grand and roaring days,
Of Buckingham and William Fox and likewise Bully Hayes;
When Warden Pyke and Nugent Wood administered the act,
And goods along the Skippers Trail by horse and man were packed;
When gold lay on the beaches like a crop of yellow wheat,
And sturdy miners swaggered down the little Arrow street,
Those days have gone but still the hills eternally look down
Upon the river and the trees in tranquil Arrowtown.

In 1864 Hayes left the Arrow with his wife and son, and her brother George. Nothing was heard of them until August that year, when a boat containing Hayes, his wife and son, George and a nurse capsized near Nelson. All drowned except the gallant Captain Hayes, who was unable to save any life but his own. He went into deep mourning, showing every sign of sincerity, but as always was the master of deceit.

Hayes turned up in Sydney soon after, as master of the *Black Diamond*, roaming the South Pacific, leaving a trail of debts and compounding his distasteful reputation. He frequently visited New Zealand at this time, where he stole a cutter in Akaroa and sailed off with a kidnapped sixteen-year-old girl. A few months later in Wellington he commandeered an American schooner, the *Shamrock,* and sailed her into the Pacific, returning to Lyttelton with a cargo of fruit and handicrafts from the islands. Proceeds from this cargo netted him enough money to live respectably in Lyttelton for a while. He married yet again and fathered twin daughters, before returning to sea to follow his chosen path. He took up smuggling guns and ammunition to warring Maori in the North Island, then left New Zealand for the last time to embark on the most nefarious chapter of his career. So far he had confined his activities to piracy, larceny and fraud, but a new business opportunity beckoned — selling human beings.

Throughout the Pacific, plantation owners were crying out for labour and Hayes believed he could provide virtually free labour by capturing and enslaving Pacific Islanders. The trade became known as 'blackbirding', and for a decade Hayes reigned as the most notorious blackbirder of the region. No one knows how many thousands he enslaved or how many died of sickness, starvation and beatings in transit. He was never brought to account for these vicious crimes and degradations.

In what might be termed poetic justice, Hayes finally met his demise in a brawl with a feisty ship's cook, Dutch Pete, at the Marshall Islands in 1877. When Bully lunged towards him, Pete drew a pistol and shot him, then hit him over the head with an iron tiller. He stood and watched Bully Hayes topple overboard and disappear beneath the surface. Without a pause, the schooner *Lotus* sailed on into the night, closing the book on the career of the worst scoundrel in the annals of the South Pacific.

> I've been a blackbirder ten years and a day,
> And I've plundered the ocean like old Bully Hayes.
> I curse all bad company that led me astray,
> Now gin and the devil relieve all my pain.
>
> Blackbirder, blackbirder I always will be,
> The Hellfire has got me and won't set me free.
>
> *from 'Blackbirder' ~ Lloyd Montgomery*

The Maungatapu murderers

Our pioneer history, unlike Australia's, has few instances of bushranging or robbery under arms. Australia, with its vast distances, gave such criminals every opportunity of evading the law, whereas New Zealand is much smaller. The back country was too inaccessible and inhospitable for many fugitives to remain at large for any length of time.

Because the risk of detection was too great for any undesirable immigrants, even in the lawless days of the gold rushes there were few really serious crimes, but one of the most sordid and senseless ever recorded was the 1866 Maungatapu killings in the Nelson province. I have touched on this subject in 'The Golden West' chapter and tell the full story here.

On a winter's day in June 1866, four men set out from Deep Creek in Marlborough for the tranquil town of Nelson, with a packhorse and a grubstake of £300 in gold dust and notes. They had decided to try their fortunes on the West Coast, but none of the men would reach their destination. They were killed and robbed in a brutal ambush on the Maungatapu Ridge and their bodies hidden in the bush.

I will use Neil Colquhoun's song 'Murderers Rock' to illustrate salient points about this incident:

> Murderers Rock stands on the track,
> And watches all that passes:
> Victorian miners, hard old-timers,
> And wash-a-bit, move-along asses.
> For the Dunstan, just as the Tuapek' did
> That gave us all gold fever,
> Has little that's left that's payable dirt,
> And we are bound to leave her.

Four strangers had been noticed in Nelson at that time; three of them, Richard Burgess, Thomas Kelly and Joseph Sullivan were old lags, men who had already done time in Australia for crimes in England. The fourth, Philip Levy, was a 'fence' — a receiver of stolen goods — who had become their ablest accomplice. Burgess and Kelly had already done time in Dunedin for bushranging and armed robbery on the Otago goldfields in 1861, and Burgess had established himself as one of the most dangerous and stubborn criminals in the gaol.

These verses are from Ross McMillan's poem 'Bushrangers':

> Sullivan, Burgess, Levy and Kelly,
> These were the names in the gang,
> They lived by the gun — bushrangers each one,
> With three of them destined to hang.
> They bailed up the pubs and looted the stores,

Relieved the miners of their pay;
At Sullivan's Rock on the Dunstan Track,
They 'stuck up' the travellers one day.

Back in the old days when Central was young,
And Gold was King of the land,
Desperate, dangerous, these were the men,
Who rode with the bushranging band.
They roamed through the ranges, hid in the hills,
Left terror behind in their wake,
The price on each head — alive men — or dead,
They boasted that no one would take …

While in Dunedin gaol, Burgess led a mutiny for a week and for his trouble was shackled in irons, placed in solitary and given 32 lashes with the cat. Kelly and Burgess were released in September 1865 and made their way to the West Coast diggings, mainly to escape the irksome supervision of the Otago police.

Arriving in Hokitika in 1866 they met up with Sullivan, who was destined to become the most notorious criminal in the country over the next few years. He was a vicious man, considered viler than the majority of the hardened criminals who were his usual confederates. More than willing to betray even his closest associates, he would perjure without compunction if he thought lying might serve better than the truth. The three men were well suited to each other.

Burgess was soon arrested and convicted for stealing firearms. On his release the party made for Greymouth, where Burgess hatched a plan to rob a banker named Fox. They botched the plan when they met a young man eight miles from Greymouth and mistook him for the banker. After realising their mistake, they strangled and buried him in the bush, lest he identify them. Their luckless victim was actually George Dobson, a government surveyor.

The gang fell under suspicion for Dobson's death, but with no direct evidence against them and fearing an enquiry, they left Greymouth and headed north. They were joined from Hokitika by Levy, whom Burgess already knew as a professional receiver of stolen property who could help the gang dispose of any booty that might be obtained. Unlike the others, he had left England as a free emigrant and set himself up as a trader in Dunedin, until he became known to the police as a fence. He followed the gold rush to Hokitika and was doing business there when he threw in his lot with Burgess.

The gang arrived in Nelson on the steamer *Wallaby* from the West Coast on 6 June 1866, fully armed but looking to all and sundry like ordinary diggers bound for the goldfields. Nothing in their appearance aroused suspicion, but they were desperately hard-up. They set off for the Wakamarina diggings to rob any digger who might be carrying gold.

Let your ears flap as they hears
A tale that'll certain displease you,
About four wild colonial men
Begetting their gold at leisure.
Dick Burgess, Kelly and Philip Levy
That now stand trial in the dock,
They butchered poor Mathieu and friends
For their gold, at Murderers Rock.

The gang's *modus operandi* was to kill their victims so that information could not be laid against them. They travelled up the Maitai Valley and over the Maungatapu, down Pelorus Valley and on to Canvastown. Still short of money, they were unable to stop at the hotel but obtained leave from the landlord to camp in an empty building. Next day they sent Levy up the Wakamarina Valley to spy out the territory. He returned with the news that four or five diggers, plus some others, would soon be leaving for Nelson, carrying money and gold with them.

The men retraced their steps, bent on repeating the ghastly method that had proved so successful already — murder and robbery in the lonely bush, enabling quick and easy disposal of victims. They had plenty of time to make their arrangements, and settled on an ambush site halfway up the Herenga side of the ridge which divides the upper waters of the Maitai from the Pelorus Valley. This ridge is the Maungatapu (sacred mountain) which had received its name in an interesting manner, as described in *The Trial of the Maungatapu Murderers*:

> A tribe of Maoris living where Havelock now stands were at feud with a tribe at Motueka and determined to attack their enemies by surprise. Consequently they formed their taua (or war party) and moved up the Pelorus River (Hoehere) till they came to the junction of the Herenga Stream. Here their chief halted them while he went to consult the omens and pray to his gods. Climbing up the ridge, from the top of which he could look towards Motueka, he set up his tuaahu (or sacred place selected by a tohunga for purposes of divination) and recited his karakia. After a time he returned to his followers and said, "The signs are favourable, the gods will give us success. Follow me."
>
> The taua then climbed the ridge and, avoiding Wakatu (Nelson), travelled down the Aniseed Valley into the Waimea Plain and so over the Moutere Hills. Stealthily making their way to the back of their enemy's pa at Motueka, they took it by surprise, in the early dawn, and extracted their utu (revenge, payment). Without delay they returned the way they had come, and when they reached the ridge where their chief had prayed, the conquering warrior said to his followers, "This is Maungatapu, the sacred mountain. Here I set up my tuaahu. There will I go and offer thanks to the gods. Pass on, and henceforth let no man set foot on the mountain, for it is tapu!"

It was almost at this same spot that the men lay in wait for their victims — Kempthorne, Pontius, Dudley and Mathieu.

The four had planned their evil work
When Mathieu spoke up louder
And told the company in the bar,
Hard savings — no man prouder.
They travelled ahead to wait and rob,
And not one was fair fighter,
If a single robber had stood with fists,
My story could have been brighter.

The track across the Maungatapu was a lonely one. It ran five miles through rugged bush and easily lent itself to such deeds as were being contemplated by Burgess and his mates. Thomas Galloway, a Picton draper, was travelling over the Maungatapu that day and passed the bushrangers *en route*. He met Mathieu and his friends and warned them about the gang he had encountered. Although hold-ups were not unknown in Nelson province, the four companions had set off happily enough on that fateful morning. It had been arranged that Henry Moller, a German storekeeper from Deep Creek, would follow his friends on foot to Nelson, so he could bring back the packhorse. Moller left the township early the next day and made good progress, travelling light. On the way he met several people who had passed his friends on the road, but when he came across John Boun, a Pelorus Valley farmer, near the great rock on the Nelson side, Boun told him he had seen nothing of his friends. The nature of the track was such that he must have met them had they been on the road.

Moller became alarmed and made for Nelson, reaching the town that night. Finding no trace of his friends, he returned to Canvastown and reported the strange occurrence to Jervis the storekeeper. Jervis remembered the suspicious-looking Burgess and his cronies and suspected the men might have been the victims of foul play. He rode to Nelson the next day, intent on seeking any sign of the men or their packhorse as he went — but in vain. He reported his suspicions to the authorities, who sent policemen out to look for the missing men along the Maungatapu track.

Simultaneously, two miners from Deep Creek came to Nelson to search out the suspected men, in particular Levy, who had briefly visited the mining township. The miners had only been in Nelson a day when they recognised Levy in a hotel bar and had him arrested. Searched by the police, he had over £60 in his pockets. He denied having any companions, but they were found and arrested the following day and charged in connection with the murder of the missing men.

Fifty volunteers combed the bush for the missing men. First they discovered the packhorse, shot in the head. The swags of the missing prospectors were found nearby, along with a loaded musket and a shovel, but this was hardly enough evidence to prove the case against the four strangers. Kempthorne's brother arrived from Dunedin and posted a £200 reward for the recovery of his brother's body, and the

Crown also offered a full pardon and a £200 reward to any accomplice who had not been involved in the actual murders and would turn Queen's evidence. In addition, the provincial government offered £400 for the bodies of the missing men.

Volunteers renewed their endeavours and eight days later there was a breakthrough. Proving that there is no honour among thieves or murderers, Joe Sullivan took the government bait and confessed to being the lookout man for the gang. He disclosed the location of the bodies — two having been shot, one strangled and the other shot and stabbed. In his confession Sullivan revealed yet another crime — the murder of a whaler, James Battle, on the Maungatapu track as he was returning home with just under £4 in his pockets.

Acting on Sullivan's information, searchers returned to the site known as Castle Rock and found the bodies exactly as he had indicated, in the bush above the track. They were retrieved, wrapped in canvas and taken to Nelson for burial in a large grave in the cemetery.

> Hang down your head, Dick Burgess,
> 'Twill make no difference further.
> You know you'll hang from the gallows tree
> And pay for your terrible murder.
> For Kelly too I haven't much time,
> Though for Levy I am warmer,
> The jury has to make up its mind,
> On the evidence of an informer.

On their way to and from the court the villains were booed by a crowd which had gathered to see them. From the outset there would be no doubt as to the final verdict; Sullivan's testimony tied the nooses firmly around his companions' necks. But Sullivan wasn't in the clear yet, for under cross-examination it emerged that he had probably killed James Battle. He too was charged with murder, escaping the gallows only by turning Queen's evidence. He was sentenced to life imprisonment. His partners, however, were

from Ross Gore's
It Happened in New Zealand

ON JUNE 13, 1866, FOUR MEN SET OUT FROM *CANVASTOWN* FOR *NELSON* VIA THE LONELY *MAUNGATAPU MOUNTAIN TRACK.* THEY CARRIED *GOLD* FROM *DEEP CREEK* DIGGINGS.

THEY WERE *JOHN KEMPTHORNE & JAMES DUDLEY,* STOREKEEPERS, *FELIX MATHIEU,* PUBLICAN FROM MARSEILLES, & *JAMES DE PONTIUS,* GOLD PROSPECTOR OF NEW YORK, U.S.A.

THERE FOLLOWED ONE OF THE MOST *SENSATIONAL TRIALS* IN THE HISTORY OF N.Z. CRIME. *THE RESULT?* ~

~ AT 8·30 A.M. ON OCTOBER 5, 1866, AT NELSON JAIL, THE SIMULTANEOUS *TWANG* OF *THREE ROPES* ANNOUNCED THAT *BURGESS, LEVY & KELLY* HAD PAID THE *SUPREME PENALTY.*

136

hanged in Nelson gaol on 5 October 1866. Their executioner was another prisoner, who was then released and deported to Sydney.

> Murderers Rock stands on the track,
> And watches all that passes:
> Victorian miners, hard old-timers
> And wash-a-bit, move-along asses.
> My story's ended, I am done,
> And all take warning from it:
> Don't take another man's life for gold,
> Or the gallows you'll hang upon it.

In 1867 Sullivan was transported to Hokitika to appear as a witness for the Crown in the murder of George Dobson, the surveyor killed the previous year. Revelling

in his notoriety, Sullivan swaggered into court dressed as a gentleman of fashion, riling townsfolk who believed that he was the real culprit. Sullivan was returned to Nelson gaol, where he continued to build roads with the other convicts, but townsfolk were incensed that he should be allowed to work so publicly and agitated for his removal to Dunedin. He petitioned for a pardon because of turning Queen's evidence, without success, but Governor Sir James Fergusson visited Dunedin gaol in 1874 and granted him a pardon on condition that he leave the colony immediately. Fate took yet another twist — Sullivan was placed on board the *Mikado*, sailing to the USA by way of Auckland. On arrival at Auckland, the American consul and the ship's passengers protested his presence on the voyage. The captain refused to sail from Auckland with Sullivan aboard, so he had to disembark. As soon as he was known to be in Auckland a public protest had him placed under police protection until his hair and beard had grown sufficiently to disguise him. This scoundrel was then shipped off with utmost secrecy to South America.

Eight lives were lost as a result of the Maungatapu killings and all for £300. It was a pointless and sordid crime perpetrated by the dregs and wretches of colonial society, who were themselves victims of an abominable system of punishment. The gang are known to this day as the Maungatapu Murderers or the Kelly Gang, while Castle Rock has undergone a name change — to Murderers Rock.

Minnie Dean

Minnie Dean holds the dubious honour of being the only woman ever to die on the gallows in New Zealand. Although the crimes she committed were particularly repellent, the repressions of Victorian society contributed to her infamy.

Minnie Dean was born Williamina McCulloch in 1844, the daughter of a Presbyterian minister in Scotland. She was the fourth in a family of eight girls and emigrated to New Zealand in 1868. She arrived in Invercargill in the goldrush era as Mrs McCulloch, a widow with two young daughters, and later met and married Charles Dean, a well-known local settler, in 1872. After their marriage they continued to live close to town, where Minnie found work as a school teacher. They eventually shifted in 1886 to The Larches, a two-storeyed house on twenty acres at Winton, nineteen miles north of Invercargill by rail. Shortly after their arrival the house burned down and was replaced by a two-room shanty with a lean-to. The family lived in this shack, with children ranging in age from six weeks to ten years. Minnie set up a 'baby-farming' business, offering a home to unwanted children or to adopt them out — for a fee. Before 1900, illegitimacy was seen as a major threat to public morality, and unmarried mothers faced humiliation in homes for 'fallen' women. Baby-farming provided quick and confidential disposal of illegitimate children, and hid family shame.

She dressed in black and she carried a hat,
In her hatbox when early to the court house she came.
But on her way back, she'd always wear the hat,
Invercargill to Winton on the 5 o'clock train.

Chorus Minnie Dean, Minnie Dean, she's gonna catch you,
And take you away on the afternoon train.
Oh, you'd better be good or Minnie Dean's gonna getcha
And you'll never ever be heard of again.

She's so sweet and gracious to the girls and the ladies,
Twenty gold guineas was a small price to pay.
To be freed from all shame and be maidens again,
She wrapped up their little ones and took them away.

Here lie the children nobody wanted,
Minnie died for her sins and the people all cried.
They cried for themselves and cried for the children,
And they cried for Minnie for closing their eyes.

She dressed in black and she carried a hat
In her hatbox, when early to the courthouse she came.
I'm innocent she said, the children just disappeared,
But they hanged her from the gallows until she was dead.

'Ballad of Minnie Dean' ~ Helen Henderson

Whenever her house became intolerably crowded, Minnie seemed to secure permanent adoptive parents for one of the children. On several occasions she told Mary Cameron (her young adopted dressmaker) that she had found a nice home for a child. Sure enough when Mary got home, she would learn that Willie or Henry or Cyril had been collected by "a lady in a buggy" or "a lady from Wallacetown" or some other highly suitable "lady."

Minnie went to great lengths to hide her true identity whenever she accepted unwanted children, using assumed names and always taking lengthy train journeys to avoid unhealthy police interest. Following the earlier deaths of two of her small charges, police investigations had decided that natural causes were responsible, but Minnie was being kept under close scrutiny as part of ongoing investigations into the baby-farming trade.

Minnie's nefarious activities were uncovered in May 1895, when a vigilant railway guard reported that a woman answering Minnie's description had boarded the Lumsden train with a baby and a hatbox, but alighted carrying only the hatbox. Because Minnie was well-known locally, the police questioned the railway worker who had carried the hatbox onto the train. He stated it originally felt light, but seemed heavy when offloaded. Further enquiries led them to a Mrs Hornsby, who lived in Dunedin and told police that she had handed over her one-month-old granddaughter Eva, with some money, to a lady matching Minnie Dean's description at Milburn, just north of Milton. The police brought Mrs Hornsby to the Larches, where she identified Minnie Dean. A search of the house unearthed a tiny red dress, which Mrs Hornsby insisted Eva had been wearing. Minnie Dean denied any involvement despite Mrs Hornsby's identification, but finally admitted it when confronted with the evidence of the child's dress.

Janice Gill's 'Disguising the Grave'.
Telling Stories Steele Roberts 2009

Minnie was arrested and taken to Dunedin, while police searched The Larches and surrounding grounds for the missing girl. They ascertained that Charles Dean was responsible for the vegetable patch, whereas Minnie looked after the flowers, her pride and joy. One of the detectives noticed that flowers in a recently-dug plot looked as if they had been pushed into the ground rather than planted. He bent down and pulled one up easily; it was simply a flower on a stalk, like others surrounding it. On further investigation they found the bodies of two baby girls wrapped in oilcloth.

Charles Dean arrived home amidst these discoveries and protested his innocence, but was arrested and taken to Invercargill, while the children were put into protective care. The missing Eva Hornsby was identified as one of the dead children and the other as Dorothy Carter. Police searched until a further body was found nearby. In accordance with the law of the day, Minnie Dean could only be charged with one death, and that was the murder of Dorothy Edith Carter. It was soon established that Charles Dean had known nothing about his wife's activities and he was discharged, with Minnie to stand trial in Invercargill in June 1895. She walked stoically from the Invercargill railway station to the courthouse on the appointed day, braving the crowds who had already judged her guilty with shouts of "Where's the rope?"

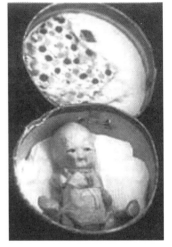

Miniature Minnie Dean hatbox sold outside the courthouse.

Throughout her trial, miniature hatboxes with baby dolls inside were sold by ghoulish hawkers outside the courthouse. Forty witnesses were called, and it was established that Minnie had bought laudanum from a Bluff chemist before going away for a couple of days carrying a tin hatbox. During this time she picked up two children, both seen with her at various stages of the journey. The hatbox had been empty when she left home, but by the time she arrived back at Winton it undoubtedly contained two bodies. It was left outside, while Minnie explained to her husband that it was full of bulbs and earth which she would deal with in the morning. When the hatbox was seen again later it was empty, but for traces of earth.

Mary Cameron testified that she had seen Minnie give laudanum to another child on the day he was to be collected by "a lady in a buggy", but he was never seen or heard of again. The fatal flaw in the defence was that Minnie could not account for the whereabouts of all the children who had been collected by "ladies in buggies." She was unable to supply one name or address to support her story that the children had been adopted.

The verdict was guilty of murder of one baby at least, with the judge ruling that any evidence relating to the disappearance of so many other children was admissible.

This probably helped seal her fate, for she had probably accounted for over twenty children in this way. She was sentenced to death by hanging and is the only woman in New Zealand ever to be hanged by the law.

Minnie Dean was a woman of contradictions, and it was widely believed that she had killed the other babies with hat pins, before throwing the bodies into streams. At the same time she seemed capable of demonstrating warmth and affection to her wards. Letters she wrote to women with children for adoption are full of religious fervour and benevolent concern.

The public automatically assumed that Minnie Dean was both insane and money-fixated. Was she guilty as charged, or did the weight of public condemnation press too heavily on the police, judge and jury to help unbalance the scales of justice? Was the Winton baby farmer a mercenary cold-blooded killer or a scapegoat for Victorian hypocrisy?

Minnie Dean was buried in a corner of the cemetery just outside Winton. Locals have steadfastly denied her a headstone, while folklore says grass never grows on her unmarked grave … though a local farmer told me it was probably due to the spraying of Roundup in the vicinity. For years afterwards it was common practice for Southland parents to tell their naughty children: "You'd better be good or I'll send you off to Minnie Dean."

Minnie Dean's name has been given to a Southland wildflower, which became the source of a widely believed superstition that it only ever grew on her grave. Many southern folk have grown up haunted by this irrational fear and its association with Minnie, leading them to rip out any plants and burn them, if they should appear in a domestic garden. A further piece of macabre folklore has the hangman turning Minnie's feet around on the gallows, to prevent her returning to haunt all and sundry.

Mike Fallow, a reporter with the *Southland Times*, recently told me how he used to be scared by a morbid tale recounted whenever the family drove past the Winton cemetery. Southland folk believed that the ghost of Minnie Dean would attempt to lure young children into the cemetery by calling for help, waiting to snatch any unwary child foolish enough to investigate her plaintive cries. This grim story gave him nightmares as a child.

Minnie Dean — Her Life of Crimes

At Winton Larches, vile and mean, there lived the wife of Charlie Dean,
Who gathered babies to adopt, no questions asked a daughter's lot.

An intellectual through and through, she taught at many Southland schools,
A doctor's widow she had been, until she married farmer Dean.

With two rooms and a small lean-to, and kids in boxes, quite a few.
But as two deaths had drawn the law, there really was no room for more.

She came from Edinburgh town, her usual fee was just ten pounds.
But when from business she arrived, her hatbox had a corpse inside.

When as the talk and rumour flew, a train guard more suspicious grew.
And when they dug her garden ground, some corpses and some bones were found.

O baby farmer Minnie Dean, a dreadful creature you have been.
You stifled babies all forlorn, and put them down with laudanum.

Some say your score was twenty-two, they changed the laws because of you.
And on your grave no growth is seen, except the plant called Minnie Dean.

~ by W.G.P., published by Lynley Hood in 'Minnie Dean, Her Life & Crimes'

Controversy surrounding Minnie Dean continues to this day; in true folklore tradition, her legend refuses to lie down. She made the news again recently when after 113 years, in a 'final' twist to her ongoing story, an unofficial rhyming headstone appeared overnight on her grave, inscribed: "Minnie Dean is part of Winton's history, where she now lies is now no mystery."

The unsanctioned marker was removed to make way for an officially approved headstone donated by family members back in Scotland. The new gravestone shows her name as Williamina McCulloch, wife of Charles Dean — no mention of Minnie, which may be seen as an attempt to dilute her notoriety and diffuse shame felt by family and community. From a folklore perspective this is all good meaty stuff, which can only further cement her place in Winton's folklore and help generate interest in Southland's Southern Odyssey heritage trails project.

Stan Graham

The legend of Stan Graham started on 8 October 1941 at Kowhitirangi on the 'Wild West Coast', which confirmed its reputation for thirteen days as the events made front pages throughout New Zealand and across the world. I'll illustrate this section with my 'Ballad of Stan Graham':

It's of a man Stan Graham, whose story I will tell,
How he became an outlaw and through misfortune fell.
Stanley was a cocky, who farmed the wild West Coast,
His shooting feats were legendary and that's no idle boast.

Stan Graham was a farmer with a passion for hunting deer in the Southern Alps. Familiar with the surrounding countryside, he was often called on to help police find people lost in the mountains and bush. He was not a particularly law-abiding citizen, however; he also kept a collection of fighting cocks (a practice long outlawed in New Zealand) which were obviously not just pets.

This almost unbelievable affair began after Graham had been quarrelling with his neighbours about the perceived poisoning of his cattle. One sunny morning he threatened a Danish neighbour, Anchor Madsen, with a rifle. Luckily for Madsen he was rescued by Alex Jamieson, who drove by at an opportune moment. Madsen lodged a complaint with the local policeman, Edward Best, who paid Graham a visit, intending to threaten him with arrest. Unarmed, Best found himself looking down the barrel of the same rifle and left the property when ordered to by Graham. He drove to Hokitika and reported the incident to the sergeant in charge.

Sergeant Cooper, on relief duty from Dunedin and unused to the ways of West Coasters, determined that under no circumstances should Graham be allowed to threaten anyone with a rifle. Taking Best and two other constables (the entire staff on duty at Hokitika that day) with him, Sergeant Cooper headed for Kowhitirangi to deal with Graham. They were greeted by Graham at his front door, still carrying his rifle. The police entered the gate and immediately Graham fired, wounding Best in the hand.

The two constables charged the front door, but were shot at point blank range, falling dead at Graham's feet. Sergeant Cooper also charged towards the house until he too was shot several times, dying just a few paces from the constables. Graham now tried to make Best write a statement, even though his hand was wounded, to the effect that the police had come with the sole purpose of shooting him. They argued for a time before Graham shot Best again and he later died in Westland hospital.

It was in 1941, when Stanley made his name,
By shooting four policemen who from Hokitika came,
To confiscate his weapons they drove to his front yard,
Trying to stop him threatening neighbours with reckless disregard.

The noise of the shots coming from Graham's house caused concern in the surrounding district. At the nearby schoolhouse, an agriculture instructor named Ridley investigated what had taken place. Borrowing a rifle and accompanied by Thomas Hornsby, a carpenter working at the school, they made for Graham's house. As soon as Graham saw them coming he shouted "Put down that rifle!" and Ridley complied. As Graham began to remove the bolt from the rifle, Ridley rather incautiously moved, so Graham promptly shot and seriously wounded him. Hornsby stood there awhile until Graham yelled "Take him out of here!" Hornsby carried Ridley away from the bloody scene, while Graham kept a close watch. Ridley died from the wounds he had received. Graham selected 2000 rounds of ammunition and, taking his favourite rifle along with the dead sergeant's pistol, departed into the dense bush nearby.

He got supplies together and set off for the bush,
With guns and ammunition to Mount Doughboy made a push.
But the job of catching Stanley was too much for the law,
So they called in extra help from the Home Guard and Army Corps.

But they hardly worried Stanley, who twice returned alone,
In search of food and clothing from his family home.
The night watch was on duty, when much to their surprise,
He shot two of their number, but was wounded in reply.

Kowhitirangi became a hive of activity as doctors and ambulances were called to the scene and messages were sent to the police at Greymouth. All available police rushed south, but no immediate action was taken. Next morning the whole of New Zealand was reading about the incredible happenings of the previous day.

Police were called in from around the country, along with members of the Home Guard, three members of which spent the following night in Graham's house in case he returned. Others took up positions across the road. Gregory Hutchinson was one of the home guardsmen entrenched in the house. Shortly after 8 p.m., when it was extremely dark, a footstep was heard outside the front door. Hutchinson challenged the visitor, who responded "I'm Stan Graham, can't a man come to his own house?" As soon as he had finished speaking, Graham fired, shooting Hutchinson through the stomach before creeping away into the darkness. The others in the house could do nothing but try and assist Hutchinson, who lay mortally wounded.

The men posted across the road guessed that someone else had been hurt and two of them, farmer Max Coulson and sawmiller Amuri King, dashed towards the house. They shouted to the men inside to hold their fire, but a shot rang out and Coulson fell, fatally wounded. King, however, was able to get off a shot at the fugitive in the darkness. Next morning they discovered a bloodstained rifle and 700 rounds of ammunition; Graham had been hit, but had escaped.

Seven men had been shot in only two days and the atmosphere was tense throughout the district. People didn't know what to do, and worried when Graham might strike next. Throughout the day army reinforcements poured into the area — even the Air Force was asked to keep a bomber ready at Hokitika in case it was needed.

A manhunt now was started and a hue and cry begun,
With the armed forces, police and militiamen.
But Stan he knew the country, every nook and cranny round,
Though the weather was against him, he proved a bushman of renown.

Not far from Graham's house was a large stand of bush. The men gathered near his home guessed he was hiding in it, and suggested the Air Force bomb it to force the fugitive into the open. Finally a group of home guardsmen rushed the bush, but Graham wasn't there, fortunately perhaps for them. Guards were posted throughout the area for the next ten days and armed men encircled Graham's home. One cloudy night he came back. The men heard footsteps on the road, with visibility almost nil. It had to be Graham. Suddenly the moon broke through the cloud and there he was, about to vault the front gate. One man fired, but before he could fire twice, Graham had vanished. In the morning they found bloodstains on the gatepost — the wanted man had been hit again.

Farms in the district had been evacuated by now and just as well, for Graham had started breaking into dwellings, helping himself to food. Tensions ran high among the waiting men and nerves were frayed. At night the slightest movement resulted in shots being loosed off in all directions.

A joke went the rounds that Hitler sent Graham a telegram, asking him to hold the South Island; he would send another man so Germany could capture the North.

Before the end of the second week everyone was sick and tired of the affray.

> For twelve days he defied them with all their expertise,
> Before they finally caught him and brought him to his knees.
> They shot him in the open, not far from Doughboy Creek,
> As he came in to surrender, his body bent and weak.

The end was almost an anti-climax. Late one afternoon a group of police and Home Guard members spotted a lone figure crossing open ground, a couple of miles from their position. Using binoculars they recognised Graham, and three constables set off after him. They got to within twenty yards when he stopped to lean on a fencepost; a policeman levelled his rifle and fired. Graham fell as the bullet hit a brass buckle on his belt and this, along with the bullet, entered his body. He was mortally wounded, but his first words to the approaching police were: "You've got me! What sort of ammo were you using?"

Apart from this final wound, Graham had two other wounds from his previous sorties. One in his hand was turning gangrenous. He gave this as his reason for being in the open: "There was no need for that last shot, I was coming in anyway." In hospital, although Graham was dying and knew it, he talked to his wife and answered police questions. He remained conscious for nearly twelve hours before succumbing.

When he died there was criticism that he had been shot in cold blood without being given a sporting chance to shoot it out. The police, though, felt that more than enough people had been killed and no risks were to be taken. Many people thought Graham insane, but this wasn't the view held by coasters, because it didn't seem consistent with his statements as he lay dying. They felt that Graham, showing true logic, had decided that after shooting one policeman, he might as well be hung for a sheep as for a lamb.

> Now my song is ended, there's not much left to say,
> Stan, he was an outlaw and for that he had to pay.
> Though his skill in hunting might have served well elsewhere,
> His memory will linger for many long and bitter years.

After the drama, morbid curiosity-seekers descended on Kowhitirangi as daytrippers, annoying locals who wanted to put the whole business behind them. One night in the rainy season the Graham homestead mysteriously burned down, leaving nothing for sightseers to gape at. The spectacular blaze that lit up the surrounding countryside was said to have resulted from spontaneous West Coast combustion.

The Graham affair passed into history, if not folklore and legend. Over the years a few songs and stories have made Graham out to be a hero in the Ned Kelly mould. Some say that local residents were friendly towards him and sympathetic to his disputes, and had even helped him after the murders. It has been said that the original cause of the whole affair was the theft of one of Graham's fighting cocks. To locals, then and now, it all seems fantastic and unbelievable.

The best-known Stan Graham song is by Jim Case of Kumara in 1943–44, 'The Hero of the Coast', sung to the tune of 'Yellow Rose of Texas' while the chorus changes to the tune of the Tex Morton favourite 'Mandrake'.

> Now you've heard of old Ned Kelly and other outlaws of fame,
> But now we have a new one, Stan Graham is his name.
> Stanley was a cocky, from the old West Coast;
> He was a famous shot and that's no idle boast.
>
> But one bright sunny morning he crossed it with the law,
> He shot four coppers standing outside his ranch-house door.
> He got supplies together, guns and ammo too,
> And set out for Mount Doughboy to hide out from the blue.
>
> *Chorus* So pick up your guns, Stan, go it while you can;
>   The cops are all around you, they're out to get their man.
>   You know the country over, you know the best of spots;
>   So all you've got to do, Stan, is watch out for the cops.
>
> Now the job of catching Stanley was too big for the law,
> They had to get the Home Guard and the Army Corps.
> They even got Bob Semple's modern army tank,
> Machine guns, a bomber, and formed in four-like ranks.
>
> Now before my song is finished there's something I'd like to say,
> I wish we had a million like poor old Stan today.
> The Japs would not be game to come within our shores,
> And we would live in quietness for now and evermore.

147

VIII

From Illustrated New Zealand News 1883

WOOL AWAY JACK

The folklore of shearing

"All aboard! All aboard!" is the cry.
They're a ripping lot of shearers in the shed;
Big Mick the Speewah ringer, must make skin and trimmings fly
This season if he means to keep ahead;
For Barcoo Ben will run him and half a dozen more
Of the lank Australian crush upon the board,
And it ain't no use to tell us of the tallies that he shore,
There'll be records broke this year, you take my word.

"Wool away! Wool away!" is the cry,
And the merry game of busting is begun!
They're going sheep and sheep, for Big Mick will do or die,
And the fleecy boys are kept upon the run.
It ain't no kind of joking, it's a game of killing men —
Up the neck and down the shoulder like a flash,
And the scruffing and the rattle on the battens of the pen
As to gain a catch the ringer makes a dash.

"Sling 'em out! Sling 'em out!" is the word
You can hear the grinding pinions of the press,
Snipping shears and flying brooms upon the board,
And the sheep are growing wonderfully less.
The shepherds' dogs are barking in the yard,
And the penner-up is cursing at the back,
And the boss is looking savage at a long Australian card
With a look that means it's odds he gets the sack.

"Clear the board! Clear the board!" is the shout,
And Barcoo Ben is caught upon the tail!
Big Mick is smiling grimly as he takes the cobbler out,
With a lead of two at breakfast he can sail.
The shearers laugh like schoolboys as they hurry from the shed,
There's a clinking of the pannikins and knives,
There's the 'barrack' at the table and the clever things are said,
And yet all those blokes are shearing for their lives.

'Shearing' ~ David McKee Wright

'SPEEWAH' IS A TERM FROM THE AUSTRALIAN shearing tradition for a mythical place where the shearers are champions. Sheep farming weaves a common thread throughout Australia and New Zealand, one which has given rise to a fund of shared songs, balladry and tall stories that have become firmly entrenched in the folklore of both countries. Sheep shearing invented a language of its own, creating colourful turns of phrase that became commonplace. These were the days before the Anzacs, when Australian and New Zealand ties were closer than in modern times of sporting and shearing rivalry. Men regularly criss-crossed the 'ditch' looking for work, treating the Tasman as if it were a mere stream separating the two countries.

The huge influx of Australian shearers in the 1890s had a big impact on our shearing industry. Working the high country stations on a contract basis, they brought with them songs, verse and stories, influencing local versifiers and rhymesters along the way. The shearers treated both countries as one and it was no surprise when New Zealand was invited to become a state of Australia in 1901. Many people on both sides of the Tasman thought there should be an Australasian federation of seven colonies, but New Zealand, under the leadership of 'King' Dick Seddon, declined. New Zealand politicians found the 'ditch' politically unbridgeable, despite being perfectly amenable to deferring to a more distant parliament at Westminster.

When the early settlers first drove sheep into the hinterland of the South Island they thought their greatest problems would be in trying to overcome the large, cold rivers and snow-covered alps. Yet shearing the sheep and getting the wool down to the ships soon became their life's work. As their flocks increased they found that the European method of shearing in the open, at the rate of a few dozen a day, was unsatisfactory. They improvised on the new Australian methods of fencing large flocks of sheep near the homestead and using gangs of men working in big covered sheds. Previously, shearing as a trade hadn't existed; now men who had seldom seen a sheep prior to emigrating had to learn new skills. Shearers became key workers in a thriving new industry, and as the sheds grew increasingly larger they were soon fleecing the wool off a hundred sheep or more in a day, using the 'blades', i.e. hand shears. Before long, a thousand head or more were being counted out in a day, encouraging experienced Australian shearers to come to our shores, looking for work on the high country stations. When shearing machines arrived on the scene, new techniques doubled and eventually trebled tallies. Because the high country can be cold even in summer, however, many stations still use the old blade shears, because no one has yet devised a machine that will shear far enough above the skin to leave that vital half-inch of wool which can mean life or death for the newly-shorn sheep.

There's a sound of many voices in the camp and on the track
And letters coming up in shoals to stations at the back.
And every boat that crosses from the sunny other side,
Is bringing waves of shearers for the swelling of the tide.

Chorus   For the shearing's coming round boys, the shearing's coming round.
        And the stations of the mountains have begun to hear the sound.

They'll be talking up at Laghmor of the tallies that were shore,
And the bloke that broke the record is remembered at Benmore.
For the yarns of strikes and barneys will be told till all is blue,
And the ringers and the bosses will be passed in long review.

The great Orari muster and the drafting of the men,
Like a mob of ewes and wethers will be surely told again.
And a lot of heathen places that will rhyme with kangaroo,
Will be named along with ringers and the things that they can do.

At last the crowds will gather for the morning of the start,
And the slowest of the jokers will be trying to look smart.
And a few will get the bullet and high hope will have a fall,
While the bloke that talks the loudest stands a show of looking small.

from 'The Shearing's Coming Round' ~ David McKee Wright.
Laghmor (Gaelic for large fields) is in the Ashburton district.

I remember performing this song at a concert in the Canterbury Museum circa 1968–69, and after I'd finished an elderly lady came up to me wiping tears from her eyes. She had been born on Benmore Station in the early 1890s and the song had rekindled strong memories for her. This would not be the only time my singing of Kiwi songs has managed to stir powerful feelings among my audience (generally of an older generation), many of whom come forward to tell me I have either just sung about their family history, or that a member of their family had experienced a similar situation. Moments like these, when audiences identify with and relate to the songs, make the collection and preservation of our musical heritage and oral history truly worthwhile.

The shearers brought a new way of life to the country — their life was hard, their day long and although accommodation often left much to be desired, the cheques were big, especially if one could attain 'ringer' or 'gun shearer' status. From exposure to the visitors' yarns and ditties, local rhymesters and poets found inspiration to create their own songs and verses recording the new lifestyle, while documenting their responses to the growth of this new and viable industry. They developed their own heroes, such as the champion shearer or fastest man in the shed, who became known as the gun or ringer and was idolised by all. Even those who possessed an insatiable thirst for hard liquor were celebrated in home-grown song, verse and yarn.

> An old shearer stood at the cookshop door, bleary and weary and stiff,
> He'd been on the queer stuff a week or more, his noodle was all skew-whiff;
> And he vowed 'by hell' and the shirt he wore, no more on the booze he'd go,
> By his old bay nag and his swag he swore that this was his farewell blow.
>
> With his 'Burgons' then to the shed he tore, where into the sheep he bogged,
> And while there was fleece to shear, he shore, and sweated, and swore, and slogged;
> And never, he vowed, with oaths blood-red, as the cobbler he undressed,
> Would he 'grind' again or ring a shed for 'Bung' at the Shearer's Rest.
>
> He set the shearers a sizzling pace, where only the 'guns' could stay,
> And he ripped and tore and he chipped and swore, and he snorted, "Wool Away!"
> He trimmed those wethers of every ounce, and he cursed and blazed ahead,
> He shore like hell, and he shore them well, and he 'rung' the blinkin' shed.
>
> Then he gathered his cheque and rolled his swag, and hopped on the old mare's back;
> With a "Cheerio, boys!" he lit a fag, and made for the bridle-track;
> For his hopes ran high but his nag went slow, and the sun was five hours down,
> When he ambled in with his hard-earned tin, and camped in the old bush town.
>
> And became a squatter, grew rich in time, as most fiction heroes do?
> No! — this 'ere little tale in ragged rhyme is perched on a fact, and true,
> And this shearer's roll and six quid as well — from the sale of his old bay nag,
> Went over the 'crow' at the bush hotel for a riotous non-stop jag.
>
> *'Wool, Wether and Wine' - George Meek*

The early shearing sheds were rough-and-ready affairs, some nothing better than corrugated iron shanties with canvas spread over them to help keep the wool clean.

The shearing itself was a relatively simple affair. Men turned up and were given shears and ointment for cuts inflicted. Sixty to eighty sheep were considered a good day's work. A record 321 were shorn by Jacky Howe in Australia, but such achievements were hotly debated, and only a few shearers reached the glorious tally of a 'century'.

After taking off the fleece, the shearer himself carried it to the sorting table and called to the overseer or boss of the board, "One for Bill Jones" or "One for Mick Kelly" whatever his name happened to be. Each call meant a move for the little wooden peg on the tally board.

George Meek wrote of an actual happening in an Otago shearing shed:

Joe Rogan had a lifelong set on all the parson chaps —
    He'd a notion that hard, honest toil they shirked;
To hear him slather up the crowd as slackers, stiffs and saps —
    You would think that Joe was the only one who worked;
"A rough diamond" said his neighbours, and the title p'raps was right,
For there never was a worthy cause for which Joe wouldn't fight.

One day the parson made a call at Rogan's grazing run,
    Joe was shearing in the woolshed on his pat;
As shearer, roller, picker-up, and broomie all in one,
    And the parson scented hellfire in their chat;
As he blew into the woolshed from a nor-west's howling roar,
Joe's first salute was "Curse you man, shut that blasted draughty door!"

The parson shut the blasted door, and saw it didn't slam,
    Then strolled silently along the shearing board,
Where, parked in perfect silence, listened meekly as a lamb
    While Joe Rogan ripped and ranted, reared, and roared
"You parson chaps are all the same — like them talking salesmen mob,
Wasting the cockie's blasted time, when he's sweatin' on a job."

"May be, I could assist you," said the Christian man of peace;
    "You could!" roared Rogan, with murder in his look —
"If I don't get these sheep shorn they will all be double fleece,
    If you want to help then take your blasted hook."
But, the parson unperturbed by Rogan's woolly-lined salutes,
With an outsize twinkle in his eye, was taking off his boots.

Joe knew he hadn't scared him, and this sort o' pleased him, too,
    For he liked a man who showed that he was game;
Old Joe was plainly wonderin' what the parson chap would do,
    And his eyes blazed like a fiery, furnace flame
When the parson donned a pair o' pants, old Joe had thrown away,
And a pair o' yolky moccasins that sure had seen their day.

Armed with a vet'ran pair of blades, he stepped in for his catch,
   Joe was speechless, as he grunted, chewed and spat;
He had a sort o' feeling he had somehow met his match;
   With his first sheep off, the parson said, "That's that!"
The parson's second sheep told Joe, his penmate was a gun;
His third went through the port-hole as Joe undressed number one.

But Rogan wasn't touchy — he could take it with the best;
   As the day wore on the goodwill spirit grew;
Joe had tallied just on thirty, then knocked off for a rest,
   While the parson chap had barbered eighty-two;
Said Joe, "You wouldn't like a spot? — you've made a damn good show!"
"Too right, I would," the parson said — that spot converted Joe.

The tales about Joe Rogan were both novel and profuse;
   Tales of toughness, roughness, honest toil and sweat;
Of wild and woolly nights he drank and spat tobacco juice,
   But one true one, those who knew him won't forget —
Of the record-breaking shearing, when scarce a blinkin' word was said,
When Joe played the role of drummer, and the parson rung the shed.

'The Parson Rings the Shed' ~ George Meek

'Wool Away Jack' is an accurate, blow-by-blow description of shearing. An old-timer, Jack Frost, was picking up the wool and each time a shearer finished a sheep he would call "Wool away Jack!" or when his pen was getting empty of sheep, he would call out to Joe Charles — "Sheep ho, Joe!" This song does for New Zealand what 'Click go the Shears' has done as the definitive shearing song for Australia:

Who would be a shearer a-sweating in a shed,
If I had to be a shearer, I might as well be dead.
For bang goes the bell and it's out upon the floor,
Take up your stand there by the swinging door.

Chorus   Singing *Wool away, Jack and sheep ho, Joe,*
        Drive in the woollies with a loud Ho! Ho!

Then it's grab a daggy ewe and drag her to the board,
Pick up your hand-piece and pull on the cord.
Down through the belly and around the back door,
Up on the neck and swing her on the floor.

Down on the shoulder and up the long blow,
Whip off the last side and let the blighter go.
Here come the flies to hang around you now,
Swimming in the sweat as it trickles down your brow.

Here comes the boss too — he's bound to have a moan,
For he worries on his troubles, like a dog upon a bone.
One drop of blood and he has a dozen fits,
For he spends half his time now counting all the tits!

Here comes the cook, she's a sight we like to see,
With a basket full of scones and a billy full of tea.
So it's knock off, Jack, and it's knock off, Joe,
We'll all sit around for a long smoko.

adapted from 'On Shearing at Four Views' by Joe Charles

Many of the shearers were nomadic or 'on the swag', travelling from station to station, where they camped nearby or in the swaggers' hut (the station owner's labour exchange). All were waiting for shearing to commence and hopeful of gaining employment. Author Anthony Trollope described it thus after a visit here:

> The bulk of the labour is performed by seasonal workers or swagmen, who wander in search of work and are hired for only a short time. They come and go and are known by strange nick-names and sometimes by no name at all. They are rough to look at, dirty in appearance, shaggy with long hair and when on the job live in either huts or tents, hardly knowing what a bed is.

How times have changed. Shearers' quarters now are generally equipped with all the conveniences of the modern age. Most sheds boast electric power, and even fans for a touch of class. Many modern New Zealand gangs employ women as rouseabouts and sometimes as shearers.

John Archer of Waiouru sent me this version of 'The Shearer's Lament' after getting it from George Black, a shearer and bush poet who became a reporter for the *Waikato Times*. It is a variant of 'The Dying Bushman' or 'Bushman's Lament', which is hardly surprising given the 1930s timeframe (signified by mention of the Lister engine which used to power shears until electricity finally reached farms in the Taihape district circa 1935), and the transient nature of bushmen.

I am just a worn out shearer and my shearing days are done,
My gear I've left behind the whare door.
For the ewes and rams and wethers have got so mighty tough,
That I just can't seem to shear them any more.

In all of the Taihape there was none to work like me,
And I long again to hear the Lister roar.
For the ewes and rams and wethers have got so mighty tough,
I just can't seem to shear them any more.

In the early days of isolation and poor conditions, men in these camps were wont to dream of better working conditions, good times (past and future) and to indulge in the universal male fantasies of wine, women and song:

I'm just a poor old shearer and I'm stationed on the board,
I've got my little hand-piece in my hand.

Chorus   But I'm happy as a clam in this land of ewes and lambs,
      In my tick-bound, bug-bound dug-out in the true.

Oh, the place is strewn all round with sheep wool and sheep dags,
Of rouseabouts there are so very few …

Oh, the walls are made of iron and the windows made of bag,
The doorways let the howling rousies through …

Oft times I wish I had a girl to sit upon my knee
And relieve me of the pain that I am in.
That girl how I would love her, if she'd come and live with me,
In my tick-bound, bug-bound, dug-out in the true.

'Dug-out in the True' – Anon

Or this more modern fantasy, 'The Shepherd's Dream' by Ross McMillan:

I must have dozed for I dreamed that we were away where the sun shone hot,
Where the wide blue sky from snow was free and sheep and hills were not.
No need for the rough old shepherd's swag nor the heavy hob-nailed boots,
Feather beds instead of sleeping bags and the dress was tailored suits.

Our meals were cooked by a chef in white with oysters and eggs for free,
And steak that melted under a bite and wine in the place of tea.
While every bloke had a serving maid clad in white bikini,
To fetch and carry, while music played and the prettiest one served me.

Her hair was dark as a blackbird's wing, her eyes were a mountain blue,
Her voice held the lovely lilt of spring as she said that her name was Sue.
I woke when an arm went round my neck, 'twas only my old mate Lew,
In the old tin hut, way out the back, to hand me a plate of stew.

Tall stories travelled easily throughout Australia and New Zealand with these itinerants, to be retold in huts from one end of the country to the other.

The legendary shearer Jacky Howe, in company with a mate, turned up at a fairly small run. The owner said, "Are you looking for shearing work?"
    They replied "Yes, have you got some?"
    It transpired there were 500 sheep waiting to be shorn.
    Howe says to his mate — "You'd better boil up the billy while I cut them out, and we'll move on this afternoon!"

Few of these itinerants had any family, or any hope of making sufficient capital to settle on land of their own. With their cheques in their pockets after months of hard work they would make for the nearest shanty where, as one squatter said,

"They could be seen in a brutal state of intoxication, more like a dog than a human being" — typical of the 'work and bust' procedure.

After the turn of the century the alcoholic excesses of shearers became rarer. Some now had wives and families tucked away in country towns, while others were cockies' sons seeking to further their experience before returning home to the family farm. The minority still 'cut out' their cheques, but often in more sophisticated ways than in the past.

> I'm what you call a New Chum and you will understand,
> Through assisted immigration, I'm here in Maoriland.
> I came out to make a fortune and on work I'd set my mind,
> But had no end of bother a decent job to find.

from 'The Embryo Cockatoo/The New Chum'

First published on a broadsheet by the *Temuka Leader* in 1907, this comes from the pen of 'The Wanderer'; probably Micky Laracy, an Australian shearer who became the first secretary of the New Zealand Shearer's Union.

Here we have another breed of shearer that can't be ignored — the new chum, often an immigrant who depended on Stockholm tar to cover up damage inflicted on the sheep as a result of his unskilled efforts. New chums were despised by the skilled tradesmen, who lost no opportunity to ridicule them, as in:

> When shearing comes lay down your drums,
> Step on the board, you brand new chums.
> With a ra-dum, ra-dum, rub-a-dub-dub,
> We'll send you home in a lime juice tub.
>
> Now you have crossed the briny deep,
> You fancy you can shear a sheep,
> With a ra-dum, ra-dum, rub-a-dub-dub,
> We'll send you home in a lime juice tub.
>
> There's brand new chums and cockies' sons,
> Who fancy that they are great guns,
> They reckon they can shear the wool,
> But the beggars can only tear and pull.
>
> They tar the sheep till they're almost black,
> Roll up, roll up and get the sack.
> Once more they're on the wallaby track,
> Once more to look for work out back.

from 'The Lime Juice Tub' (Australian folk song)~ Anon

Micky Laracy also wrote the following piece, 'Snowed In', collected by Elsie Locke from a shearer at Castle Hill in Canterbury in 1950. It took Australian shearers a little time to acclimatise to weather conditions and work practices, but once they did, Maoriland was the place to be. Elsie passed this on to me in 1969.

I heard Australian shearers talk in good old days gone by,
Of being snowed in in Maoriland and I used to wonder why.
Well last year I came over, I had a decent run,
I then took on the harvest, when the shearing was all done.

I cut a dash in Christchurch, I had a merry time,
Fell in love with a Maori maid and pressed her to be mine.
Well now my fun is over, for I've squandered all my tin,
My Maori maid has jilted me, so here I am snowed in.

My mates have crossed the Tasman and are on the Sydney side,
While some are shearing now beyond the Great Divide.
While I must be a rabbiter, or else take on a team,
And to an outback shearer you know what that would mean.

Now to winter here midst snow-clad hills, where the sun does seldom shine,
And wood's as scarce as diamonds are out on the Condamine.
I find my garments far too light and my blankets far too thin,
So now I've got a good idea what it's like to be snowed in.

And should I get acclimatised, it's here I'll make my home,
In search of shearers' fleeting cheques, I never more will roam.
For this is a land of plenty, where droughts are quite unknown,
And a democratic government that we would like to own.

The people are so friendly here they'll take you by the hand,
I can vouch for the treatment you'll receive in Maoriland.
And if a bloke is careful and takes care of his tin,
While Seddon steers his little craft, he'll never get snowed in.

A shearer had to abide by rules or he didn't get the job. Frequently agreements had to be signed in advance and would vary from place to place. One such agreement states:
* Payment seventeen shillings and sixpence per 100.
* Food to be purchased from the station owner at a fixed price.
* Hours of work from 6a.m. until half an hour before sunset.
* One hour for breakfast and lunch and three short smokos during the day. [On Saturdays they worked till 3 in the afternoon]
* Any shearer breaking a fleece, is not to be paid for shearing in such a manner.

Eventually shearers refused to accept these conditions — especially travelling from station to station without certainty of employment and never knowing what wages would be on offer. The continuing prospect of rough and dirty accommodation, coupled with astronomical food prices, paved the way for a shearers' union which did much to improve their lot throughout New Zealand and Australia.

> There are shearing sheds I shore in that are scattered by the way,
> And I seem to hear the clatter of the cutters making play.
> And the laughter of the shearers from the days of long ago,
> When they called me Jim the Ringer down a country road I know.
>
> How I raced to hold the ringer's place and shear at number one,
> Chased by the shearers in the gang and every bloke a 'gun'
> The white wool seemed to fall away 'neath every perfect blow,
> With just half a sheep between us, down a country road I know.

Shearing terms

Blow	A cutting stroke
Bluey/drum	Swag or blanket roll, named for the colour of the blanket
Board	The floor of a shed on which the sheep are shorn
Broomie	A shedhand who sweeps the board
Burgons	Burgon & Ball — hand shears with a single bow
Century	Total of 100 sheep shorn in a day
Cobbler	The last and roughest sheep in the catching pen
Clip	The total amount of wool shorn
Cocky (cockie)	A small-scale farmer (from cockatoo)
Cockie's joy	Golden syrup
Cove	Squatter or station owner
Crow	The counter in the bar of a hotel
Cut out	When a shed is cut out it means the shearing is over
Daggy sheep	Sheep with excrement stuck to the wool of the tail and backside
Damper	Coarse bread made with baking soda for leavening
Drummer	Shearer with the lowest aggregate tally of shorn sheep
Gun	A crack shearer
Jag	An extended drinking bout
Johnny cakes	Flat cakes of flour and water paste toasted on a bed of glowing embers
Jumbuck	A sheep
Lime juice tub	English immigrant ship on which lime juice was served to prevent scurvy

The rouseabouts were running from the table and the board,
With the fleeces and the pieces that the classer binned and stored.
While the bloke who worked the wool press, how he made the levers go,
As the bales were sewn and branded down a country road I know.

When the hard day's work was over and the sun was in the west,
And the vivid flash of evening stained that far off mountain's breast.
We'd share a smoke and bottle while we watched the shadows grow,
As they lengthened into darkness down a country road I know…

from 'Down a Country Road I Know' — Ross McMillan

Long blow	A shearing movement running down the full length of the sheep
Moccasins	Shearers' footwear made of jute & cut from a woolpack
Nobbler	A measure of liquor
Nudist	A shorn sheep
Pannikin	A tin drinking mug
Pen mate	Two shearers sharing a catching pen
Picker up	One who picks up the fleece and carries it to the wool table
Pink	To shear a sheep too close to the skin
Port hole	A swinging door through which the shorn sheep were passed out into the counting-out pen
Ringer	Champion shearer of the shed, with the highest tally of sheep shorn
Rousey	Rouseabout — a shed hand/general hand, who may be called on to undertake any job in the shearing shed
Sawbees	A type of hand shears
Shoulder cut	A blow cutting off the main portion of the fleece
Siding blow	A cutting thrust made with the shears
Slummed a pen	Shorn a pen full of sheep hastily and carelessly
Snagger	A clumsy shearer
Stand	When a shearer is engaged to shear, he is said to have booked a stand
Tally	Number of sheep shorn by a shearer in a day
Tar	Antiseptic Stockholm tar, dabbed on sheep cut by the shears
Three spot	A cheque for £100 or more
Wet sheep	Sheep too wet to shear
Wool bale	A jute pack in which the wool is baled — also called a woolpack
Wolseleys	Machine shears

VIIII

HUNGER IN THE AIR

Hard times

NEW ZEALAND BEGAN TO EXPERIENCE hard times and harsh conditions with the onset of the first major Depression. As the gold boom collapsed, affecting financial institutions and farming, it created a severe job shortage which culminated in the economic recession of the 1880s and '90s. This period became known as 'The Hungry Years' and thousands took to the roads in search of employment and security. Thousands more departed for Australia in this period — which became known as 'The Exodus' — looking for a better way of life, unfortunately arriving just in time to experience a similar recession in that country.

A comparable exodus would occur almost a hundred years later, as an economic recession hit our shores once again in the 1980s.

And when skies are grey above us, it's getting hard to bear,
The feeling that the country has of hunger in the air.

from 'Hunger in the Air ~ David McKee Wright

The Hungry Years lasted from 1879 through to 1895, inhibiting growth in the new colony, despite a proliferation of fresh ideas which included tax reforms, workers' rights, trade unionism, temperance and votes for women.

Somehow, the Auckland economy remained unaffected by the recession in the south, despite the burgeoning population drift northwards. However, the final reckoning came in 1885~86, when the economy collapsed fast and hard, beginning a ten-year banking crisis which affected the whole colony. Leading businessmen went under, previously solid businesses closed their doors and hundreds were declared bankrupt. Poverty could be seen everywhere, with the unemployed on the streets, clamouring for help to emigrate. Husbands deserted families so their children could receive charitable aid. Soup kitchens sprang up and men took to the roads seeking work. Men were encouraged to shoot rabbits for a pittance and there was a resurgence of interest in gold mining. Northland became an attractive proposition as hordes of men migrated northwards to search for kauri gum.

The economic conditions shook people's thinking as unemployment and uncertainty opened their eyes and ears to radical new ideas such as socialism. Soon many were talking about a new social order based on co-operation and brotherhood. This led to the growth of friendly societies and trade unions, the latter becoming a popular remedy in the battle against privilege and exploitation.

> Who robs the widow of her right
> By work that takes her day and night
> To earn his poor starvation mite?
> The sweater.
>
> Who is it makes girls go astray
> To earn their bread in sinful way
> Because for work he will not pay?
> The sweater.
>
> Who is it that will cheat and lie
> And every cunning trick will try,
> His greed of gain to satisfy?
> The sweater.
>
> Who is the vilest, meanest thief,
> That trades in flesh and blood and grief,
> Till from his fangs death brings relief?
> The sweater.
>
> Who has the rings and jewels on,
> And gloats o'er money he has won
> By dirty business he has done?
> The sweater.
>
> He is society's disgrace
> And must be told so to his face.
> So out with him! Leave him no place,
> The sweater.

'The Sweater' ~ Anon

Women in clothing factories were paid very little for long hours stitching in poor light. After this song was published in the *Lyttelton Times* in 1889 public meetings highlighted further concern, which led to the appointment of a Royal Commission and the formation of a tailoresses' union.

When the economy finally climbed out of its doldrums in the mid-1890s, new pastoral industries paved the way to national prosperity. The price of wool picked up, while fat-lamb farming and dairying also began to flourish. Meat refrigeration, still fresh from its beginnings at Totara Estate in 1881, was poised to underwrite the country's standard of living for the next hundred years.

Chorus Sailing the ocean wide and blue, let the winds blow fair and free,
The shipping of meat to London town will go down in history.

'Twas in the year of eighty-one — sail oh sail away,
Bill Davidson unveiled his plan — to seek a bright new day

Tom Brydon built a slaughter house — sail oh sail away,
On the farm estate at Totara — to seek a bright new day…

They mustered sheep from all around — sail oh sail away,
They railed them to Port Chalmers town — to seek a bright new day.

Once the mutton's chilled and stowed — sail oh sail away,
Dunedin's anchor can be raised — to seek a bright new day…

John Whitson is her captain bold — sail oh sail away,
He'll fight to keep this cargo cold — and seek a bright new day.

When they've docked at London town — sail oh sail away,
Smithfield Market is the place — they'll find their bright new day…

Bill's golden dream has been preserved — sail oh sail away.
As a tribute to the export trade — that built a bright new day.

The Totara story's no mean feat — sail oh sail away,
Let's raise a glass to frozen meat — that built a bright new day…

'Bright New Day' ~ Phil Garland

New Zealand was becoming a land of abundance and hope — sometimes called the 'Britain of the South Seas' or the social laboratory of the world. Nationalism was on the rise and the term 'God's Own Country' had been coined. But all this peace and prosperity was about to be shattered by the onset of two very different wars.

An outpost of the empire, New Zealand was culturally, emotionally and economically tied to Britain. The price of 'Empire' proved small when New Zealand soldiers underwent their baptism of fire on the battlefields in South Africa, but in the Great War of 1914-18 New Zealand's innocence ended on the bloody shores of Gallipoli and in the fields of France and Belgium.

Few New Zealanders did not lose a relative, friend or neighbour in the war, and many who did return were physically or mentally scarred for life. The government spent considerable money to help returned servicemen train for new careers, buy houses or farms, although the country seemed anything but a land fit for heroes. Many disgruntled 'diggers' gravitated towards the camaraderie and mateship of the Returned Soldiers Association, which became one of the country's most influential pressure groups. As if the war hadn't done enough, Spanish influenza swept the world in 1918 and arrived in New Zealand, in all likelihood brought home by returning troops, to devastate the population.

Those years after the Great War were a worrying time for New Zealanders trying to overcome the price of war and the cost of the influenza pandemic. A short sharp economic recession in 1921~22 only added to the country's woes. Fortunately some stability was near at hand with good progress being made. The country eagerly embraced new technologies such as electricity, motor vehicles, radio, talking movies and aeroplanes. The overall trend was one of modest expansion, despite an unstable economy and the approaching dark clouds of Depression.

> We shall come the unemployed,
> The disinherited of this earth,
> We shall come into your temples
> And your marble halls of mirth.
>
> We shall come as you have made us,
> Ragged, lousy, pale and gaunt,
> You the House of Have, shall listen
> Unto us, the House of Want.
>
> We are measuring the weed-chip gangs,
> That stretch from coast to coast,
> We shall come, us, the rightless
> Us, the God forsaken host,
>
> We shall come in all the madness,
> Born of hunger, pain and strife,
> On our lips the cry for vengeance,
> In our souls the lust for life.
>
> We shall swarm as swarmed the locusts,
> That on Pharoah's kingdom fell,
> And sling your politicians
> And your damned police to Hell.

An anonymous worker, 1932

The Great Depression impacted on the lives of millions around the world, but proved most severe in countries such as New Zealand, where a reasonable standard of welfare had already been attained. Wool and dairy prices fell and unemployment rose as the world crisis deepened. New Zealand lived by exporting primary produce and needed more of its income to meet overseas debts, making us extremely vulnerable to market fluctuations. As export prices fell, government revenues shrank as well. Despite measures already in place for unemployment relief, they weren't enough to cope with the effects of government policy. The early 1930s saw the worst of it and the government was finally pushed into real action, setting up a fully-fledged relief scheme for the unemployed.

My man's gone now — he had to go,
He couldn't find no work around this town.
Not for ages — used his wages,
Got up this morning and he was gone.

Monday morning, it starts to rain,
Around the curve there comes a south-bound train.
Under a tarpaulin rides a bum called John,
He was a strange man, but now he's gone.

Morning sunshine, the rooster crows,
Along the highway walking to where, goodness knows.
Where's John sleeping? How's he keeping?
When will he take the homeward road?

My man's gone now, he had to go,
He couldn't find no work around this town.
Not for ages — used his wages,
Got up this morning and he was gone.

He was a strange man but now he's gone.

'My Man's Gone' ~ Anon

The Depression treated all walks of life equally. Wealthy investors and businessmen found themselves penniless and jobless, sharing the unemployment queues with the chronically poor. People were being denied a decent life amid our 'pastures of plenty' while unemployment continued to grow in the presence of underutilised resources. The deprived became as despairing as their leaders, watching as material and mental bankruptcy walked side by side through the growing calamity.

Wand'ring above a sea of glass
In the soft April weather,
Wand'ring through the yellow grass
Where the sheep stand and blether;
Roaming the cliffs in the morning light,
Hearing the gulls that cry there,
Not knowing where I'll sleep tonight,
Not much caring either.

I haven't got a stiver,
The tractor's pinched my job.
I owe the bar a fiver,
And the barman fifteen bob.
The good times are over,
The monkey-man has foreclosed,
The woman has gone with the drover,
Not being what I supposed.

I used to set things spinning,
I used to dress like a lord,
Mostly I came out winning,
Now all that's gone by the board.
My pants have lost their creases,
I've fallen down on my luck,
The world has dropped to pieces,
Ev'rything's come unstuck.

Roaming the cliffs in the morning light,
Hearing the gulls that cry there,
Not knowing where I'll sleep tonight,
Not much caring either.
Wand'ring above a sea of glass
In the soft April weather,
Wand'ring through the yellow grass,
Close to the end of my tether.

'Down on My Luck' ~ ARD Fairburn

With unemployment rising and rural income falling, government applied the old-fashioned cure of trying to make costs follow the downward movement of prices. This cure-all only added to the bankruptcy of farmers, storekeepers, manufacturers and tradesmen, creating more problems throughout the country.

A desperate and out-of-touch parliament passed legislation that intensified the problems it was seeking to address. Each act of deflation pitched more and more people into want and hopelessness, because the government still believed in economic rules that were no longer relevant. People were starving and real hunger was in the air when this story did the rounds:

> A hungry bloke went up to the Hospital Board to get his handout and he received an old flap of mutton. The fellow behind the counter said to him, "Well, that'll keep the wolf from the door."
>
> "Keep the wolf from the door!" the bloke answered. "We dragged him in months ago and ate him!"

As the new wage and retrenchment policies increased so too did the number of unemployed, many of whom could take it no longer. Men decided to strike in Auckland, and on 14 April 1932 nearly 20,000 hungry unemployed marched up Queen Street to the town hall, which could only hold 3000. When the doors were shut and police were called to prevent more entering the hall, the biggest riot in New Zealand's history occurred. Blood was spilt when the police drew their batons and the unemployed countered by tearing pickets off the fence of the Auckland City Mission. Thousands moved down Queen Street, smashing shop windows and looting. Despite naval reinforcements being called in to assist, another riot took place the next night in Karangahape Road which heralded the start of civil disobedience throughout the country. The new poor had started to revolt. The unemployed lay down on tram tracks in front of the largest grocery store in Dunedin, stones and bricks were hurled through tram windows in Christchurch and a riot (nearly as big as Auckland's) took place in Wellington on 10 May.

Arrested men were far better cared for in prison than they were on the dole.

Frightened authorities opened more country camps, separating more husbands and sons from wives and homes. The extent of human suffering and bitter misery has never yet been recorded in full.

> I struck for better wages and they said I was a fool,
> And the crafty agitator merely used me as a tool.
> And when the kids was starving and we hadn't sup nor bite,
> They only shrugged their shoulders and they said it served me right.
>
> For it's 'ruin to the country' and it's 'wickedness and crime'
> But it's 'sacred rights o' labour' just about election time.
> Just about election time, my lads, just about election time,
> Oh, it's 'sacred rights o' labour' just about election time.

from 'I Struck for Better Wages' – Anon

Half of New Zealand's farmers were bankrupt and many more had been reduced to subsistence level, so the authorities detailed thousands of unemployed to aid rural development. It was considered more prudent to keep farmers labouring on a subsistence budget than to re-possess farms. Some farms were abandoned, but on the whole farmers preferred poverty on their land to poverty on the dole.

> I was farming in the foothills, when the bank paid me a call,
> To tell me that I'd have to quit this place.
> "Sorry, mate, to do this, but we're going to foreclose,
> Your credit's used up all of its good grace."
>
> *Chorus* Standing in the dole queue's a lousy place to be,
>   I can't believe that I can't find a job.
>   It's a bitter pill to swallow for a working bloke like me,
>   To end up taking welfare from the Mob.
>
> They're calling me a bludger through no fault of my own,
> Because I'm taking hand-outs from the state.
> This never should have happened if they'd settled on a plan,
> To ease our plight before it got too late.
>
> We can't afford to stay here with so little left to gain,
> Unless we get relief we'll soon be gone…

from 'Walking off the Land' – Phil Garland

People became poorer and dispirited. Wives wondered when their husbands would return from the unemployment camps to share the burden of bringing up the children. With shabby clothes, some home-made from flour sacks and sugarbags, many — especially women — were loath to venture out. Elderly men and women with reduced pensions wore threadbare garments, as their counterparts had done in the days before Seddon had established the old-age pension. Girls were victimised and forced to work for little more than shelter and clothing. There was disillusionment everywhere, with many afraid their standard of life might sink even lower. The unemployed had absolutely no faith in Parliament. A resolution was carried by 3000 people in the Auckland Town Hall "That this meeting of unemployed workers hereby declares that the people of New Zealand should form a dictatorship of the Proletariat." From north to south, people signed petitions calling on the government to resign.

At the ballot box people turned to the Labour Party, who won in a landslide in the 1935 election. The gloom seemed to be over as the conservative coalition was swept from power, and any economic slack that remained would soon be taken up by our involvement in World War II.

Perhaps some good came out of the Depression, as a political and economic watershed was crossed. More people became politically-minded as they realised that living within their financial means was not enough, and the financial system had to be altered. The Depression taught people the value of money as they learnt not to waste anything, and to have a go at any opportunity. If someone had a couple of bob they'd lend it to another who was worse off.

The suffering of people had bankrupted any old-fashioned ideas of finance as the nation began to provide greater security of jobs, health and welfare. Thousands of lives had been wrecked in the process of learning a vital lesson — hunger is no cure for plenty.

> The country's looking not so bad, the prospect's pretty fair,
> But for coves that's out of collar mate, there's hunger in the air.
> For it's when God's hand is open most with plenty and to spare,
> That the swagger feels it roughish when there's hunger in the air.

from 'The Swagger' ~ David McKee Wright

[Thanks to Tony Simpson's The Sugarbag Years for some of the material in this chapter.]

Barn dance
at Diamond
Harbour,
2008.

CLEAR THE BOARD

Colonial barn dancing

Match today if you can, the grace of the mazurka, the dignity of the maxina, the liveliness of the polka, the swinging rhythm of the schottische and the grand old square dances; the vigorous lancers and the quadrilles; the graceful languorous d'alberts. Listen to the music — watch the instant response to the orders of the MC:

"Top and bottom couples visit to the right — swing corners — ladies to the right — gentlemen to the left and swing partners — waltz to corners and waltz the room ..." all done to the sobbing of the old accordion and later to the challenging rally of the fiddle. There was a little roughness sometimes, a bit of horseplay perhaps, 'but the swing 'em off their feet boys' soon suppressed by the MC if it threatened to get out of hand, but no vulgarity. Compared with the black-bottom and the big apple, with their obscene suggestiveness, our wildest romping was decorum itself.

Jean Boswell, 1876–1963

COLONIAL BARN DANCING HAS BEEN WITH US since the pioneering days of European settlement and has recently enjoyed something of a revival. It derived from the peasant dances of Europe and the country dances of the British Isles, which were once more complex, coming from times when dancing was an integral part of life. Dances had a serious purpose as part of rituals for hunting, planting, harvesting, along with religious, fertility, processional, courtship, wedding, and seasonal ceremonies. Because of the intense enjoyment people got from this indulgence, recreational dancing became a logical development, remaining with us long after the original social circumstances had disappeared.

The Circassian Circle and Lucky Seven, for example, both descend from the closed circle, most commonly used in worship and magic rituals. Later, as the rituals became more complex, so did the circling, with the dancers moving in and out of the circle as well. Our colonial dancing had such basic origins, but is separated from them by a process of development which has taken hundreds of years.

> Last Monday afternoon Mrs Studholme gave the first of a series of dancing afternoons. It was a fine day and the rooms were crowded. There was some very enjoyable singing … Italian songs … and when the music was over we all went to the dining-room and danced. It is a lovely room for a good spin, it is so long and the floor perfection. We danced in our hats and bonnets, our jackets and, no, not parasols, we put them out of sight first, but we did not discard our muffs. It is odd what fun there is in this … twilight dancing, for the rooms were not brightly lit, and no one, [un]less they took some trouble to ascertain, could tell how often one danced with the same partner …"
>
> *'A Southern Gentry' - Stevan Eldred-Grigg, quoting a gossip columnist*

Recreational dances which arrived 'Down Under' with the pioneers have been modified and added to by further migrant arrivals, giving us what we have today. These dances are sometimes unjustly deprecated because they don't appear unique or indigenous to New Zealand, but any study of folk dance through the ages shows that the social conditions for development of a characteristic style of dancing only exist for relatively short periods. In our case that was the time between the settlers' arrival and the changed society brought about by the advent of the motor car.

People have always wanted to dance. In our pioneering days, when women were scarce, solo jigs and hornpipes by lonely males were commonplace. Eyewitnesses have told of shearers and swaggers performing solo whenever the fancy took them. And goldminers, as in this picture from Gabriel's Gully, 1862:

> By daylight the town was as repellent as its vices, but in the evening, when the gullies were ablaze with candles, flares and lamps, the scene became invested with a romantic quality to which the miner, at heart a sentimentalist, readily succumbed…later when the lights of the tent dwellers would be slowly extinguished, the sound of fiddles and concertinas half muffled by dancing and the rhythmical stamp of heavy booted feet … told of a revelry that would last far into the night.
>
> *- James Robertson, digger*

Dancing solo wasn't always a viable option, and men on the West Coast goldfields in 1865 frequently had to dance with one another:

> In a room 14 by 20, I found some 40 or 50 diggers standing about, smoking, chatting and a few dancing. There were only three dance girls and those who were fortunate enough to secure one as a partner must have found it hard work dancing on a floor fully an inch thick with mud. It struck me as a queer sight to see hairy-faced men in pea jackets, long boots and with pipes in their mouths, dancing together. The dance room was a great attraction — at first there were growls innumerable, there being so few girls — it was impossible for all those who wished to dance to get partners. However, those who were not fortunate enough to obtain a lady partner

simply had to take a hairy-faced gentleman or not dance at all.:~ *Banking Under Difficulties — George Preshaw*

Swaggers and shearers were seated round the fire under the shelter of a Canterbury plantation…. The Shiner could dance an Irish jig, but wanted much persuasion, which came in the form of whisky. There was only short grass to dance on — no place for a jig, but the jig was in the heart and the fire was bright and glowing. Concertina Charlie tried an air and the Shiner was at it…he sang as he danced and the concertina went at it to show him the way — the Highland Chief whooped at each pause as though it were a Scottish reel and not a jig the Shiner was engaged in.
~ *Shining with the Shiner — John A Lee*

Much of this dancing was performed in country areas, at a time when the social divisions between town and country life were not as great as they are today. This was the heyday of the woolshed or shearing shed dances, when people came from miles around to attend — for it was open house to everyone regardless of their social standing. Food and liquid would be in plentiful supply, fulfilling a definite need, while the band performed energetic jigs, reels, polkas, mazurkas, quadrilles, lancers and waltzes. When the festivities ended, usually in the wee small hours, the revellers would return home, in readiness for a new day's work.

Shearing was followed by a 'shearing shed dance,' which opened with a quadrille, followed by sets of the lancers, polkas and country dances, with a caller to instruct us when to set partners and swing. Occasionally one of the Irishmen present obliged us with a jig.
~ Lady Barker, *Station Amusements in New Zealand*

During those early times the settlers would every now and again take some enjoyment in the form of barn or woolshed dances. I can still remember the first such ball held in the north and how everyone really enjoyed themselves. Mothers left their sleeping infants on the floor at one end of the barn, while they danced and what's more they could really dance! There were no two-steps or foxtrots in those days — just square dances, waltzes, polkas, reels, schottisches and other good old dances and everyone had a good time. There was a splendid supper about 11 o'clock and after supper dancing continued until sun-up. Then we all left for home in drays and spring-carts and some on horseback, but how tired and happy we all were.
~ *Reminiscences of a Colonial Pioneer*

The music for these occasions was often provided by itinerant shearers and farm labourers. As they arrived, greeting friends old and new, they would sing, yarn, reminisce and recite poetry, sometimes even dancing to impromptu musical groups playing in unison whatever instruments came to hand — accordions, concertinas, fiddles and harmonicas. All manner of percussive devices would come to the fore — bones, spoons, lagerphone, bush bass, along with the readily available gumleaf. Consequently, such spontaneous groups could find themselves providing the music for the dances and other special social occasions.

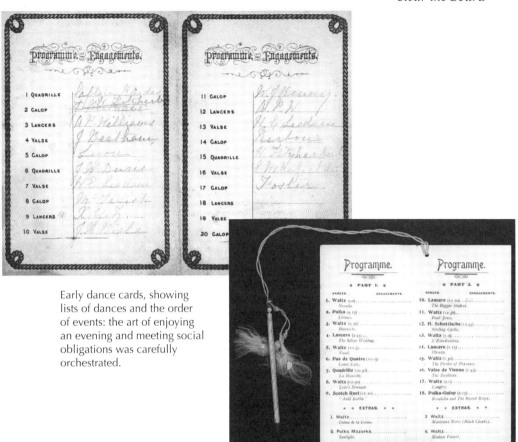

Early dance cards, showing lists of dances and the order of events: the art of enjoying an evening and meeting social obligations was carefully orchestrated.

There was often a dance held in a neighbour's barn, when both young and old would roll up from miles away. I often used to attend these dances and being able to play the concertina I was made a very welcome guest. On one occasion I was staying with friends at the time and the family got an invitation to a wedding about a mile distant. The invitation included myself — ah me, what a time we had.

The large barn was decorated for the occasion and there were seats all round the room. A barrel of beer and a cask of wine held conspicuous positions. How happy and jolly everybody was. Old and young danced till daylight. I nearly forgot to mention the roast fowls, joints of meat besides puddings and cakes galore and the family and I walked home in the morning and as we walked through the scrub how we all sang... ~ *EJ Foreman*

The decorations were green boughs tied to posts in the woolshed. The endless waltzes and lancers were not as stately as the old order, but of a more rousing kind. One of the shearers would play a concertina — another, a fiddle and sometimes singing would swell up from the dancers. This was only for the very strong, for no half-hearted waltzes or polkas went on here. ~ *A shearers' ball, 1890s, source unknown*

Woolshed dances haven't undergone many changes over the years, as may be seen from Merv Addenbrooke's memories of dances at Mangamahu in the 1920s. The following abbreviated observations are taken from his book *Home from the Hill*, edited and published by John Archer in 1990:

> At Mangamahu we used to have quite big woolshed dances. The wool room and shearing board were ideal for dancing, the moving of wool bales and fleeces over the years had made the floor quite greasy.
>
> We used to drag a big bag of sand with cloth around with a motorbike and with the flaked candle grease it made a slippery, shiny, glossy floor. Tarpaulins were used around the catching pens to cover the walls for the ladies and gents dressing rooms. What with all the decorations of ferns and leafy branches from the bush, one would hardly know they were in a big woolshed.
>
> I used to play the accordion now and then to give the pianist a spell. The accordion was especially good for waltzes, polkas and the schottische, the timing beat of the music was distinct and the waltzing kept the dancers in an easy timing rhythm. The accordion seemed to get a great hearing. For the lancers, the energetic males, when wound up, used to swing their partners off their feet amongst a noise of happy screams. There was always some alcoholic drink etc ... but nobody seemed to get out of order.

The one thing that truly distinguishes 'colonial' music from British country dance is the instrumentation so frequently used by local bands. The instrumental line-up is similar but for the ingenious bush bass, which can take many forms — an up-ended packing case or tin bathtub, kerosene tin and even the ubiquitous jug or glass flagon. Australian groups, and Kiwi revival groups to a lesser extent, make extensive use of the highly distinctive lagerphone, Murrimbidgee Rattler or Jingling Johnny as it is also known.

Until the turn of the century England's military bands used a similar percussive device which may well be the forebear of the lagerphone, which in turn has other names in different locales. This device consisted of a metal rod with two or three cross-pieces and a pagoda top. The whole thing was covered with jingles from a tambourine and shaken as well as beaten to provide a percussive rhythm. The lagerphone as we know it today is usually an up-ended broomstick complete with head (bristles or hair removed) with numerous bottle tops attached by either nails or screws driven through their centres. A clear space is normally left on the stick, just under the head, as a hand grip and sometimes another is left about 15cm further down to allow free contact for the ratchet or rattle stick. As many adornments and noisemakers as desired may be attached in addition to the bottle tops. The ratchet, which appears to be an Australian invention, is made from a cut-down axe handle or strip of hardwood fashioned into a handle at one end, while the edges are serrated so that when it is drawn across the lagerphone the sound of massed bottle tops shatters the silence like a host of tambourines. Alternate bowing, scraping and tapping with the ratchet accompanied by the bouncing of the instrument on the floor can provide the player with any rhythm desired.

> The swell dances in the woolshed (Ah! I think we'd best forget) —
> When the ringer called the figures, for the Lancers and the Set.
> And we sat around on wool bales, or just squatted on the floor,
> While some shearer sang a ballad of the golden days of yore.
>
> And we all joined in the chorus, just to give the bloke a hand;
> While the cook's mate led the music, with his concertina band;
> The girlfriends took round the supper, and the boss he gave a pound;
> As the rouseys in their shirt-sleeves passed the pannikins around.

from 'Station Days in Maoriland' ~ George Meek

Barn dances, bush dances, woolshed balls, shearing-shed hops or shindigs — whatever you wish to call them — are always popular. What's more, they're helping to make people aware of their musical heritage and, most important of all, for the interested collector or researcher, here is the folk process or oral tradition still at work and developing.

While Irish music heavily influenced Australian music, song and dance, the Scots infiltrated New Zealand with a more regimented style of music and dancing which can still be seen today, particularly in the South Island. This influence manifests itself in many of the modern tunes composed by such people as Charlie Jemmett and John Allan, who have both been involved with pipe bands, Scottish country dance and barn dance music, all of which draws heavily on their Scottish influences.

In 1971 I made a pilgrimage to Diamond Harbour on Banks Peninsula to meet 89-year-old musician Oliver Hunter, born in 1882 of Welsh and Shetland Island parentage. His father had been a seaman on the *Blue Jacket* and became a digger during the Australian and New Zealand gold rushes. Oliver told me that his grandfather had been a harpooneer on whaling ships off the Greenland coast. As well as writing poetry about New Zealand country life, Oliver played the accordion and used to perform for local dances just before World War I, but reckoned he could hardly remember much of his repertoire let alone their titles 60 years on. However, after encouragement he was able to oblige with 'The Ship that Never Returned' plus a few medleys. Coincidentally I later met up with his grand-daughter Marion Coxon when she was teaching in Hanmer Springs. She showed me an unpublished biography of her grandfather, which makes considerable mention of his musical prowess and dedication to the planting of trees in the area, and relates how he used to bike from Lyttelton to Amberley in North Canterbury when courting his wife-to-be in the early 1900s.

Since its inception in 1910 the Kokatahi Band has been a unique and evocative link with New Zealand's colourful past. In their bright uniform of the old-time miner's Sunday best, and playing an unusual array of instruments such as accordion, melodeon, saxolin, violin, banjo, harmonica, triangle, kettle drum and bass drum, they have long been associated with reviving and preserving the music of the West Coast goldfields. When the New Zealand Folklore Society first made contact with them in Hokitika in 1967–68 the band was at the height of its popularity. We made two trips to record them and especially their leader Percy Crough, who amazed us with his ability on the saxolin and banjo, and provided interesting variants of tunes such as the 'Drovers Dream', 'Father O'Flynn', 'The Irish Washerwoman' and 'Bonaparte's Retreat'.

There are a few hilarious stories about members of the band, and Billy Ritchie features prominently. Billy played triangle in the band and began to lose his hearing as he got older. The band had finished a bracket of tunes and when the leader announced to all and sundry that the next piece would be 'It's a Long Way to Tipperary', Billy spoke up and said "I just played that one!"

Billy's deafness became legendary. At a school reunion on the Coast he met up with an even older district nurse, who said that she used to change his nappies when he was but a babe in arms. Old Billy completely misheard her and replied, "Yes, you wouldn't recognise the old place now!"

The Kokatahi Band was in constant demand for barn dances and weddings up and down the Coast, even making the occasional foray over the ranges into Canterbury. I caught up with them again at the Hokitika Wild Foods Festival in 2004, where I found the band dynamics had changed, with women now comprising half their number. This was a natural progression to enable the band's survival; it was getting harder to attract young men into the fold. Mind you, it was quite difficult to spot the women because they were dressed exactly the same as the men, in the band's traditional uniform.

Chorus Let's hear it for the boys in the band
What a colourful sight to see.
Still going strong after all these years,
Let's hear it for the boys in the band.

The Kokatahi was formed a century ago,
Wearing miners' Sunday best,
Their Crimean shirts and moleskin trews,
Have made them the pride of the West.

Stories abound from the days of the gold,
When two-up and forty-fives held sway,
The boys are keeping the past alive,
Playing music from a bygone age.

See them in a circle ready to start
Playing those songs from yesteryear,
The band strikes up and the music begins,
Drawing people from far and near.

There's saxolin and banjo, bass drum and bones,
Together with some buttons and bows,
Their performance is truly unique,
And they keep playing till the whistle blows.

'The Boys in the Band' ~ Phil Garland

A band at Puhoi,
north of Auckland, circa 1940s
Alexander Turnbull Library F36252 ¹/₂

No study of music and dance in New Zealand would be complete without mention of Puhoi, where music and dancing have been a way of life since settlers arrived there in 1863. Among the scant possessions the Bohemians brought with them were instruments that have enabled them to make their unique music down the years. Traditions died hard and amidst all the turmoil of settling into a new country, music and dance played a huge part in the social structure of the new community.

As more and more settlers arrived the number of musicians grew, and soon the area lacked for nothing in musical entertainment. While it is generally accepted that the dudelsack and violin arrived with the Bohemian immigrants, there is debate as to whether or not the accordion actually arrived then. It has been suggested that a local brand of button accordion was introduced and played by several families.

Over the years they have been replaced by the piano accordion as dance orchestras became a valuable asset to the district. The focal point is the Puhoi Pub with its many artefacts of days gone by and featuring regular performances by the Puhoi Band. This unusual combination features the dudelsack bagpipes and is always popular for local celebrations.

> Early settlers from Puhoi brought with them from Bohemia a musical instrument, which resembles bagpipes and to the uninitiated ear sounds like nothing on earth. The Bohemians love it and will listen for hours. They call it the dudelsack. The instrument at Puhoi is more than 100 years old and is believed to be the only one in the country — the player, with the bellows part of the dudelsack attached to his right arm, pumps the bag full and places his fingers over seven holes to produce music. One of the two horns produces the bass notes and the other the melody.
>
> *New Zealand Herald, 1963*

There was always music in Puhoi and there were two bands. The older one of accordions, violin and dudelsack, played the traditional tunes of Bohemia. Today it is the traditional music that has survived. Dancing was always popular, but it was the waltz, schottische, polka and the lancers etc, that filled most programmes.

> When attending dances in the hall at Puhoi as a little fellow, I was wrapped in a blanket and put to bed under the old forms in the dressing room. Other children were sleeping there too. I couldn't see what dances were done as I was only a little fellow. ~ *Anon*
>
> A newspaper report at the time confirms the local legend that in 1883, Yesensky played the fiddle for three days and nights at a wedding dance. They danced the finger polka, the sprat polka and the Reichstachel and in the tradition of Bohemia they drank lager beer by the barrel. ~ *Auckland Star, 1957*

There has been a recent revival of interest in the music of Bohemia and particularly the dudelsack, inspired by Roger Buckton of Canterbury University who frequently leads musical tours to its original homeland.

The current folk dance revival was spearheaded by the Woolly Daggs Bush Band in the 1960s before morphing into the Canterbury Crutchings Bush & Ceilidh Band in 1972. Our dance repertoire was largely influenced by one of the accordionists, Charles Jemmett, who alternated between his own Scottish country dance band and the Crutchings. The Crutchings lasted only five years before disbanding by mutual consent, when Barrie MacDonald was transferred out of town and Charles Jemmett found his Scottish Country Dance Band was booked solid for the next twelve months. However, such was the demand for barn dances that we had to re-form the band as Canterbury Bush Orchestra just a few months later. Two new

www.leiermann.com/Musik_dudelsack.htm

members were recruited to augment the four remaining 'Crutchings'. This band has continued playing to the present day, though changing their name to Shindig in the 1990s.

After leaving the band in 1987, I moved to Australia, where I formed another band, Bush Telegraph, in Perth in 1988, travelling and playing regularly throughout Western Australia for the next eight years. Returning home in 1996 I brought the band name with me and so the Kiwi branch of Bush Telegraph was born. Ten years on this band is still successfully performing for festivals, woolshed and barn dances throughout the South Island.

Bush bands had sprung up around the country, with the Ginger Minge Bush Band from Dunedin joining the revival in the 1970s. They would eventually form the backbone of the long-serving Pioneer Pog'n'Scroggin Bush Band which became well known throughout Otago and Southland.

> The hall was well filled and the guests were sitting on chairs and forms, around three sides of it. One or two dances went by, then the MC called, "Take your partners for the Alberts, please." There was a burst of clapping and everyone rushed to form their sets.
>
> The floor was a veritable cat's cradle of dancers — "Honour your partners" — we did that. We all bowed while the band played a long chord, then away we went; first and second couples — half right, half left, swing your partners and ladies chain. First gents solo, swing corners and promenade, all ladies to the centre, gents hands across and swing. This was really dancing! You took hold of people, of hands and arms and shoulders and waists and the liveliness inside everyone you touched flowed through you. Better than wine!
>
> If sometimes I got lost a bit, it was only for a moment, someone always put me right: on and on we went till at last my wife and I were together again, simmering down in the circular waltz …
>
> Kids! There were kids everywhere, all having a whale of a time. Unlike city people attending a party or dance, it never occurred to these country folks to leave their children behind in charge of a bored babysitter. Not on your life, they all came too. Fathers waltzed with schoolgirl daughters, eager to be grown up; mothers manoeuvred their shy sons about the floor; while children danced with their grandparents. Everybody danced, even the hall itself, as the streamers swayed overhead and the floor bounced under the dancers' feet — After we'd waltzed the Grand March to a finish, supper was served outdoors under the gleam of scattered stars and so we ate standing up and walking about.
>
> We ate roast chicken, bacon and egg pies, salmon and oyster patties, potatoes roasted in their jackets, trays of savouries, chocolate cake or wedding cake, topping it all off with large helpings of fruit salad and pavlova.
>
> Gradually, in twos and threes, we drifted back inside the hall and the dancing began all over again. Sometimes in the course of this figure or that, I found myself with Margaret for a partner, but for the most part I danced with other men's wives and when I could manage it without being too obvious about it, with their pretty

daughters. Oh dear, the years fell away from me and I almost convinced myself I was 22 again. But if my heart imagined I was 22, my legs didn't and by one o'clock I was weary and so was Margaret. We'd had enough and so, after saying goodnight to more people than we'd said good evening to, we found the car and drove back to the city at an easy pace.

You'd like to know where and when that wedding dance was? Only two years ago, here in South Canterbury! *~ Asquith Thompson, Otipua 1961*

The closing song 'And When They Dance' was written by Roy Abbott, a bush band musician in Perth, Western Australia. The inspiration for the song came while Roy was playing for a school graduation ball, watching the young lasses spinning around in their new gowns. There must be any number of musicians in either country able to identify with similar scenarios. I have taken the liberty of changing his Australian place names to fit the Kiwi situation.

Chorus And when they dance their dresses spin round,
They travel so light that they ne'er touch the ground.
And the smile on their faces would win any crowd,
The lasses who dance till the morning.

I've played many dances, I've seen lots of towns,
From the North Cape to Bluff as I travel around.
And it warms up my heart every time I look down,
On the lasses who dance till the morning.

I've played for the gentry, I've played for them all,
From a small country gig to a debutantes ball.
If there's one thing that joins them the big and the small,
It's the lasses who dance till the morning.

At the end of the dance, the folks leave the floor,
Their feet must be tired, so tender and sore.
But who are the ones who call out for more,
It's the lasses who dance till the morning.

So long may I travel and far may I roam,
From Auckland to Christchurch, a long way from home,
And I'll stare at the people who I'll never know,
Those lasses who dance till the morning.

Canterbury Crutchings Bush & Ceilidh Band, showing the bush bass and lagerphone. (Phil Garland second from right.)

New Zealand bush band revival

An almost-comprehensive list of revival bush bands:

Christchurch	Woolly Daggs Bush Band, Canterbury Crutchings Bush & Ceilidh Band, Canterbury Bush Orchestra, Bush Fire, Rimu Rattlers, Mainland Swag Band, Bowyang Bush Minstrels, The Pheasant Pluckers Bush Band, University of Canterbury Folk Music Club Bush Band, Cock'n'Bull Bush Band, Murphy's Law, Colonial Fayre, Shindig, Bush Telegraph, Bantam of the Opera.
Dunedin	Ginger Minge Bush Band, Pioneer Pog'n'Scroggin Bush Band, Puc Na Horne, Mountain Oyster Band, Bog Boogie Bush Band, Ambush, Lost in the Bush, Shiner
Cromwell	The Dunstan Rangers
Wanaka	(including Cardrona) Snowgrass
Geraldine	Boru Bush Band
Blenheim	EPNS
Nelson/Motueka	Dun Mountain Distillery Bush Band, Jiggery Folkery
Nelson Lakes	(including Murchison) Captain Moonlight, Highly Strung, Rural Newz
Wellington	Southern Cross Ceilidh Band, Mug Wumps Bush Band, Celtic Plus, Famous Plimmerton Bush Band, the Jimmy Cook Band
Palmerston North	Battered Hats Bush Band
New Plymouth	Gumboot Tango
Auckland	Gumdiggers Bush Band, Colonial Two-Step, Twisty Willow, Titirangi Barn Stompers

Bleeding a kauri tree for gum, Northland c. 1913.
Northwood Brothers, ATL PA1-q-180-16

XI

SWEAT IN THE SUN

Kauri timber & gum

"Sweat in the sun, mate, you can't rest in the shade." ~ Peter Cape

NORTHLAND WAS THE CRADLE of European settlement in New Zealand, for it is where the first Christian service was held and the country was proclaimed a British colony. The Treaty of Waitangi was signed here, the first capital set up and the first newspaper established. I am drawn to approach the story of kauri timber and gum not only because of its inherent interest, but also by dint of early family connections with our northernmost province. My forebears on all sides came to Northland in 1823, Wellington in 1839 and Canterbury in 1854. Descending from the Reverend Nathaniel Turner, who established the Wesleyan Mission at Kaeo in 1823, and Captain William Mein Smith who was surveyor-general with the New Zealand Company in 1839, has certainly heightened my interest in our folklore and music.

New Zealand is blessed with a unique range of timber trees and among them the kauri has few equals in the world. At maturity it dwarfs most other trees with its massive clean trunk and spreading crown. Maori knew the value of the kauri long before the arrival of the Pakeha, and used it to make canoes. No tree played a more important role in our economy in the early days. Since sailors discovered it in 1772, until the decline of the industry on which it was based, around 1908, kauri and its by-product, gum, were major contributors to the nation's wealth. For well over a century kauri was practically the only natural resource to be exploited to its fullest potential in Northland, Auckland and the Coromandel, despite settlers also using rimu, matai, totara and kahikatea for many purposes. From the first days of settlement, sawmills were established throughout the country. One of the strongest softwoods known, kauri became a leading building timber in the colony, durable and useful for all types of construction including furniture, bridges, wharves, mining tunnels and railway carriages. It was outstanding for ship and boatbuilding — ranked by the British navy as the best timber for masts and decking, its reputation has never been surpassed.

Come all you jolly seamen bold and listen to my song,
I'd have you pay attention and I'll not detain you long.
Concerning of a voyage to New Zealand we did go,
For to cut some lofty spars to load the *Buffalo*.

Chorus   Cheer up my lively lads, to New Zealand we will go,
          For to cut some lofty spars to load the *Buffalo*.

When at New Zealand we arrived, our hands were sent on shore,
Our tents were then all pitched well, and provided with good stores.
At six o'clock we all rouse out, then such a precious row,
Come quick and get your grog m' boys — unto the woods you go.

With saws and axes in our hands, then through the bush we steer,
And when we see a lofty tree, unto it we draw near.
With saws and axes we begin to lay the tree quite low,
With cheerful heart strikes every man to load the *Buffalo*.

Now eight o'clock is drawing nigh, All off! All off's the sound,
All through the trees it echoes loud and makes the woods resound.
Then every man lays down his axe and through the bush we come,
To get their jolly breakfast, every man does nimbly run.

Our breakfast being over, then to work we do repair,
Our work it is all pointed out, for every man his share.
There's roughters and refiners and there's jolly sawyers too,
To lop and trim those lofty spars to load the *Buffalo*.

When twelve o'clock is drawing nigh, "All off!" again's the cry,
Then every man lays down his axe and through the wood does hie,
Our cook has got a dinner that will make all faces shine,
With pork and murphies smoking hot on which we tars do shine.

"Grog ho!" is the next joyful cry, we drink it up with glee,
We light our pipes when time is up and smoking go away.
Unto the woods to finish well the spars that we began,
And when the afternoon's expired, then home comes every man…

from 'Voyage of the Buffalo' ~ Anon

Not surprisingly, the first forest to all but disappear was the kauri of the north. The value of kauri had led to the establishment of some of the first settlements and provided early exports. The manner in which this forest was sacrificed and laid waste was described by an early observer, Ernst Dieffenbach:

Noble trees which had required ages for their perfection were thus recklessly destroyed in great numbers, as, in consequence of the great quantity of resin around this pine, the fire always spread rapidly. The cupidity of new settlers too often occasions the destruction of the forests, to the irreparable injury of subsequent colonists. A great many of these first settlers, doubtful of being able to maintain their claims to their immense purchases, have no other object than to clear the greatest possible amount of profit in the shortest possible time, even at the sacrifice of a large and invaluable forest. It is utterly impossible ever to make good the damage thus done to the real interests of the country at large, as the kauri-land is so exhausted that scarcely anything will grow on it but fern and manuka. Unless the strictest measures are immediately taken to prevent this reckless destruction, it is very certain that the forest of this noble tree will be greatly and irreparably reduced, as the kauri is already a scarce tree and is confined to very narrow limits.

As Dieffenbach predicted, removal of the kauri and destruction of forests meant that Northland became for the most part a great wasteland of difficult soils growing only tea-tree and weeds. It would be a long time before modern farming techniques would convert it into productive farmland.

Marion du Fresne had been the first European to discover kauri, when his crew cut spars for masts on the shores of Whangaroa Harbour in 1772. Once a penal colony was established at Botany Bay in Australia, the trade in kauri spars increased, with ships frequently calling in to cut large quantities of kauri from Whangaroa's hills and valleys. On the opposite coast, the shores of the Hokianga were also covered with kauri, but not until the harbour bar was successfully negotiated in 1822, was a timber settlement established there. Ships arrived regularly from England, Australia and even South America to trade in kauri. Meanwhile, the dense forests around the vast Kaipara Harbour remained untouched until the mid-1830s, due to the treacherous bar at its entrance. Once the bar had been successfully traversed, the Kaipara hosted an export trade larger than all the other ports in the colony, for a quarter of a century.

> It's not for nothing that they call this place the graveyard,
> Every fisherman on the harbour's lost a friend out on the bar.
> I thought I heard screaming, but perhaps it's just the seagulls,
> A man can rest forever, out on the Kaipara Bar.
>
> A man can rest in safety, in the shelter of the harbour,
> But many a man has lost his life, crossing the Kaipara Bar.

from 'Crossing the Kaipara Bar' ~ Bill Worsfold

A new era of forest exploitation began when New Zealand was proclaimed a British colony and Auckland chosen as its capital in 1840. Land was urgently required for settlement and the kauri forest became an obstacle to be removed as cheaply as possible. The forest was the farmer's enemy and had to be cleared. Axes were used at first, but felling the giant trees was a huge job so it wasn't long before the crosscut saw was put to work. The felling of a large kauri was described by a *Weekly News* writer, cited in AH Reed's *The Story of Northland*:

As the sawyers pursue their work they occasionally drive in with heavy mauls the iron wedges inserted in the cut in order to throw the weight of the tree on that side, which has been 'scarfed' or cut into, to guide the descent of the bush giant. As the work progresses and the eyes of the expert bushmen note the first quiver in the ponderous barrel, the saw is stopped for a moment, while the stereotyped cry "Below in the gully!" is sent forth, echoing from tree to tree. This is a timely warning for those working below to betake themselves to a spot of safety from flying limbs; and shortly afterwards, to further full-throated cries, the great kauri leans slightly, the wedges are driven further home and with immense sweep the stately monarch, New Zealand's timber pride, with tremendous concussion crashes to earth. The falling of such a tree is awe-inspiring, the deafening crash is unexpected and for a while the air quivers, birds shriek in fear and nature seems to protest against the outrage.

As the demand for kauri grew, large sawmills were built, many on tidal flats to enable direct loading onto ships. Further inland, kauri logs were hauled to creeks and rivers for floating or transporting downstream, with the aid of dams, to the nearest mill. Sawmillers lit fires to clear passageways for logs to be easily moved and uncontrolled burning off became all too common.

> The man who hauls the logs along, a brainy chap is he,
> Unto his team of bullocks he discourses fluently.
> We bark the logs and butt them square and roll them up the skids,
> The cocky chap's impatient and he's waiting with the quids.
>
> The sawdust heaps up day by day, the scantling's piling high,
> And weatherboards and four-by-twos are in a stack close by.
> And still the bark heap grows apace, while cant-hooks slip and grab,
> And logs lie on the cradle which is just a long pine slab.
>
> Old Sam the cook has packed his pots, the tents are down and rolled,
> The bench is on the wagon and the engine fires are cold,
> The cocky chap can build and wed, the pine tree clump is gone,
> The good old sawmill and its crew are moving further on.

adapted from 'The Pine Mill' ~ CW Winter

Moving the logs to the nearest waterway was done by primitive methods. In some cases a rolling road was made — a broad track taking every advantage of the natural incline, so that the logs could be rolled downhill crosswise. Another method was the chute, built in the shape of a cradle and used to send logs down steep hillsides to the creek below. The sides were built higher to prevent the logs from slipping over the side and they raced down the hillside with terrifying velocity.

The rolling road was superseded by the bullock team. At first the logs were attached to the bullocks by chains, but this method was replaced by teams of seven or eight pairs of bullocks pulling a contrivance called a catamaran, or 'cat' for short. This was a kind of sledge with the skids greased for easy running. When the command 'Walk away' was given, a good bullock team could move ten thousand feet of timber, sometimes weighing up to twenty tons. A perfect understanding developed between a humane driver and his bullocks. The team would naturally respond to whatever language their owner or trainer adopted, a situation portrayed by Andreas Reischek in his book *Yesterdays in Maoriland*:

> Never in all my life have I heard such fluent cursing! When I asked one burly fellow why he let off such a string of oaths, he replied: "Try it yourself, then and see if yon bullocks'll get a move on without!" Every bullock responded to its own name, no reins were used, guidance being given entirely by the whip and the voice of the driver.

A similar occurrence is described by H E Von Haast in his *The Life and Times of Sir Julius von Haast*:

> If the English sailors have acquired a not undeserved reputation for their curses, surely the New Zealand bullock-drivers must be reckoned superior to them in this accomplishment, for such an assortment of fantastic oaths from all kingdoms of Nature, heaven and Hell, I have never heard before from mortal lips. Astounded I listened to this blue-eyed son of Albion and was at last impelled to ask him why he cursed so horribly; it could serve no purpose and only made the beast more stubborn. "You don't understand, Sir" the young man answered. "I'm only speaking the bullock language. The animal certainly wouldn't understand or obey me if I spoke to him as I would my horse. The bullock has been brought up to carry in this way and if I want to get on fast, I've got to talk to him like this."
>
> To this argument advanced by the driver with a good-natured smile, I naturally could find no reply…

Bullock team hauling a kauri log in the Kohukohu area, circa 1912.
ATL PA1-q-180-039, part of Northwood album 4

A writer in the *North Auckland Age* describes an almost legendary picture-book scene in 19th-century Northland:

> A long reach of white dusty road stretched away and vanished in the tea-tree. The sun burned above me from a blue cloudless sky. The rider followed the ribbon of road towards the two little hills in the distance, but the two little hills evermore retreated. At last he reached them and began to climb. Strange voices met him coming forward. The crack of a whip, the rattle of clumsy wheels, the clink of chains and between walls of tea-tree appeared the leaders of a bullock team. At sight of him they stopped and the twelve workers swerved from the road. The driver walked beside his team, cracked his very long whip and commenced to swear. He cursed the leaders and he cursed all the other bullocks in the team, calling each one by name. Then he briefly cursed the man in his way, who listened as to something new and was so astonished at the picturesqueness of the language that he forgot to make any comment. He watched the driver get his team under way again. "Gerrup! Poley, you gory blank! Hi Flincher! Into it, you son of a greenstone tiki! Now Snider! You crimson heifer!" Slowly the team drew on to the road again and the load, three immense kauri logs, creaked past the horseman. The road was a rough one, a mere path in the tea-tree widened by constant use.

This inspired me to write the song 'Bullocky Joe':

> I hail from Matakohe and Joe Sheehan is my name,
> To drove a team of bullocks is my game.
> I carry kauri logs so fine and I never lag behind,
> You'll find no better teamster on the road, on the road,
> I swear there is none better on the road.
>
> I draw timber from the bush, where the mighty kauri grow,
> Many's the log I've drawn steady and slow.
> Hauling timber down the line builds a thirst for beer and wine,
> You'll find no better teamster on the road, on the road,
> I swear there is none better on the road.
>
> I'm always on the go, come rain, hail or shine,
> There's never been another team so fine.
> For I can draw a thousand feet, turn around on any street,
> 'Cause you'll find no better teamster on the road, on the road,
> I swear there is none better on the road.
>
> Young Billy's always ready to skite and to blow,
> About his skill with a whip on the road.
> But I tell you it's no slander and I really raise his dander,
> When he hears the crack of my whip, along the road, along the road,
> I swear there is none better on the road.

'Bullocky Joe' – Phil Garland

The next development would be the tramway, which ran for miles into the bush, climbing hills and crossing creeks. On easy grades the trucks were drawn by locomotives, but were taken up and down hills by endless steel ropes operated by steam.

Despite all these methods, most logs were transported by damming the creeks and then releasing or 'tripping' the banked-up water to carry thousands of logs downstream to the harbour or river mouth. One bushman recounts the tripping scene thus:

> The sound of innumerable logs thudding against each other, driven by the violence of the water. Then a wall of water and logs, many feet in height, came into sight and beneath the westering moon we saw thousands of logs go past. They seemed to be alive, grumbling and complaining in their discomfort and agony. Great logs were driven high on the band, swung round and torn away again. Long logs, their butts driven into the bank of the creek, rose up on end and fell over again, until the whole mighty mass had gone thundering down the main Wharekawa to the salt water.

After reaching tidal water the logs were roped together into rafts and floated or towed to the mills.

Forests were systematically destroyed to feed the waiting mills and the export market as if there was no tomorrow. Before long there were too many mills, all vying for work, so the larger companies began amalgamating smaller units. The timber trade fluctuated wildly and was seriously affected by the recession of the 1890s. To break the depressed market conditions, the larger companies increased output while still trying to find more outlets. In 1890 kauri being sold in Melbourne left no margin for profit and production slumped. Demand slowly picked up, however, and mills were soon at full capacity once more. The industry peaked one last time in 1906 before declining until the 1950s, by which time it had shrunk to a tiny percentage of the total timber milled. The industry's demise is captured by Peter M Gross in his recently-written song 'Kauaeranga Kauri':

> The kauri bush is finished, the last big trees are gone,
> The fantail and the tui no longer sing their song.
> Mist-clad hills are quiet now, the valley sleeps below,
> As ghostly forms of bushmen past, move silent in the dawn.
>
> The axe-man and the sawyer, masters of their trade,
> No timber could withstand the touch of axe or mighty blade.
> Trees that stood a thousand years come crashing to the ground.
> To feed the want of man and beast, the width of this great land.
>
> From bush to mill the road is long, by flooded creek and dam,
> By bullock team and tramway, through mud and driving rain.
> On down through the valley by road and rail and sea,
> Mighty trees that once stood proud brought down by man's great need.

The bushlands where the trees once stood with head up in the clouds,
Now sit in silent witness of man's influence and greed.
The wants of man above all else, don't let this power sway you,
Leave the bush to beast and bird, the future will repay you.

The old-time kauri bushmen were rough-and-ready individuals. Bush life was harsh and the men needed to be able to survive and cope with the conditions. The typical 19th-century bushman has been described as a huge, muscular, hardy fellow, but one who had earned a reputation for honesty. Camp stores could remain open with no shopkeeper in attendance, and when goods were needed they would simply be taken and noted by the purchaser on a large slate for settlement later.

Vast tracts of kauri were devastated by logging or ravaged by fire. There were no young forests to replace the old and only isolated pockets remained. Today the surviving stands of mature kauri are in state forests, reserves and sanctuaries. The need for conservation has finally been accepted and kauri saplings are being protected for future generations of New Zealanders to appreciate and enjoy.

'Twas the year of 1940, the day was calm and still,
When an old-time kauri bushman wandered up a northern hill.
With an axe upon his shoulder and his coat upon his arm,
He was making for the kauri tree that stood above his farm.

He thought "I'm getting older and it's time I had a spell,
For there's no more kauri standing but the one I'm going to fell.
The kauri bush is finished and my cobbers are all gone,
Jobs are getting fewer as the years go rolling on.

"I will hire a motor lorry and I'll take that tree of mine,
To the mill down in the valley, where they're cutting up the pine.
And I'll build a little cottage with my good old kauri tree,
To give me rest and shelter for the time that's left to me."

He reached his precious kauri and put a scarf in low,
Then backed it with another, stood back and watched her go.
Then he felt a little weary, so he thought he'd rest a space,
Sat down on the tree stump, where the fern would shade his face.

And there they found him lying, his head upon the chips,
His axe was there beside him, he'd a smile upon his lips,
For they both had died together, the last this world would see
Of this old-time kauri bushman and his dear old kauri tree.

'The Old-time Kauri Bushmen' ~ Anon

Kauri gum

As the black billy boils at the end of the whare,
I remember the time when I lived in a hurry,
With my hand on a line tied to a bundle of money,
And I was a very young new chum.

As the black billy boils at the end of the whare,
I look back on the days and how they seemed so very funny,
Now I've ended my ways and I never have a worry,
And it's thanks to the kauri gum.

'As the Black Billy Boils' ~ Anon

No study of the kauri can ignore its by-product — a true resin always referred to as kauri gum. The gum was formed by the hardening of resin bleeding from wounds or injuries to the bark, branches and leaves of the tree. There are two types of kauri gum — tree gum and fossil gum, which is dug from the ground. Tree gum played a lesser role in the industry because it could be collected only from living trees, whereas fossil gum was collected from areas where forests had once grown plentifully. This gum was dug from the beds of shallow lakes and swamps, with the best coming from the open fern land north of Auckland. Inferior grades were obtained from swampland. These swamps, however, provided some of the richest gumfields and also the worst working conditions.

Ways of collecting fossil gum began with 'paddocking' — picking it up off the ground. After that the men dug deeper, using a gum spear made from fencing wire attached to a wooden handle so the digger could thrust it into the ground to locate gum deposits. A longer spear called the 'joker', invented around 1910, proved useful in locating deeper gum. Dalmatian diggers often worked together as they found it more economic to drain the swampland first.

Sod-wall shanty, chaff-sack for a door
Fernstalk mattress, packed earth floor
White clay country, white clay and scrub
Seventeen miles to the nearest pub.

Chorus   Gum-spear and pikau, slash-hook and spade
          Sweat in the sun, mate, you can't rest in the shade

They say that the kauri grew here long ago
Mebbe they're right, but a joker wouldn't know
Only know the feel of gum on the spear
Gum for me flour-sack, gum for me beer

Mend me own moleskins, cook me tucker too
Black tea and damper, eel-meat stew
Fine fat tuna swimmin' in the creek
Sometimes it's so quiet here, you can hear the beggars speak

They're sayin' … (chorus)

Sit of an evening, cleaning up me gum
Mebbe in a year or two a better price'll come
Gum for your varnish, varnish for your door
Sweat from the brow of the gum-digging poor

'Gumdigger' ~ Peter Cape

The gumfields were generally a desolate, unromantic and often harsh environment, best described by James Cowan:

> Sombre patches of undulating country, sparsely covered with bracken fern, or with manuka and dotted everywhere with upturned heaps of clay — the marks of past diggers.
> Here and there clumps of native forest, their fringes sentineled by black logs and gaunt, half-burned dead trunks, far-stretching level swamp land, waving with the long sword leaves of the native flax … or with the white flags of the toi toi [toetoe] or the whispering ranks of the light green raupo sedge, in sheltered nooks the white tents of the nondescript huts and sod and corrugated iron chimneys of the diggers — these are the gumlands of North Auckland.

For all their desolation and unattractiveness the gumfields were of considerable economic importance to the area. Next to gold, kauri gum contributed more to New Zealand exports than any other mineral.

The End of the Earth isn't far from here,
And it's getting much darker year by year.
The gum's getting smaller and deeper down,
And never again will I see a town
With pretty white houses all in a row,
And women in aprons to and fro,
And the bar in the pub down by the sea,
Where a ship is waiting there to carry me
Back to the land from where I come,
Where I was born, where I was young,
With a ruddy good tingle on my young face,
And money to jingle all over the place.
Aye but then I'd punch my foreman's nose,
And run to sea for the "There she blows"
And get caught out for the homeward cruise,
And end up working in moleskin trews;

And get a little drunk and get a little sore,
And end up fighting it with the law,
For what are them bright shop samples for?
When a man is hungry and a man is poor,
And's got no work worth working for,
And's running up north away from the law.
Aye walking up north like everyone,
To end up sitting out in the sun,
At the door of a shack with a hole for a lum,
Scraping up clean a hundredweight of gum.

'The End of the Earth' ~ Anon. 'Lum' is a northern England term for a chimney.

The gum industry was investigated by a commission in 1898, which found three categories of diggers: the diggers proper, whose living depended entirely upon gum; part-timers, who occasionally dug to supplement their earnings; and Maori, who only dug when their crops failed or provisions were exhausted.

The gumdiggers comprised university graduates, remittance men, clerks, accountants, secretaries, shopkeepers and unemployed labourers. They were a mobile population which attracted the misfit, the nonconformist, the recluse and the itinerant. Despite some being solitary individuals, many congregated in camps, often near running water and firewood and a storekeeper for disposing of gum. Some diggers were itinerant, pitched tents and moved on quite frequently, while others banded together and built themselves a whare, with sod or slab walls, a chimney and a tent fly or raupo-thatched roof. A digger's life was laborious but he was independent and free. Come midday he boiled his billy and rested in the shelter of a tea-tree, while evenings, by candlelight, he scraped dirt off the gum dug during the day, to make it more saleable.

The restless shadows by me flit and day will soon be o'er,
As in the dying light I sit outside my whare door.
Away across the east I see the black swans homeward come,
Through sunset skies that gleam on me, a digger scraping gum.

Mid hills of grey and brown, I live here in the scrub,
Full fifty miles from any town and ten from any pub.
Through winter's rain and summer's drought, this life maybe suits some,
I grind a scanty living out, digging and scraping gum.

And if you want the way you've gone, hid from the friends you've lost,
As slow the years of life steal on and turn the hair to frost.
Then see across the eastern sky the black swans homeward come,
'neath sunset skies that gleam on my hard scraping of the gum.

'Black Swans' ~ EL Eyre

The *North Auckland Age* continues its description of 19th-century Northland:

> For a mile or more he continued to follow the road which taking a sudden turn, there was revealed to him, cut off from the world, on the edge of a reedy swamp, a dozen or two of small shanties. A mixed group of men were sitting in a cleared space of ground, chipping away with knives at pieces of kauri gum. The journalist descended from his horse. Greetings from many languages fell upon his ears; Austrian, Maori, English. Tomorrow the packhorse train would be in and take the gum to the sorting shed, where it would be classed and branded according to quality, ready for shipment to the city merchants.

Drunkards were all too common and indulging in such intemperate habits could make many a digger an employment liability. Some storekeepers were still willing to advance a week's provisions without payment until the end of the week, enabling the digger to get back to work — and obliging him to conduct all his business with that storekeeper. This situation is mentioned by Bill Worsfold in his song 'Fields of the Gum'.

> The storekeeper staked us with gum-spear and spade,
> Diggers soon taught us the way of the trade.
> We'd sore backs and blisters, but boy we were keen,
> And soon we'd a fine stack of gum-lumps to clean.
>
> By lamplight, by moonlight, scraping our gum,
> No thought of the past or the years to come.
> Sam played a squeezebox and I beat a drum,
> As the years rolled by on the fields of the gum.
>
> Friendships were easy with the blokes that we met,
> Hard cases and misfits, but some of the best.
> A hardship's no hardship with a friend at your back,
> And I'd good friends a-plenty on the old northern track...

An unwritten code of respect and practice was common among diggers. If one struck gum, no other digger could go near him unless invited. If men drained a swamp, no one else could dig there without contributing to the labour of draining. If a man cleared a gully by fire, it was his and his alone to dig.

Antagonism developed, however, between the diggers and settlers struggling to make a living in Northland. The stereotypical view of gumdiggers as reckless and lawless can be attributed in part to attitudes expressed by the settlers. Although some settlers dug part-time to help maintain their farms and homes through hard times, they believed the full-timer diggers threatened their livelihood by destroying farmland. Roads needed by the farmer to get produce to market were cut up and damaged by the hauling of gum to ports. It was inevitable that the nomadic digger would incur the wrath of the seemingly more stable, but struggling settlers and farmers.

Chorus This is the song of the digger, the song of the seeker of gum,
           Sung in a kerosene twilight, to the sound of the kerosene drum.

The hooking is done in the summer, it's done in the winter as well,
The finer the weather the better, for the scrub when it's wet gives you hell.

It's hard, bloody hard is this scraping, which goes on for most of the night,
If ever you sat round just waiting, you'd never get the damn thing bright.

'Song of the Digger' ~ William Satchell

Dalmatians were integral in the development of the gum industry. Escaping hardship and conscription at home, they began arriving in New Zealand in significant numbers around 1892. Within a few years Northland locals felt threatened by their influx and agitated for protection. Following a 1898 Commission, the government introduced digging licences which were obtainable only after three months' residency in the colony, to discourage Dalmatians from coming to New Zealand to dig for gum.

The majority of Dalmatians came to Northland because gumdigging was an unskilled occupation, needing little contact with locals and therefore little English. In many respects the Dalmatians' reasons for being on the gumfields were similar to the Chinese on the goldfields — they didn't come to settle, but to make what was to them a substantial fortune and return home. They banded together in groups, worked hard and saved their money, remitting most of it home. They lived frugally and paid their debts to the storekeepers, but once they had met with some success they could live as well as anyone else on the gumfields.

After the 1898 legislation, things quietened down on the gumfields until World War I. As more and more diggers were either conscripted or volunteered to serve overseas, the industry fell increasingly into the hands of the Dalmatians, and if it hadn't have been for them it might well have collapsed before 1918. The industry, regardless, did not survive long after the war, particularly once synthetics replaced kauri gum in the manufacture of varnish. There was interest in rebuilding the industry in the 1930s Depression, but it never again achieved economic importance.

Many Dalmatians regretted having come to the gumfields, because of the local antagonism, the dreary landscape and the need to work constantly and so hard. All these disadvantages mitigated against a ready acceptance of New Zealand society. Dalmatian gumfields poet, Ante Kosovich, summed up a common reaction as he told his countrymen not to forsake their homeland for the hell of the gumfields.

Dalmatia, I have news to give you now,
Of your poor sons who suffer here and now.
This wild hard country beats them down…

Legislation turned many Dalmatians away from gumdigging and towards other occupations, while others left the country. Those who stayed, took up mining in the Thames district, or settled on the land and initiated viticulture. Increasing urbanisation would also result in many Dalmatian immigrants becoming fully integrated into New Zealand society.

AH Reed, talking about the export of kauri gum in *The Gumdiggers* tells this delightful story:

> Kauri gum was packed in big wooden cases for export to England. The boxes in the early days of the trade were all of kauri boards, mostly a full inch or an inch and a quarter inches thick and the timber itself of the highest quality and much of it figured …
>
> Forty years ago I was being entertained in the home of an elderly English couple, where I noticed and could not help but admire, a sideboard, a table and odd pieces of furniture built of kauri, with much of it mottled and French polished. Observing my interest they told me they had brought the furniture all the way from England. I said "But that's New Zealand kauri!" They agreed and then proceeded to explain how they had come by it. My host as a young man had been employed in a linoleum factory using large quantities of kauri gum … he used to buy the big boxes in which the gum was packed, for firewood, at sixpence each, but in taking them to pieces would select and save all the prettily marked boards. He had a friend who was a cabinet maker and together they worked in exhange, timber for labour and labour for timber.

I'll give the honour of the last word on gum digging to Bill Worsfold with a verse and chorus from his 'Farewell to the Gumfields':

> Farewell to the gumfields, I'm not sad to leave you,
> Farewell to the whare of tea-tree and sod.
> The dirt floor at last is a thing of the past,
> No more through your mud-fields I'll plod.
>
> It feels that I've wasted my years on the gumfields,
> Far from my family and the friends that I knew.
> But now we've a farm on the edge of the town,
> Oh, gumfields, I'm glad to leave you.

XII

BARDS AND BALLADEERS
Colonial & contemporary poets

N EW ZEALAND CAN BE PROUD OF ITS BALLADEERS, rhymesters and poets who have contributed to our rural and high country heritage. Their body of work shows that our folk heritage is alive and well, as people are still reciting their work and setting it to music.

Over the years suggestions have been levelled that New Zealand and Australia (to a lesser extent) suffer from a contrived musical heritage. The songs and verse of our rural balladeers and bush poets give the lie to such claims. New Zealand has a strong tradition of reciting bush poetry. It was once more common to find bushmen, shearers, drovers, farmhands or swaggers in a bar (or indeed any social gathering) reciting poetry and spinning yarns than singing — especially from 1890 through to the 1930s. Many of our bush poets, however, wrote to a rhythm or metre ideally suited to singing — the best example was Henry Lawson, who is perhaps better known for his Australian work but who has been frequently described as a songwriter rather than a poet. I mention Lawson because he spent time in New Zealand both writing and carrying the swag, and because he, along with Banjo Paterson, greatly influenced their Kiwi contemporaries and succeeding generations of poets.

New Zealanders who come to mind in this regard are David McKee Wright, George Meek, Hamilton Thompson, CH Winter, Dennis Hogan, Tod Symons, Joe Charles, Willow Macky, Peter Cape and more recently, Ross McMillan. Most have stated that their rhymes and verses were meant to be sung, while Joe Charles in particular (who incidentally was tone deaf) wrote his ballads to a musical rhythm that was in his head at the time, which is why much of his verse easily lends itself to a tune or melody.

I'll leave it to readers to make up their own minds as to whether we have a contrived musical heritage. My own opinion is that time and acceptance by the 'folk' will make the decision for us and future generations of Kiwis, regardless of how any of us may feel.

FACES IN THE FIRELIGHT

Henry Lawson

Henry Lawson is probably the best known and most loved of all the colonial Australian poets and writers, deserving of more than a passing mention here because of his itinerant life and lasting influence on early New Zealand poets and writers. He was very much a minstrel of the people and his verse was highly regarded by all and sundry on both sides of the Tasman. He was the voice of Australia, and in a lifetime of writing he sentimentalised 'mateship' and the 'dauntless Australian spirit' which endeared him to working class society, especially swaggies and rural farm labourers of Australia and 'Maoriland.'

Lawson contributed much to the *Bulletin,* the leading Australian magazine and review paper, avidly read throughout Australasia. No writer was considered successful until they had been seen in the *Bulletin*, an outlet for New Zealand writers as much as for Australians. In truth it was the *Bulletin* that renamed New Zealand 'Maoriland', a term that found a ready acceptance from the 1890s to the days of World War I and beyond.

Lawson was born in 1867 on the Grenfell gold diggings, where his father (a Norwegian ship deserter) was working a claim. Much of his childhood was spent around Gulgong and Eurunderee, surrounded by life on the diggings, which made a lasting impression. His father later struggled with farming and despite building a homestead, the life proved too tough and demanding in the end. Henry's parents were unhappy together and he led a rather solitary life, showing little affection for his mother Louisa, despite her encouraging him to develop an interest in poetry. When his parents separated he moved to Sydney, and while working as a painter in the Blue Mountains he began to concentrate on writing. His first poem was accepted by the *Bulletin* in 1887.

Lawson's popularity grew with his contributions to the *Bulletin*, but unable to make a living from them, he travelled around the country trying to survive as a free lance journalist. The 'Hungry Years' were starting to bite in Australia, and finding little work he returned to Sydney, where the *Bulletin* gave him a rail ticket to Bourke in outback New South Wales. There, he began tramping with a mate, looking for casual work on shearing boards from Bourke to the Queensland border. Without enough work to earn a decent living, he returned to Sydney "fed up with the bush". As the Depression deepened, Henry joined the hordes of Australians who were leaving for New Zealand to chase paying work.

I've just received a letter from a chum in Maoriland,
He's working down at Auckland, where he says he's doing grand.
The climate's cooler there, but hearts are warmer, says my chum,
He sends the passage money and he says I'd better come.
I'd like to see his face again, I'd like to grip his hand,
He says he's sure that I'll get on first rate in Maoriland.

An' tho he makes the best of things (it always was his style)
You mostly get on better in a new land for a while.
An' when I see the fading line of my own native shore,
I'll let it fade and never want to see it any more.
I'm tired of Sydney pavements and the Western scrub and sand,
I'd rather fight my troubles for a change in Maoriland.

I'm off to make enquiries as to when the next boat sails,
I'm sick of all these colonies, but most of New South Wales.
An' if you meet a friend of mine, who wants to find my track,
Say you "He's gone to Maoriland and isn't coming back."
An' should it be the landlord or the rates, you understand,
Just say 'You'll find him somewhere knocking round in Maoriland."

'The Emigration to New Zealand' ~ Henry Lawson, recorded as 'Gone to Maoriland' by Phil Garland

The Union Steam Ship Company donated a first class fare to Auckland, but Lawson came steerage instead, described in his short story 'Coming Across'. He couldn't find work in Auckland and spent his last pound on travel to Wellington, where he ran into "old-chums on every corner." His reputation had gone before, helping to introduce him to men of influence who were able to help him get a painting job while writing for local papers. In an article entitled 'New Zealand from an Australian's point of view' he refers to New Zealand's national joke:

> The national joke of New Zealand, which has not been immortalised yet, is that you can always tell a Wellingtonian by the way in which he grabs his hat when going round a corner. Sometimes you hear it on the boat coming over; the boarding house runners will tell it to you as soon as you step ashore; men to whom you have letters of introduction will fire it at you as soon as they decently can; chance drinking acquaintances will tell you; perfect strangers will take you aside and try the damned old joke on you; and if you meet an old friend over here, you will find him bursting to introduce you to the national joke of New Zealand.

The windy hills of Wellington were black and cold that night,
The rain came down at times enough to drown the 'lectric light.
'An like a hymn of hate an' want from black misfortune's choirs,
I heard the cruel spiteful wind go snarling through the wires,
An' from the winches by the wharf a rattle and a clank,
While sitting by a Sydney chum who'd drawn New Zealand blank!

He'd sent for me in all the land the only chum he knew,
His health and hope and cash were gone — and he was going too.
His frame was shrunk and his face was drawn, his eyes were bleared and dim,
For drink and poverty and want had done their work for him;
And when I came, he turned to me, his features pale an' lank —
'I'm glad you've come, old chum' he said 'I've drawn New Zealand blank'…

The breezy hills of Wellington are fair as they can be,
I stand and watch a Sydney boat go sailing out to sea.
And while the sun is setting low on blue and brown and green,
I think of cruel things that are and things that might have been.
And while the same old sun goes down in clouds a golden bank,
I sadly think of my old chum who drew New Zealand blank!

Lawson worked on and off throughout the lower North Island as a lineman, bushman and bullocky, but with unemployment on the rise he sailed across Cook Strait to join a gang overhauling the telegraph line between Picton and Kaikoura. This outdoor life suited him and he would recall this time with great affection at the close of his brief autobiography penned in 1896:

I think the most pleasant days of my life were spent on an old telegraph line in New Zealand. Am inclined to prefer New Zealand of all the colonies.

I take pleasure in reminding my Australian audiences of these comments, whenever the opportunity presents itself.

The newly launched *Daily Worker* in Sydney offered him a job and so he returned to Australia in 1894. The job didn't last long, and as the paper slowly went down the tube Henry longed to return to New Zealand. His first visit had been a real success, for it had yielded him ten stories and sketches and a few poems as well.

The wild wet waves of wintertime were drifting o'er his head,
He wrote to her from Maoriland and this is what he said.
'It's hard to make a living, but whatever fate may bring,
I'll come to meet the summer in the latter end of spring,
I will come to meet my darling in the latter end of spring.'

She wrote and if she waited, then she waited all in vain,
The spring went by and summer and the autumn came again,
The autumn passed and winter, and the youth of whom we sing,
Was felling bush for tucker in the latter end of spring,
Oh it's weary weary waiting in the latter end of spring.

She wrote, but ah his hopes were crushed as often as they came,
(Otago's winds blow mighty cold through old Australian clothes)
The year went round again and he — what sorrows love can bring,
Was digging gum in tatters in the latter end of spring.
'Twas a brown-eyed girl that loved him in the latter end of spring.

But luck will change however and wherever you may roam,
An uncle left him money and the calf grew fat at home,
Then never ship can sail too fast, when love is on the wing,
He came to claim his sweetheart in the latter end of spring,
But she was married to a banker in the latter end of spring.

His brow went cold with pain and then with anger it grew hot,
'I'll love the girl who loves me, since the girl I loved forgot',
He turned to her unto whose soul his love was everything,
And married her in Maoriland before the end of spring,
And it's jolly jolly living in the latter end of spring.

'The Latter End of Spring' ~ Henry Lawson

Lawson didn't return to New Zealand until 1896. He stayed only briefly before returning to Sydney posthaste to marry a trainee nurse, Bertha Bredt. They joined a gold rush to Western Australia, with Henry still struggling to make ends meet from his freelance writing. Despite the recent successful publication of 'While the Billy Boils' in Sydney, he was becoming steadily depressed at the lack of opportunities afforded him in Australia. His reputation had been established throughout Australasia and his books were being noticed overseas, so Lawson might reasonably have expected some form of security to eventuate from his full-time writing career, but it was never to be.

The couple returned to Sydney where his uncertain writing income led him to indulge more frequently in serious drinking bouts, while Bertha struggled to keep him away from alcohol and his drinking mates. The *Bulletin* came to the rescue once more, providing two steerage tickets to New Zealand, so the Lawsons set sail for 'Maoriland' in 1897. On their arrival at Wellington they announced they were intending to settle here and Henry began writing for the *New Zealand Mail*.

With some influential help, the Lawsons obtained joint positions as teacher and sewing mistress for a Maori school at Mangamaunu, just north of Kaikoura. The Education Department advanced them the fare and they sailed on the *Wakatu* for Kaikoura shortly thereafter. They were warmly welcomed into the community, but were dependent on Maori help from the beginning. Their relationship with the local community was more informal than had previously been the case, and at first everyone seemed to get on well together. Henry continued to write his stories, through which he had already created his own legend.

Life deteriorated when Bertha became pregnant and they missed the companionship of their own people. This desire was exacerbated when a Maori girl they had taken into their home gave away their hard-earned groceries to her extended whanau. By and large it was a cultural misunderstanding, but it was enough to hasten their departure for Wellington. The Lawsons travelled around the North Island until their son was born, but despite Henry being offered another

Maori teaching post in Auckland, they left New Zealand in 1898. Some of his most successful and enduring stories were written at Mangamaunu, and New Zealand folklore has it on good authority that he met with David McKee Wright during his time in the South Island.

> Fern and tussock and flax, range and river and sea,
> A strain on my heart that will not relax — a heart that will never be free.
> Promises fair in the future rise; what are they all to me?
> She haunts me still with her great brown eyes, over the leagues of sea,
> Beautiful Maoriland — Dreary Maoriland,
> Oh my heart! for my heart lies dead in desolate Maoriland.

from 'Beautiful Maoriland ~ Henry Lawson

Lawson continued to struggle with his writing, and the lack of adequate recompense for his work led to an increasing dependence on alcohol and the charity of friends, one of whom was Andrew Barton (Banjo) Paterson. He was often broke and frequently underwent treatment for his alcoholism. He died in 1922 and was given a state funeral by the New South Wales government. It is somewhat ironic that this great Australian poet, a man who constantly struggled to rub two pennies together, should wind up honoured by his depiction on the Australian ten dollar note.

David McKee Wright

> For it's boys of the mountain and gully
> And it's chaps of the bush and the plain,
> Draw your seats to the fire and here's your desire,
> We're going a-rhyming again, we're going a-rhyming again
> Of the south in its pleasure and pain.
> There's no one before us, so join in the chorus,
> We're going a-rhyming again!

from 'We're Going A-Rhyming Again' ~ David McKee Wright

McKee Wright was born in 1869 in County Down, Ireland. His father was a Presbyterian minister and a well-known author. After finishing his schooling Wright emigrated to Australia, then moved to New Zealand for health reasons in 1887. He spent a few years on stations in the Otago back country and in 1890 began writing verse about the local life and characters.

While rabbiting on Puketoi Station he took the advice of a friend, Robert McSkimming (Crockery Bob) and submitted verses to the *Otago Witness*, where they were published. This body of material soon earned him the title 'Outback Laureate of New Zealand'. Here is his 'Old Mates':

I came up tonight at the station, the tramp had been longish and cold,
My swag ain't too heavy to carry, but then I begin to get old.
I came through this way to the diggings — how long will that be ago now,
Thirty years! How the country has altered and miles of it under the plough,
And Jack was my mate on the journey — we both run away from the sea,
He's got on in the world and I haven't, and now he looks sideways on me.

We were mates and that didn't mean jokers who meets for a year or a day,
We meant to go jogging together the whole of the blooming long way.
We slept with one blanket between us the night that we run from the port,
There was nothing above us but heaven, yet we took it as jolly good sport.
And now he's boss of a station and I'm — well the bloke that you see,
For he had the luck and I hadn't, and now he looks sideways on me.

We pegged out a claim on the Dunstan, there used to be gold in them days,
There's blokes still sticks to the diggings, but Lord only knows how it pays,
For the country as far as I've seen it's as chock full of holes as a sieve,
With the Chinkies [sic] a-mullocking through it and yet them coves manage to live.
But when Jack took me to the cradle, the place was a wonder to see,
We washed out a fortune between us and now he looks sideways on me.

We both fell in love with one woman — she worked in a pub for a spell,
It ain't the best place for an angel, but angels ain't better than Nell.
For she was as good as they make 'em and hadn't a notion of ill,
It's long years and years since we parted and seems I'm in love with her still.
But Jack was the handsomest fellow — I saw how things had to be,
He got the best wife on the diggings and now he looks sideways on me.

I left him, I just couldn't stand it — I knew it was better to part,
I couldn't look on at the wedding with a pain like a knife in my heart.
I never said nothing to no one — we didn't whack out all the gold,
I wanted my mate to be happy without my own yarn being told.
So I went to the coast by the steamer and now I'm the bloke that you see,
He told me to go to the whare, it seems he looks sideways on me.

There's steps coming down to the whare — some other bloke on the road,
'Taint nothing to him to get growled at, the boss ain't a bloke that he knowed.
Too dark to make out who's coming — he's crossing the plank at the creek,
The years and the whisky are telling, my eyesight begins to get weak.
What's the odds? It ain't like me to whimper and all that's gone by had to be,
But the old times come crowding around me, to see him look sideways on me.

What, Jack! Why, old man, you don't mean it? You didn't right know it was me,
Well I'm altered — it ain't for the better — never mind, never mind, let it be,
O mate, the long years since we parted — there's a blooming great lump in my throat,
I ain't been as glad, mate, I tell you, since that time that we run from the boat.
You ain't a bit altered — you're crying — why Jack don't be sorry for me,
I'm that glad that I think I'll go cranky — and I thought you looked sideways on me.

I first chanced upon David McKee Wright during my research into early copies of the *Otago Witness* in Dunedin's Hocken Library. Trawling through these pages, I stumbled across verse he had contributed to the newspaper in the 1890s and became more and more excited as I read his work, realising that here was a real voice of colonial New Zealand.

His first fully published work was *Aorangi and Other Verses* in 1896, then came *Station Ballads,* which soon sold out. Deciding to follow in his father's footsteps, McKee Wright began study for the Presbyterian ministry, but he wanted to marry, and finding the course too lengthy, joined the Congregational Church. For the next couple of years he preached at Alexandra, Clyde and Oamaru, but the church failed through lack of congregation, mainly due to the population drift, causing him to resign in 1899. He returned to writing and his next work *Wisps of Tussock* was published in Oamaru in 1900.

The speargrass crackles under the billy,
And overhead is the winter sun,
There's snow on the hills and frost in the gullies,
That reminds me of things that I've seen and done.

There was blokes from many the shed I shore in,
That I would have liked to call me mates,
But we said our farewells and laughed and parted,
For good and all at the station gate.

I remember the time when snow was drifting,
And Billy and me was out for the night.
We lay in the lee of a rock and waited,
Hungry and cold for the morning light,

Then he went one way and I the other,
We'd been like brothers for half a year.
He said "I'll see you again in town, mate
And we'll blow the froth off a pint of beer."

He went to a job on the plain he knowed of,
And I went poisoning out at the back.
But I missed him somehow — for all my looking,
I never could knock across his track.

He never came back and he never wrote me,
I wonder how blokes like him forget.
'Cos a chap like me makes friends in plenty,
But they slip away and I loses them yet.

'While the Billy Boils' ~ David McKee Wright

He moved to Wellington then on to Nelson in 1901, where he continued his ministry in the Congregational Church until his eventual retirement from the church in 1905. He now devoted himself to literary work by becoming a journalist and editing his own weekly *Te Rauparaha,* alternatively known as the *Nelson Times*, which had a brief albeit useful existence.

Anxious to find a wider field for his versatile pen, McKee Wright returned to Australia in 1910 and joined the Sydney *Bulletin*. While working for this prestigious magazine he won many prizes for his poetry, gaining fame as a critic and for his able prefaces to some of Henry Lawson's poetical works.

He had wide-ranging interests, being a collector of coins, stamps, china and precious stones as well as a keen gardener. He built his own house at Glenbrook in the Blue Mountains of New South Wales in 1926, but died suddenly at his home just a couple of years later.

David McKee Wright's works live on. He captured the life of the camps and shearing sheds and the spirit of those pioneering days, when men and manners were both free. He wrote of the tussock country, where men were employed as rabbiters, felt the warm glow of the campfire and saw the beauty of the New Zealand bush and countryside in all its different moods.

His poetry appealed to the heart and the head, readily finding a sympathetic audience. Old-timers still recall his verse being recited by individuals in pubs, while others remember seeing station hands, seated round a campfire, listening spellbound to someone reciting his poetry. John A Lee mentions this very same occurrence, when he tells of the Shiner and shearers reciting David McKee Wright's poetry in both his books *Shining with the Shiner* and *Shiner Slattery*.

During the Otago Centennial in 1948 it was recorded with much regret in the local newspapers that no school of 'bush' singers had succeeded him in New Zealand.

> The sun shines bright on Arlington, the drowsy sheep creep by,
> The water races seam the hills, cloud shadows line the sky.
> New fences climb the warm brown spurs to guard the scrubber ewes,
> Because the run is broken up for hungry cockatoos,
> The township sleeps below the hill, the homestead on the plain,
> But the last days of Arlington will never come again.
>
> The working men are seen no more in hut or rabbit camp,
> The stockwhip never will be heard about the river swamp.
> No more the mighty fleeces crown the bins like drifted snow,
> No more the princely rams go down, the wonder of the show,
> The swagger on the weary tramp comes o'er the summer plain,
> And sighs for rest at Arlington, yet knows he sighs in vain.

There's little work on Arlington since the old station days,
The hawk-faced owners groan to tell sheep farming never pays.
They build no homestead on the runs, they pay no wages out,
The station style was different when money flew about,
The rabbits flourish on the hills and burrow all the plain,
The stock that ran on Arlington will never run again.

The good old boss of Arlington was everybody's friend,
He liked to keep the wages up right to the very end.
If diggers' horses went astray they always could be found,
The cow that roamed across the run was never in the pound,
He was a good man through and through, cheery, fair and plain,
And now he'll never ride the rounds of Arlington again.

And yet the talk is evermore 'The people want the land'
I tell you that the workers cry is 'Let the stations stand!'
The greedy few will clamour loud and clamour to the end,
A dummy grabbing what he can is not the people's friend,
And heaven's curse is on him still in all his schemes for gain,
He falls and yet old Arlington will never rise again.

'Arlington' ~ David McKee Wright

George Meek

Born the son of a railwayman in 1881, George
Meek grew up in Dunedin. At 14 he went
to work on Benmore Station in the Waitaki
district, before taking a job in 1906 as clerk
with Galloway Station, just across the hills from
Puketoi Station where David McKee Wright had
worked. At Galloway George Meek encountered
local characters and rural folklore, along with the
verse and song of David McKee Wright, which
struck a responsive chord with him. He would
later pay tribute to his mentor:

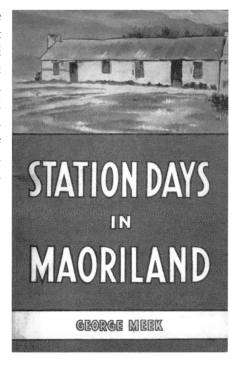

> Clear on the air tonight there rings,
> A voice that breathes of bushland joy,
> A song of honest worth it brings,
> Across the hills from Puketoi.
>
> A song that lightened many a load,
> On lone nights played a human part.
> For like a crystal stream it flowed,
> Straight from a friendly human heart.

Hale, happy roving station hands,
Passed merry rhymes of wit and cheer,
With homely pride in Maoriland's
Big-hearted singing pioneer.

On bridle-track and tussock top,
Where storm-swept ridges sweep along,
Mem'ry waits there for those who care,
For one who fashioned these in song.

The tolling of an old church bell,
Steals through the trees in yonder glade,
A tale of worthwhile works to tell,
To fan a mem'ry lest it fade.

Lest Maoriland a son forget,
Who blazed with song the bushland way…
This mem'ry of the torch he set,
Upon his tomb I humbly lay.

'David McKee Wright' ~ George Meek

In North Otago Meek found his own voice and begin writing the songs and verse that were published in the *Otago Witness* from 1906 to 1910.

For the next thirty-odd years he worked in Oamaru with the stock and station firm, Dalgety & Company. He continued writing ballads and verse to capture the atmosphere of the early station days which had so inspired singers and writers such as David McKee Wright.

The firelight glows a cheery red, the flickering flames pop out to play,
And I am back in the shearing shed — where a voice is calling "Wool Away!"

Back where my youth had scarce begun, speeds the night to the morning sun,
I was fleet foot on the shearing board, when a voice growled softly "Wool Away!"

A day full-lit with the shearer's song, that spurs him on in the fleecy fray,
And the boss's grouching seemed all wrong, as a friendly voice called "Wool Away!"

A lonesome tang scents the evening clear, while the singing city crowds its way,
But the rabble song I do not hear, it's a far voice calling "Wool Away!"

And the silent voice I hear the best, above the sweep of the city's sway,
It's a voice I know comes from the west and it's calling clearly "Wool Away!"

The firelight glow begins to wane, the flickering flames no longer play.
But the flame of youth leaps up again as a still voice whispers "Wool Away!"

'Wool Away' ~ George Meek

Meek once said that he made no pretence of contributing to New Zealand poetry, but that his aim was to revive memories of the station days, which inspired so many singers in Australia and seemingly so few in New Zealand. Station life intensified the appeal of writing verse rather than prose — to him it was more human and he used it because it lingered longer in the memory, suiting his powers of expression.

Much of George Meek's verse was published by newspapers, farming magazines and the *Australasian* (an Australian publication). Some found its way into AE Woodhouse's anthology *New Zealand Farm and Station Verse* in 1950. This recognition led to publication of his *Station Days in Maoriland* in 1952.

> With swear and curse and oaths and worse, we sauntered to the shed,
> We 'ere sir, bawled as names were called and with a lumb'ring tread,
> Lunged off in mobs to do odd jobs and wished the sheep were dead.
>
> We sorted belly, piece and neck, we picked the locks and stains,
> We filled the tins and swished the bins and to the hectic strains
> Of wild discord we broomed the board with little for our pains.
>
> We piled the bunker to the brim, the wood for cookie chopped,
> The tables brushed & scrubbed & slushed, the battoned floor we mopped.
> And toiled, and when 'twas 'smoke-oh' then like workmen down we flopped.
>
> And rolled our fags and talked of snags, of bosses we had struck,
> The stingy sort and real good sport who'd never see you stuck,
> And that strange breed who grudge a feed to coves down on their luck.
>
> Tall yarns we spun of jobs we'd done and jobs that were a frost,
> Of roads we'd tramped and where we'd camped and places we had dosed,
> The dreams we dreamed and hopes that gleamed and chances we had lost.
>
> Gun shearers who, big tallies do, when half-shot at the pub,
> And tales we told of squatters cold, who'd charge us for our grub.
> Who met success with pet caress and us coves with a snub.
>
> Our fags we doused and grinned and groused and hoed in once again,
> When things were set, we prayed for wet and now we cursed the rain,
> And vowed each one would have a run with sheep of pure-bred strain.
>
> We stacked the bales of dingy wool, we baled up skin and hide,
> The wagon load we heave-a-ho'd, the ropes we twitched and tied,
> And washed our bags and rolled our swags and scoured the countryside.

'The Ballad of the Rouseabout' ~ George Meek

George Meek died in 1953, not long after founding the Pioneer Gallery of the North Otago Museum in Oamaru.

Cecil Winter

Our folk heritage owes much to the Australian influence, and two poets originally from Australia exemplify this: Cecil Winter, who used the *nom de plume* 'Riverina', and Thomas Henry Thompson, alias 'Hamilton Thompson'.

Winter was born at Moulamein in the Riverina district of New South Wales and from the outset felt as much a part of the bush as if he had been the hero of an Australian novel. His mother educated him at home before sending him off to a couple of bush schools. By age fifteen, his first verses were being published by the *Worker* and the *Bulletin*. After his formal education he worked as a drover, boundary rider, wool-scourer, station-hand, axeman, saw-miller, coach driver, school teacher and postmaster in a bush township, before a spell in the army fighting alongside New Zealanders, who he found to be really good blokes.

When Winter was working at Bungaree, Victoria, he got a telegram from a cousin inviting him to go on a trip to New Zealand the next day. He did so, and settled in Southland where he found more time to write, and became a regular contributor to the *Southland Times, NZ Artists Annual, The Highway* and a few notable Australian magazines. Riverina's most active writing period was in the 1920s, when he was often described as the Banjo Paterson of New Zealand, although others saw his work as continuing the Lawson tradition. *Bulletin* readers appreciated his work, which demonstrated excellent craftsmanship. Many of his most vivid pictures and highest moments of inspiration are attributed to his time in Southland, while remembering the wide days of long ago in the land of his birth, Australia.

Whereas many Australian poets hated the bush, seeing it as the oppressor and blind killer of human hopes, Cecil Winter revelled in it. He loved it with the patient, all-seeing perspective of someone who had obviously enjoyed living there and loved even more the chance to write about it. The song 'The Mill', complete with added chorus, is based on his poem, 'The Pine Mill':

Beside a clump of needlewoods, we've set the little mill,
The engine's by the blue clay tank and further up the hill
The blokes are in the pine trees and chips are on the wing,
And in the fresh bush morning you can hear the axes ring.

Chorus   With a jigger and a jemmy and a shigger and a shammy,
And there's saw-dust in the sky,
I keep thinking will he gimme up all of the money,
Or wait till the big 'uns lie.

We've set the bench and trued the saw and let her have a spin,
The benchman eyes his pet with pride and pats the packing in.
We've chocked the eight-horse engine's wheels, we've backed the water-cart,
And stacked a heap of short-length wood in readiness to start.

We have no tearing vertical, we run no twin saws here,
No clanking winches, swinging cranes, and wealth of Yankee gear.
We have no collared office staff, no multitude of men,
We've just a little clearing mill and number nine or ten.

We grease the transports, oil the trucks, the benchman gives the sign,
The engine starts, the big belt flaps, the saw begins to whine.
The sun comes out a scorcher and the bullocks raise the dust,
The water bag gets covered and our throats begin to rust.

The hill is looking strange and bare, the bigger trees are cut,
And through the gaps we catch a sight of someone else's hut,
The slope is scoured by dragging logs, the grass is put to rout,
And now it's just a few more days and we shall be cut out.

Hamilton Thompson

Thomas Henry Thompson was born and educated in Queensland before coming
to New Zealand in the early 1890s. He spent three years in Central Otago working
as an accountant for a miner before moving to Dunedin to work as a public
accountant. While there he published a magazine and collaborated in writing a
textbook about accountancy.

I came across his 1904 poem 'The Ships Sail In' (later titled 'Auckland') in the
earliest days of my folklore interest, and composed a tune for it in 1965.

The ships sail in and the ships sail out,
The tourists they come and go,
For this is the land of mystery,
Wherever the strange will flow,
And its story, say, who shall know.

The ships sail in and the ships sail out,
And they choose of the harbours twain,
With their cargoes of kauri, gold, fibre and gum,
Fruit, mutton, butter and grain,
They travel across the main.

The ships sail in and the ships sail out,
With the wealth of the southern seas,
Do they gather the meaning of what they pass,
Ere they furl or unfurl in the breeze …
Where the turbulent stand at ease.

Writing verse took up much of Thompson's spare time and he contributed prose
and verse to the *Otago Witness*, culminating in his book *Ballads about Business and
Back Block Life*. He had more than a passing literary relationship with David McKee

Wright and they taunted each other in verse form via the pages of the *Otago Witness*. A distinct Australian influence can be seen in his writing style, an influence that remains with us even today.

I met one morn near Halfway House, upon the Cromwell Road,
A weather-beaten little man, who staggered 'neath his load.
His build was slight, his beard was grey and barely five feet high
He looked, yet carried on his back a swag with tent and fly.

"Good day" said he, "Good day" said I and then produced a flask,
I ventured "Will you have a nip?" there was no need to ask.
He threw his swag upon the ground and at a wayside creek,
We wished each other "Happy days" ere more we sought to speak.

And there beneath the sunlit sky, in clear crisp morning air,
While rabbits scudded down the slopes and bounded everywhere,
And larks soared high above our heads and just a shade below,
Swept past the roaring Molyneux, with swift incessant flow.

We sat and talked for half-an-hour on topics up to date,
For he was fairly well informed, although he called me 'mate'
And Passing Notes, by Civis, he descanted on with gust,
And sketches from the *Bulletin*, hilariously discussed.

We drifted towards the personal and ere an hour had fled,
Exchanged a little history, I learned his name was Ned.
Ned Dunne, in full — 'twas brief enough and easy to retain,
But I should e'er remember it if thrice as long again.

Fossicker, fencer, rouseabout and rabbiter he'd been,
From Riversdale to Naseby, every hamlet he had seen,
He'd scaled the heights of Nevis, padded hoof to Albertown,
Tramped and coached it through Kawarau Gorge and spelled at Arrowtown.

On the eerie road to Skippers, o'er the Rock and Pillar Range,
Scarce a bend, a bluff or gully, scarce a rock to him was strange.
O'er the dreary Maniototo many a time he'd humped his swag,
From Morven Hills to Middlemarch he knew each peak and crag.

And now to Alexandra, keeping on the riverside,
He meant to walk·unless, perchance, he'd get a lift at Clyde.
He'd met a friend a week before and on the strict QT,
Confided that for old time's sake they'd got upon the spree.

Now he had not a copper left, but ere the night would fall,
At Alexandra hoped to get a couple of pounds in all.
That he had lent some months before, ere thence he shifted camp,
And on the road to Criffel had begun a former tramp.

I had some notes upon me, but of silver coin was short,
A pound I didn't care to ask, and meanly did distort
The truth, and said I'm sorry, but 'twere even half a crown,
You'd get it if I had it, but I haven't got a 'brown'.

Did Ned look disappointed? No, he disappointed me,
His thoughts were not on borrowing, but that I failed to see,
He looked at me in sympathy and said "If you are broke
I'll wire a pound to Cromwell, for you seem a decent bloke."

"Just stay there till tomorrow and I'll wire a pound to you,
When I get to Alexandra and get back the borrowed two."
I was badly clad and dusty and upon a walking tour,
And Ned from all appearances concluded I was poor.

…

Ah 'tis only in the country that such open hearts abound,
We are cautious in the city where the schemers prowl around.
But our fellow-men distrusting, where the trams and buses run,
We would not, for aye, continue if we found them like Ned Dunne.

'Ned Dunne' ~ Hamilton Thompson

Dennis Hogan

Dennis Hogan was born in Frankton Junction in 1889, shortly after his parents emigrated to New Zealand. His father was a ganger on the railways and the young Hogan's earliest memories are of living in a house not far from the soot and smoke of the railway yard. When the family shifted to Papatoetoe and later to Helensville it was time for Dennis to begin his schooling.

At eleven years of age and having gained his standard six certificate, Dennis left school to make his way in the world. He got a job on a dairy farm at two shillings and sixpence a week and most of his leisure time was spent among the sailing ships that came to load kauri timber for all parts of the world. His accommodation on the farm, a leaky one-roomed shingle-roofed hut, was the communal bedroom, change-room, laundry, wash-house and lounge/living room for three persons. The floor was covered with a mixture of cow-dung and caked clay, and when it was time to sweep the floor (once a week usually) it was almost impossible to find the floorboards beneath it all.

Dennis stayed on the farm for about six months before taking a job as cook's mate on a river boat plying its trade on the Kaipara Harbour. Here he learned the rudiments of cooking and how to polish the pots and pans, while his wages for an eighty-hour week were a paltry ten shillings.

Dennis soon found himself working as a cook for a ploughing camp, then as a stable hand in Rotorua, before ending up at Waihi where he became a fully fledged miner. There he saw men's heads blown off, mates crushed beyond recognition, and unemployed men waiting round the shaft for any job going. The impressionable lad realised that the world was not all it was cracked up to be, as he'd been taught in Sunday school. From his fellow miners' discussions and from books he began to understand that the average man was little better off than the donkey with the carrot, cajoled along for another's profit. At the same time he was introduced to poetry, which gave him the idea of stringing words together in harmony — a logical progression for him, because even in his school days he had always obtained full marks for composition, spelling and recitation.

Dennis left Waihi before the big strike and took on a variety of jobs in the ensuing years, including labourer, quarry-man, hod-carrier, barman and cook. He even spent time on the swag throughout New Zealand and Australia, a pastime he enjoyed a great deal, despite finding it a rather fruitless occupation.

I don't know where I'm going and I never reason why,
The tui's singing in the flax, the stream is running by.
I'll wander on till sun goes down and birds have gone to rest,
Then if I want to sing a song, I'll get it off my chest.

I'll boil my billy as I sing and make a cup of tea,
There's tucker in the tucker bag, the world is good to me.
I'll make a hollow for my hip and sleep among the fern,
And how the other fellow sleeps is none of my concern.

If someone offers me a job perhaps to shear or cook,
I'll rouse myself in my own time and go and have a look.
But if I have to pass a pub, my swag against the wall
I'll throw down light and easily and never go at all.

They say I am a scallywag, a loafer and a dunce,
I'm making no excuses but you should have seen me once.
A dandy on the racetracks with a lady by my side,
With people glad to know me and respected far and wide.

I married quite a pretty girl, a girl worth fighting for,
And when the bugles rang out clear I went away to war.
When I came home without a scratch, quite lucky I'll admit,
There was no welcome waiting me — my wife had done a flit.

So when you pass me on the road, footslogging in the dust,
Don't look down too superior with loathing and disgust.
For I am what you made me with your smug society,
And fate could deal the same to you as it has dealt to me.

'Driftwood' ~ Dennis Hogan

Dennis Hogan's collected work was illustrated by John Parry and published by Unity Writers as a *Fernfire* special.

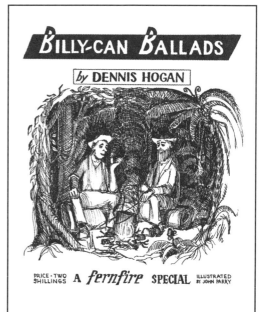

He wrote verse in the evenings after work, occasionally sending his efforts to magazines and papers. To his surprise they began to be published far and wide. He wrote his unique style of poetry for over fifty years and was occasionally described as the voice of the New Zealand countryside. His ballads lend themselves to music and I've been responsible for turning a couple into songs.

> Whenever you're out walking down busy city streets,
> Scrutinising faces of the people that you meet.
> Don't nod a casual greeting and continue on your way,
> Stop a perfect stranger and this is what you say.
>
> *Chorus* How are you, mate, how are you, mate,
> Stop a perfect stranger and say "How are you, mate?"
>
> The hand is never hard to shake if you will hold it out,
> This friendly sign of welcome is much needed round about,
> There's no such thing as being made of different kinds of clay,
> The world would be a better place if only we would say…
>
> How are you mate, how are you, mate,
> If only we would stop awhile and say "How are you, mate?"
>
> Now the heart responds to kindly words, although not understood,
> A friendly smile suffices to bring out the common good.
> So never shun the stranger hesitating at the gate,
> Extend the hand of fellowship and say "How are you, mate?"
>
> How are you, mate, how are you, mate,
> Extend the hand of fellowship and say "How are you, mate?"
>
> So when you see the stranger just arrived from Whakatu,
> Lost, staring at buildings in surroundings that are new.
> Don't bother if he's rich or poor or if his tie is straight,
> Produce your hand quite naturally and say "How are you, mate?"

> How are you mate, how are you, mate,
> Produce your hand quite naturally and say "How are you, mate?"

'How Are You, Mate' ~ Dennis Hogan/Phil Garland

Tod Symons

Tod Symons was born in 1907 on his parents' farm at Galloway near Alexandra in Central Otago, where from an early age he made friends with original goldminers in the area. From age five he was already accompanying his father on prospecting forays into the Crawford Hills and the Raggedy Range, and from that time forth he roamed the district far and wide in search of game or gold.

Tod Symons at Alexandra, 1969.

Educated at Galloway primary school and Alexandra High School, he worked for a time in Dunedin's Public Trust Office, but his father's failing health brought him home to the family farm.

The Depression of the 1930s led Tod to take up gold prospecting for a living, but after several years of its delights and despairs he abandoned this insecurity for a position with the irrigation department of the Ministry of Works based in Alexandra — a job he held until retirement in the late 1960s.

Tod didn't start writing until the late 1950s, but when he did the public response surprised him. The *Central Otago News* began publishing his verse and it won the immediate approval of readers. His deep feeling for the rugged beauty and romantic past of the Central Otago region manifested itself in his poetry and his obvious love of the gold shone through everything he wrote. He made no pretence of being a poet of note — he was only too happy to express his appreciation of the district he came to know so well.

> You can buy flowers from my garden,
> The sweetest that all central grows,
> Full with the colours of sunshine,
> But you can't buy a Red Conroy rose.
>
> This is a story of Central,
> A story not everyone knows,
> From the unwritten history of Central,
> This tale of the Red Conroy rose.

213

In the gully still named for them 'Conroys'
A man and a woman alone,
Lived away back in the sixties,
In a primitive cabin of stone.

They planted a rose by their window,
A satin-deep, love coloured rose,
And search where you will throughout Central,
It's the only one place that it grows.

Now Conroy went off to the gold rush,
That year of the great tragic snows,
Over the back of the mountains,
Where there's death where the southerly blows.

As speechless they stood in her doorway,
When they brought back his shovel and pan,
She begged of those men of the gold rush,
"Tell me, oh where is my man?"

'Twas a rough bearded miner who told her,
But his voice was a prayer as he said,
"We buried him back of the mountain,
Your husband, Red Conroy is dead."

But she cried "No! He'll live on forever,
In that one flower this harsh country knows,
He will live in the rose that he planted,
In this beautiful Red Conroy rose."

And search where you will through the country,
There's only one place that it grows,
But you can't buy a rose of Red Conroy,
They won't sell a Red Conroy rose.

'Rose of Red Conroy' ~ Tod Symons

Tod wrote not only about gold but also about hopes and dreams, especially the few that come true and the others that fade away and die. He wrote of mountains, sheep-men, wild game, people, pubs, dogs and ghosts, but mostly about the freedom that allowed a man to search for what he desired and live as he liked.

In the hush of a winter's evening in the day's fast-fading light,
I stood by St Bathans township and waited the coming night.
And I saw it again in the glory it knew in the long ago,
In the harsh raw setting of Central's hills with their tops white-skiffed with snow.

I heard the ring of shovel and pick, the clatter of falling stones,
The roar of nozzles, the shouts of men as I stood by that road alone.
Then darkness fell, the clamour died, the workings faded from sight,
And only the sound of tramping feet broke the peace of a curfewed night.

Then the hills that were dark were dotted with a thousand winking lights,
From house and cabin and canvas tent on flat and gully and heights.
Ghost lights of the days of the gold rush from the homes of its mining men,
Then the lights went out and the past had gone back into the past again.

So I crossed the road to the Vulcan of many the very last
Of the old-time pubs from its golden days and a link with St Bathans' past.
And the warmth, the lights and the laughter brought back the present again,
But we drank to the days of long ago and the old St Bathans' men.

'St Bathans' ~ Tod Symons

I met up with Tod a couple of times on my collecting trips in the 1960s and early
1970s and on each occasion he was amazed that anyone should show any interest
in his work. He was absolutely delighted when I or others set any of his work
to music. A modest and gentle man, he was blest with a great sense of humour,
frequently telling me he knew a secret place where gold could still be found. "I
know a place," he would declare, and set off alone into the Central Otago hills,
often away for days on end to visit a familiar spot. As if to prove this story true,
he showed me gold he'd previously found in the area — and mark my word, there
was plenty of it!

"I know a place" is a saying, you'll still hear where miners are,
That phrase is the opening gambit of their stories near and far.
And there never was an old-time miner, who in memory couldn't go back,
To where there was gold for the digging, could he only hit the track.

And such a one was Bill Whookey, who lay in a hospital bed,
An old-time bloke just waiting, to join the ranks of the dead.
But the spirit of old Bill Whookey was strong as in days of youth,
And the tales he told me were many and rang with the ring of truth…

He told me his great deep secret, a smile on his lined old face,
He spoke in an almost whisper "Matey! I know a place!
I know a place on the mountain, on the Old Man Range, up high,
And now is the time for going, while the weather's fine and dry."

The gold is in shallow digging, right close to a little stream,
There's a hollowed rock to camp in, it's a proper miner's dream.
There's rabbits there for the catching, a roasted rabbit's a treat,
There's matagouri for firing, oh, the smoke of it smells so sweet.

But we'll have to keep it quiet, for you know what miners are,
If they know we've gone to the mountain, they'll come from near and far.
But if no one sees us going, then none will know the way,
So we'll leave in the early morning, we'll leave at the break of day…

'I Know a Place' - Tod Symons

Tod may no longer be with us, but his memory remains in his sensitive poetry and in the interviews and recitations I recorded on those trips, which have helped foster a deep love and respect for all that is Central Otago. This piece of Tod's verse says it all for me:

Those golden days will never fade,
To the realm of forgotten things,
For to those with a love of Central's past,
The voice of Central sings.

Joe Charles

Joseph Henry Fache Charles was born in Timaru in 1916, the son of a Southland farmer descended from pioneering stock. His grandfather founded the *Dunstan Times* in the Otago gold rushes of the 1860s, so writing was in his blood.

From the outset Joe was a poor speller and tone deaf, but this didn't deter him from writing ballads. He wrote his first at age ten and showed his correspondence teacher, who expressed the wish that he would put as much effort into his schoolwork as into his rhyming ramblings. Although the ballad was written in his formative years it was not published until he was forty five.

Joe attended Gore High School and went on to his father's farm for seven shillings and sixpence a week, augmented by earning a similar amount per column for contributing to the *Mataura Ensign*. He spent much of his time round the sheds and pens and up in the hills chasing pigs and deer. He socialised with musterers, shepherds, fencers, harvesters, shearers and passing swaggers, even frisking at woolshed dances and booze-ups.

All the while he was building up a great store of memories, respect and experience for good use in the future.

> I was sitting on a shingle slide in the bush beneath the snow,
> And away down in the valley I heard a whistle blow.
> It was smoko in the sawmill and I knew it must be ten,
> So I set my watch and shook her well and wound her up again.
>
> *Chorus* Smoko! Spell Ho! Billy on the boil,
>   Light a fag and take a drag and rest your bones from toil.
>
> There's nothing like a cup of tea and time to roll a fag,
> Wet your whistle, stretch your back and squat and chew the rag.
> So whenever you hear a whistle blow or someone ring a bell,
> Whatever the note, grab your coat and wait for the boss to yell …
>
> When they are drafting in the station yard and you're just the rouseabout,
> When the dust does fly, and you are hot and dry, you will hear a shed-hand shout,
> They are banging along to beat the gong for the last sheep in the pen,
> When they give them the boot, and they are down the chute,
> You'll hear them yelling then …
>
> When you are cutting wood on contract in a block of old dead wattle,
> You are facing a loss and the clock is the boss, it's cold tea from a bottle.
> Take a bite to eat, put up your feet and rest if you can't relax,
> Ten minutes neat, then it's on your feet, and a smoke while you grind your axe.

'Smoko' ~ Joe Charles

Joe joined the air force in World War II, serving in the Pacific as a flight engineer on Catalina flying boats before becoming an instructor. After the war he went to the Nelson Downs district with the Forest Service, finally returning to farming in 1950 at Glenroy in the foothills of the Southern Alps. There he built a cottage entirely from local stone, which became one of his legacies to the district.

In the 1950s his writings began to receive widespread acclaim after a few were recorded by international balladeer, William Clauson, on one of his frequent visits to the country. Before this, Joe had read his ballads only to his family and friends. Clauson recognised Joe's ability and told him he had a duty to continue recording the history of New Zealand in song and poetry, and advised him not to go near anyone for a formal musical education.

217

Joe moved north to a farm near Wellsford in 1960, but with his wife in poor health he took up a lease of the hotel at Opononi for a few years, where he was provided with dolphin material for further ballads. After this stint, Joe moved south once again, this time to manage the Lodge Hotel at Hanmer Springs, where the New Zealand Folklore Society first made contact with him, taping interviews, stories and balladry of vital interest to folk enthusiasts around the country.

Joe retired from Hanmer to live at Corsair Bay near Lyttelton, running the Corsair Gallery with his wife Joyce. Although his first book *Black Billy Tea* was not published by Whitcoulls until 1981, folksingers and others had already recognised the importance of his work by introducing a few of his songs and ballads into their repertoires. I got to know Joe well during this time and subsequently recorded some of his songs for my albums with Kiwi Pacific Records. He became a member of the Christchurch branch of the Folklore Society and spoke about his life and work to the group on a couple of occasions.

> In Queen Street today, there's a billboard to say,
> That the *Kiwi* is ready to sail,
> Yes early next week she'll be on her way,
> With passengers, cargo and mail.
> There's gold so they say in those hills round the Grey,
> Just for digging and dragging away.
> There's a living to be made if you've something to trade,
> Men are hungry with gold dust to pay.
>
> Now if men are not liars, the captain Joe Bryers,
> Knows the Coast like the back of his hand,
> So pack up your swag and your old carpet bag,
> Let's go and wash us some sand.
> She's a tough little tub loaded down with good grub,
> Whisky, tobacco, cigars,
> So let's sing in praise of the *Kiwi* today,
> Coming home loaded down with gold bars.
>
> I've a sad tale to tell for they've just rung the bell,
> In the streets with the news of the day,
> There's one little ship on a prospecting trip,
> Is lost with all hands so they say.
> Where the mountains stand bold and the rivers run cold,
> Down to the wild Tasman Sea,
> My song is now sung, so come on everyone,
> Here's a toast to the good ship *Kiwi*.
>
> *'Ballad of the Kiwi' ~ Joe Charles*

The rhymes suggest a melody to the reader, and people respond well to Joe's material. Willow Macky, Paul Bond and I have each set his 'Ballad of the Kiwi' to music.

Joe's sensitivity to rural life put him in touch with a considerable body of folk material. His love of the land and sense of place helped him blend tall stories with genuine historical events, creating poetry that would not be out of place in any shearing shed or bar. He developed a firm sense of mission to record this country's colourful folklore in verse and song, while there were still old-timers with anecdotes to tell. His rhymes documented the stories of those unsung heroes who helped to build our nation, from the Northland gumfields to the Otago gold rushes and beyond. He continued his fine work until his untimely death in Christchurch in 1991. Before he died, Joe entrusted me with the rough manuscript of his follow-up book, tentatively entitled *Blackberry Pie*, for which he had been unable to find a publisher. It waits in the NZ Folklore Society archives, which are currently in my possession.

I've carried my swag by station and farm,
Slept under hedges, which did me no harm.
But now I've a hut and roof over my head,
A fireplace, a chair, a mattress and bed.

Chorus   Here's to the fellows who fell by the way,
Good health to the cobbers I still have today.
There's Crooked-Neck Stanley and old Ginger Jack,
The Shiner, the Clocky, all the boys of the track.

I've a neat little camp with a dog for a friend,
Some old swagger mates for a yarn now and then.
There are some who are dead and gone long ago,
And those still living like Black Billy Joe.

Don't cry for one who's too old for the road,
For I've plenty to do without humping my load.
I can visit the store for a bit of fresh grub,
Still spend a few bob with my mates at the pub.

Now the day will soon come when our paths meet again,
On that final journey when all men are friends.
There'll be time for a greeting, a yarn and a chat,
Before tramping once more with the boys of the track.

'Boys of the Track' - Joe Charles & Phil Garland

Willow Macky

Katherine Faith (Willow) Macky was born in 1921 and became one of our leading composers of folk-style songs about Kiwi towns, history and heroes. She wrote poetry very early on and by age 16 had published a volume of verse, later contributing to several anthologies. Educated at St Cuthbert's and Iona colleges and Elam School of Fine Arts, she began collecting songs from many lands as a hobby. Finding so few about this country, she wrote her own. After starting to play a Gibson guitar that her American mother brought from Texas she never looked back, writing and composing over a hundred songs and a folk opera entitled *The Maori Flute*.

In World War II she met a Jewish member of the US Army Medical Corps, but their marriage plans were halted by family opposition on religious grounds. She retained a strong interest in Jewish history and wrote a film script, *Song of Zion*. She took it to Hollywood, where producers were so impressed that she was invited to join a team of Hollywood writers, but she was unable to take this offer up as her recently widowed mother urgently required her assistance.

On a visit to Sydney in the 1950s she met the composer Alfred Hill, who was keen on folk music, and he invited her to a meeting of the Bush Music Club to hear the original Bushwhackers playing their 'dinky-di' Aussie music. Willow was enchanted by their homemade instruments, such as the bush bass and lagerphone.

By the late 1950s she was performing occasionally at the Rafters folk club in Auckland and at Mary Seddon's Monde Marie coffee bar in Wellington. She would sing her originals about the 'Waitemata Harbour', 'Tamaki Moonlight' and 'Wellington Cable-car' mixed in with blues and boogie. Her first real success came from meeting Swedish-American balladeer, William Clauson, on his visit to New Zealand in 1959. Clauson went on to record five of her songs, including one specially written to a melody he particularly liked. It had become traditional for each country he visited to supply different words to the same tune and on this occasion

it became 'The Bishop and the Tohunga.'

Meanwhile, renowned Maori bass and opera singer Inia Te Wiata was praising her as "the only New Zealand composer, besides Alfred Hill, who can capture the authentic Maori atmosphere."

While these accolades helped introduce her music to a wider audience, local folk singing groups — the Tarriers Three, the Mariners and the Voyagers — also recorded more of her songs. The best known is the Kiwi Christmas hymn 'Te Harinui', which has become recognised as the unofficial New Zealand Christmas carol. It was first published in 1957 but not recorded until 1964, when Colin Fenton sang it for

Kiwi Records on their *Bay of Islands* extended play record along with 'Waitangi', 'Marsden' and 'The First New Zealand Christmas.'

'Te Harinui' (The Great Joy) is about Samuel Marsden preaching the first Gospel in New Zealand, at the Bay of Islands on Christmas Day, 1814.

> Not on a snowy night, by star or candlelight,
> Nor by an angel band, there came to our dear land,
> Te Harinui, Te Harinui, Te Harinui,
> Glad tidings of great Joy.
>
> But on a summer day, within a quiet bay,
> The Maori people heard that great and glorious word,
> Te Harinui …
>
> The people gathered round upon the grassy ground,
> And heard the preacher say I bring to you this day,
> Te Harinui …
>
> Now in this blessed land, united heart and hand,
> We praise the glorious birth and sing to all the earth,
> Te Harinui …

The 1960s were busy for Willow as she continued to write and then tour England and the USA, appearing as a guest at the 4th Festival of British folk music in 1962. This led to her publishing an article on folk song in New Zealand in the English magazine *Folk* in January 1963. While touring America she stuck a plastic fernleaf on her Gibson to indicate her Kiwi connection. She later put this guitar aside and used a nylon-strung classical guitar. Her old Gibson is owned today by Auckland singer Graham McGregor, who says you can still see the glue marks on the body where the fernleaf once proudly sat.

> Thames it was a boom town, a hundred years ago.
> When the gold ran rich and the drink ran free,
> And the river ran to the waiting sea,
> In Thames, Thames, a hundred years ago.
>
> Thames it is a ghost town or so it seems today.
> Where are the fabled riches that caused men's hearts to burn,
> Gone, gone, never to return.

Where are the men who laboured, lured by that golden gleam?
Gone, gone, back to the fading dream,
Of Thames, Thames, a hundred years ago.

'Thames' ~ Willow Macky

Willow struck up a friendship with bush poet and balladeer Joe Charles, another who had been acclaimed by William Clauson, and the two found much common ground. She composed tunes to Joe's material, such as 'Ballad of the Kiwi', and thought I might be interested in performing them. She sent me some of her musical transcripts and corresponded occasionally with Joe and me, expressing support for the work we were doing in helping promote Kiwi folklore and music.

Willow Macky is a great exponent of writing about local experiences, history, people and places, including Maori legend and tradition.

In later years she would recall how people laughed whenever she sang the line "I love to go to old Mission Bay" in her song 'Tamaki Moonlight', mainly because of the strangeness of hearing a local place mentioned in a song or ballad. But what better example of that previously mentioned cultural cringe?

Willow's life and work are indeed an important part of the story of New Zealand music. As she had observed 40 years previously:

We have something to sing about — a land as beautiful, interesting and as worthy
as any other and we wish to pay New Zealand a tribute, which is long overdue,
giving pleasure to our people and all others who wish to hear.

Willow Macky was awarded the Queen's Service Medal for public service in the 2006 New Year's Honours. She died on 10 December 2006.

Oh young James Cook was a sailor bold,
He was brave, he was good, he was clever,
He rose to be captain in the king's navy,
And commanded the good ship *Endeavour*.

He said to his wife, "You're the joy of my life
Though oceans may roll between us,
But I must be off to the isles of the south,
To observe the transit of Venus."

Then he sailed away out of Plymouth Bay,
With his doughty crew beside him,
With a ready sail for breeze or gale,
And the faithful stars to guide him.

They journeyed that way for many a day,
This band of gallant freemen,
Far to the south in the tempest's mouth,
Till they passed Cape Maria Van Diemen.

Then "Land Ahoy" cried the cabin boy,
And eager they were to see land,
Then going ashore raised the flag they bore,
On the bush clad hills of New Zealand…

from 'The Ballad of Captain Cook' ~ Willow Macky

Peter Cape

I'm an ordinary joker, getting old before my time
For my heart's in Taumarunui on the Main Trunk Line.
Taumarunui, Taumarunui, Taumarunui on the Main Trunk Line …

The words to this song were written by probably the most successful and instantly recognisable songwriter of all our bards and balladeers; a man whose claim to be "one of New Zealand's foremost failed poets" led him to write comic verse. He later said that "If it hadn't been for Jim Henderson returning from Coromandel with a fantastic story about a little place called Whenuakite, which someone talked about as Fenackaty, I wouldn't have started writing doggerel about New Zealand place names. And if Fenackaty hadn't been such an impossible word to find rhymes for, I wouldn't have gone on to write a ballad about Taumarunui. You know, the one that starts, "I'm an ordinary joker …" We sure do!

Peter Irwin Cape was born in 1926 in Helensville, north-west of Auckland. His parents had emigrated from England after World War I and were continually on the move, travelling by caravan from the King Country to Northland. During this nomadic existence Peter became conscious of how different his parents' North Country accents were to the Kiwi voices he heard. Absorbing Kiwi vernacular would stand him in good stead once he began writing seriously. He was educated by correspondence, and after completing his schooling worked as an uncertified teacher, a cow-cocky, postman and brickworks labourer, before attending Auckland University where he completed a Bachelor of Arts degree in 1949.

Peter's publishing career began with *Craccum,* the Auckland student newspaper, which he edited in his second year as an arts student. His work was published in the university's literary review, rubbing shoulders with the likes of James K Baxter, Denis Glover, ARD Fairburn, Maurice Duggan and Keith Sinclair. Perhaps due to his upbringing he was restless after leaving university and embarked on hitch-hiking trips around both islands. He drew on his hitch-hiking experiences when he was establishing himself as a freelance journalist, writing articles and short stories.

Peter decided full-time religion would be his calling and began studying at Dunedin's Selwyn College in 1952. After his graduation, Australia offered him his first appointment — he was ordained at St John's Cathedral in Kalgoorlie in 1953. The heat and the dust of Kalgoorlie took its toll on his family and his asthma so he returned to New Zealand after only a year. He soon found himself working as a 'talks'

Peter Cape: publicity photo for one of his EP recordings.

producer for the NZ Broadcasting Service from 1955-57. Peter moved steadily onwards and upwards with radio, eventually heading a section making religious programmes from 1958-62.

During this time he wrote and recorded songs with subject matter that seemed at odds with his religious disposition. It was timely to be writing such material, with record companies and radio looking for songs expressing Kiwi identity. Tony Vercoe of Kiwi Records was the first to recognise the uniqueness of his songs and wanted to record them. 'Taumarunui' was Peter's first song and Wellington tram driver Pat Rogers recorded it with its well-known tune, because Peter's original tune had too wide a range for Pat's deep, resonant voice. Some townsfolk of Taumarunui didn't take to the song, mainly because it claimed that you couldn't get a job there. New Zealanders couldn't laugh at themselves then and it would take a few years for the locals to overcome their initial opposition. In writing his humorous ballads, Peter was probably twenty years ahead of his time.

> There's a sheila in Refreshments and she's pouring cups of tea
> And my heart jumps like a rabbit when she pours a cup for me
> She's got hair a flaming yellow, and a mouth a flaming red
> And I'll love that flaming sheila till I'm up and gone and dead.
>
> You can get a job in Wellington or get a job up north
> But you can't in Taumarunui, tho' you try for all you're worth
> If I want to see this sheila, then I got to take a train
> Got ten minutes for Refreshments, then they cart me off again

From Taumarunui, Taumarunui, Taumarunui on the Main Trunk Line.

This quintessential Kiwi song has even surfaced in Australia, where it is sung as 'Cootamundra.' Only the place names have been changed to help make it into a genuine Aussie song.

Peter was one of those early performers at the Monde Marie in Wellington, where he first met Don Toms, his mentor, arranger and backing guitarist. 1961 heralded the release of an EP, *Taumatawhakatangihangakoauauatamateapokaiwhenuakitanatahu,* which featured two songs that would prove extremely popular. Radio ZB's midday request session played 'The Inter-Island Steamer Express' almost every Sunday, while the other, 'Down the Hall on Saturday Night' has become an absolute classic. The song captured the essence of a Kiwi dance hall anywhere in the country, describing the occasion to perfection. On hearing the song, many people reckoned Peter must've been to a dance in their immediate vicinity.

> I got a new brown sportscoat, I got a new pair of grey strides
> I got a real Kiwi haircut, bit off the top and short back and sides.
>
> Soon as I've tied up the guri, soon as I swept out the yard
> Soon as I've hosed down me gumboots, I'll be living it high and living it hard.
>
> I'm goin' to climb onta the tractor, I'm gonna belt it outa the gate
> There's a hop on down the hall, an', she starts sharp somewhere 'bout half-past eight.
>
> Hey, look at the sheilas cuttin' the supper, an' look at the kids slidin' over the floor
> And look at the great big bunch of jokers, hangin' round the door.
>
> They got the teacher to belt the pianner, they got Joe from the store on the drums
> We're as slick as the Orange in Auckland, for whoopin' it up an' makin' things hum.
>
> I had a schottische with the tart from the butcher's,
>   had a waltz with the constable's wife.
> Had a beer from the keg on the cream-truck,
>   an' the cop had one too, you can bet your life.
>
> Oh, it's great being out with the jokers, when the jokers are sparkin' and bright
> Yeah it's great givin' cheek to the sheilas, down the hall on Saturday night.

In 1962 Peter moved into television production and went to England to train with the BBC. On return he became senior producer for WNTV1, making documentaries and current affairs programmes from 1963-66.

The release of 'She'll Be Right' in 1964 gave the country an unofficial national anthem, one which has endured for some time now — it has been a guaranteed crowd pleaser in folk clubs and concerts throughout the country for many years. People took the song to their hearts and added extra verses as the mood and fancy dictated. What better definition of a real folk song!

> When you're hunting in the mountains and your dogs put up a chase
> And this porker's comin' at you and he doesn't like your face
> And you're running and he's running and he's crowding on the pace
> Don't worry mate, she'll be right.
>
> *Chorus*   She'll be right, mate, she'll be right, don't worry, mate, she'll be right
>   You can get your feed of pork, when he slows down to a walk
>   So don't worry, mate, she'll be right.

When you're logging on the saddle and you're driving down the bluff
With a thousand feet of timber, bouncing right behind your chuff
And the clutch has started slipping and your brakes are worse than rough
Don't worry, mate, she'll be right.

> She'll be right, mate, she'll be right, don't worry, mate, she'll be right
> If you give all you can give her, she'll just fly into the river
> So, don't worry mate, she'll be right…

When you've had the copper going and you've boiled a ton of hops
And you've brewed your brew and bottled her and hammered on the tops
And your missus keeps on asking where you left your footy socks
Well, don't worry, mate, she'll be right.

> She'll be right, mate…
> Shove a shot of Metho in and you'll swear you're drinking gin
> So, don't worry mate, she'll be right.

When they've finished off your forwards and your backs are wearing thin
And the second spell's half over and you're forty points to win
And this hulking wing-threequarter's got his teeth stuck in your shin
Don't worry mate, she'll be right.

> She'll be right, mate…
> You won't worry who's the loser when you meet them in the boozer
> So, don't worry mate, she'll be right.

This is where Peter finished the song … "but wait there's even more." The sleeve notes on the first recorded version said, "If you don't like Peter's verses you can always write a few more." People loved them and added more. The extra verses I sing were all written by my old mate Sam Sampson (a Stewart Island identity) during his 1960s stint in Wellington, while studying to be a teacher. He was a regular follower of the local folk scene.

When you're standing in the boozer and you're supping on a beer,
And this burly great big copper comes and whispers in your ear,
You're under-age m'lad, you shouldn't be in here,
Well don't worry mate, she'll be right,

> She'll be right mate…
> Just finish off your beer and then kiss him on the ear,
> Don't worry mate, she'll be right.

Now Labour's gone and got the country in one helluva mess,
And National is no better than them I will confess.
So parliament's got to be dissolved 'cos she's all a bloody mess,
Don't worry mate, she'll be right.

She'll be right mate…
Next election vote informal, things will soon get back to normal,
Don't worry mate, she'll be right.

Peter had responded to the international folk boom by writing about what he knew, and his efforts coincided with a new quest for Kiwi identity. Songs like 'Taumarunui' and 'Down the Hall' have been credited with helping ease the way for such comedians as Barry Crump and Fred Dagg.

While still working in television, Peter scripted, sang and produced three television programmes on folk music, something we haven't seen much of since. But stress, alcohol, marriage breakdown and burnout led him to leave his job. After a period out of work he became a recruiting and publicity officer for Volunteer Service Abroad from 1968-70. He then continued to build a career as an independent broadcaster and a writer for leading New Zealand papers and journals.

Peter moved to Richmond in 1974 to live with Gladwen McIntyre, and took up subsistence farming as a sideline to his writing and publishing career. He participated in 'Writers in School' programmes and won several state literary fund grants.

As well as comic vernacular songs, Peter composed beautiful love songs such as 'Culler's Lament' and 'Drover' ('When the Rainbird Sings in the Tea-Tree'). He painted vivid word-pictures of the times with his songs, and to my mind no one has done it better than he.

Visiting Elsie Locke early in my collecting career and rummaging through her papers I came across a poem 'The Stable Boy' (scribbled in longhand). Impressed with the story and its sentiments, I asked Elsie who had written it and she replied that she thought it was Peter Cape, but couldn't be sure. I didn't know how to contact Peter at that time, but set the poem to music, calling it 'The Stable Lad' (lad

seemed to have a slightly better feel to it.) I recorded the song and attributed the words to Peter Cape. Eventually I met up with Peter at a Nelson Folk Club concert in 1977 and the first thing I asked him was if he wrote 'The Stable Lad'.

Peter's reply went as follows — "It's funny you should ask me this, because I was listening to National Radio one day, when I heard this song being played. I thought to myself, by jove that sounds familiar, I wonder if I wrote it. So I rang the announcer and asked, did I write that song? He replied that as far as he knew, I had — to which I replied, Oh, that's fine, so long as I know these things!" Peter told me that he loved what I had done with the song and I have treasured that moment ever since. The full text of the song is in 'The Golden West' chapter.

> When Cobb & Co ran coaches from the Buller to the Grey
> I went for a livery stable lad in a halt up Westport way
> I gave my heart to a red-haired girl and left it where she lay
> By the rolling Westland highway from the Buller to the Grey...

Peter died unexpectedly aged 53 at Richmond in 1979, having made a real difference to arts and music in New Zealand and leaving a lasting impression. He was probably one of the most versatile figures in his field for almost a quarter of a century and his songs have given him true immortality.

Ross McMillan

The only one of these important poets still living is Ross McMillan, who was born in the Naseby district of Central Otago in 1929, spending most of his years involved with high country life in the area. He left school in 1945 to become a horse-breaker, and in the ensuing years worked as a musterer, shearer, fencer and rousie on most of Central Otago's larger high country stations before taking over his parents' Naseby farm in partnership with his brothers Grant and Bill. His high country experiences have provided him with much of the material for his poetry.

> When it's springtime in the mountains I must saddle up and go,
> To the high country stations at the thawing of the snow.
> For the city charm has vanished and I'm weary of the rush,
> As I long to hear the singing of the bellbirds in the bush.
>
> When I hear the bawl and bellow of the cattle on the track,
> And see the dusty stockyards and the homestead way out back.
> My stock-horse answers eagerly when the spurs are driven hard,
> In the race to slew the leaders as they try to dodge the yard.
>
> Now the old camp cook is swearing and the campfire embers glow,
> Beneath the blackened oven and quart pots in a row.
> The lounging bushmen tell their yarns, while the sun is going down,
> As they dream of pretty girls like the ones they know in town.

My riding gear has gathered dust my spurs have lost their shine,
And it's ages since I caught the scent that drifts in off the pine.
Where it mingles with the wood smoke, but it's westward soon I'll go,
To join a Spring muster with some country blokes I know.

'Springtime in the Mountains', adapted by Phil Garland
from 'Country Blokes' ~ Ross McMillan

Ross started writing in 1960 while holidaying in the North Island. Homesick for Central Otago, he put into words some thoughts he'd had while droving sheep through Dansey's Pass to the Maniototo Plain. Signing himself 'Blue Jeans', he sent the work to the *Auckland Weekly* and was surprised to receive a cheque a few weeks later. Since then he has written hundreds of poems. Many have been published by the *Central Otago News*, and selections later published by the newspaper in a series of high country books. Ross is probably best known to Otago people by his 'Blue Jeans' *nom de plume* and also to Radio New Zealand listeners for the many examples of his work that have been recorded, read and recited.

Ross had no inclination to write verse or prose when he was younger, but admired Banjo Paterson and Henry Lawson from an early age and still regards them as the greatest writers in Australasia. The Lawson influence can be seen in this evocative piece:

I lay one day in the old tin hut, when the temperature was low,
And smoke was thick for the door was shut to keep out the whirling snow.
The packer swore as he tried to cook with the wood that was wet and slow
While the boss leaned back with a dirty book and read by the candle glow.

Now some were playing at poker games and cheating with every card,
While others were talking of dogs and dames, two subjects never barred.
I could hear the horses stumbling round outside in the frozen yard,
And I cursed the snow out on the ground, for my bunk was so cold and hard.

I must have dozed for I dreamed that we were away where the sun shone hot,
Where the wide blue sky from snow was free and sheep and hills were not.
No need for the rough old shepherd's swag, nor the heavy hobnailed boots,
Feather beds instead of sleeping bags and the dress it was tailored suits.

Our meals were cooked by a chef in white with oysters and eggs for free,
And steak that melted under a bite and wine in the place of tea.
While every bloke had a serving maid clad in a white bikini,
To fetch and carry, while music played and the prettiest one served me.

Her hair was dark as a blackbirds' wing, her eyes were a mountain blue,
Her voice held the lovely lilt of spring as she said that her name was Sue.
I woke when an arm went round my neck. 'twas only my old mate — Lew
In the old tin hut way out the back to hand me a plate of stew.

'The Old Tin Hut' by Ross McMillan, renamed 'The Shepherd's Dream' by Phil Garland

229

Ross wrote much of his poetry to remain sane in a troubled time. He had not long been married when his wife was struck down by multiple sclerosis, which meant he had to cope with running the farm, caring for their two young children and nursing his wife. This was his way of life for some fifteen years before she finally succumbed. It is possibly due to this difficult period that many of his poems reflect a mixture of nostalgia and regret. He has a great sense of humour and this next yarn is a beauty:

Not long after first meeting Ross on a visit to Christchurch, I spent a few days in the Naseby area chasing local verse and song. I remember setting off one morning and noticed him standing like a scarecrow in the middle of one of his paddocks. I thought this was a bit unusual, but continued on my way. When I returned later in the day he was still there and I nearly stopped to check if everything was okay.

The following morning I noticed him there again and worried about his state of mind. I very nearly stopped to check things out, but thought it's his property and he must know what he's doing. He was still there, standing quite motionless, when I came past again later in the day and by now I was getting quite concerned.

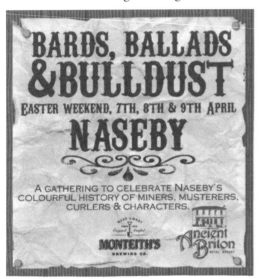

Next day, as I was setting off on my search once again, I noticed him still standing there. Finally I decided to stop, vaulted the fence, walked over to him and said "Ross, What are you doing, mate? You've been standing here like this for three days."

He replied "Well, Phil, it's that time of year."

I said "What do you mean, it's that time of year?"

Whereupon Ross replied, "It's that time of year, when they give the Nobel Prize to the person outstanding in his field!"

Some of his best poetry is undoubtedly his nostalgic verse, recalling mustering, shearing, horses and dogs, in the early days of the high country stations. Ross also has a considerable affinity with the Central Otago countryside, its mountains and its people — their sense of humour, their strengths and weaknesses — which often lifts his verse to considerable heights.

One of his most evocative and widely recited poems (especially each Anzac Day), is about the bottle of beer forever preserved in the bar of the Waihou Forks Hotel. Entitled *The Soldier Who Never Came Home*, it has been set to music and recorded by his mate Dusty Spittle.

There's a bottle of beer in the Waihou Forks bar,
From the rest on the shelves it stands out like a star.
For its shape is old-fashioned and just might perplex,
And the label proclaims that it's Ballins Four X.

It was brought long ago by a young soldier brave,
On his final leave there, these instructions he gave,
Don't sell it or break it, just keep it in store,
And we'll drink it when I come back home from the war.

He was killed overseas on the island of Crete,
When they battled it out with the German élite;
There's a headstone but nobody knows where he lies,
If he sleeps his last sleep 'neath the seas or the skies.

But the bottle still stands in the country hotel,
A memorial strange for the soldier who fell;
And travellers and locals take time out to think
Of the soldier who never came back for his drink.

For somehow a glow by the bottle is shed,
As poppies surround it and edge it with red,
And each Anzac morning a new one is there,
And they lie like a wreath round that bottle of beer.

There are many stone cairns scattered over the land,
But I wonder how many are polished by hand.
Though the cap is all rusted it outshines the chrome;
As it honours the soldier who never came home.

His work deserves a wider audience and it's only a matter of time before the country discovers his ability and contributions to our heritage. Meanwhile Ross McMillan can still be found living on the outskirts of Naseby and writing about his beloved Central Otago.

Time for us to muster up on Yorky's run,
The autumn lends a lustre to the rising sun,
All grey and gold the ranges with beauty fit to stun,
As dawn from darkness changes up on Yorky's run.

Chorus　Up on Yorky's run boys, up on Yorky's run,
　　　　　Soaking up the sun boys, soaking up the sun.
　　　　　Where ways are rough and risky, but when the day is done,
　　　　　We'll drink old Yorky's whisky up on Yorky's run.

The blue crown of Mt Ida, the downland shepherds shun,
Home of mountain riders of whom brave yarns are spun.
Home of the fiery stock-horse, the chestnut and the dun,
And sheepdogs wild and wiry, up on Yorky's run.

I can't afford to lose a sheep, I must get everyone,
As slowly down the steep incline, the way is won.
For Yorky musters by me and next beat is his son,
As double fleecers try me up on Yorky's run.

But how I love the muster, the riding and the fun,
As through the rocky clusters, the mobs of sheep are run.
Life of a mountain drover takes second place to none,
How my heart turns over on a mountain run.

'Up on Yorky's Run' ~ Ross McMillan

"A singing historian"

When I seriously started writing songs back in the 1980s I found myself heavily influenced by the writings of Henry Lawson, David McKee Wright, Dennis Hogan, Cecil Winter, Tod Symons, Joe Charles and Ross McMillan, not just as a result of field collecting, but from setting some of their poems to music. From these colonial and backblocks balladeers I learned how to approach my subject matter and turn oral history into song. Fortunately a few of my original compositions seem to have found favour in some quarters and are often requested by audiences. I'll feature three of these now, with thanks to those early balladeers who have in part influenced and inspired my writing.

The one song that is often asked for and expresses my feelings for the land beyond the cities where the real New Zealand lies is 'Wind in the Tussock'. I have always been fascinated by fields of wheat or tussock grass blowing in the breeze — something that seems so relaxing and soothing. One day I noticed some grass gently waving in the breeze on the Pisa Range up the Cardrona Valley, and that fascination was rekindled as it provided me with the inspiration to write this song.

Chorus   There's snow on the hills and frost in the gullies,
Where winters are keen and the air tastes like wine,
My heart feels the pull of the wind in the tussock,
Calling me back to the mountains again.

The scent of the speargrass is drawing my heart in,
As I long again for the high country air.
The wind in the tussock is calling me homewards,
To the valleys and ridges that I love so dear.

There's a fragrance in the tussock fire as it's burning,
Wisps of smoke curling up to the sky.
The dew in the dawning of a clear spring morning,
As the sun warms the tops all white skiffed with snow.

There's pleasure in working the snow-crested mountains,
In boiling a billy and watching stars fall,
To be lost in a world remote from the city,
With the mist far below like a great rolling sea.

When the old man nor-wester blows hot down the valley,
Reminds me of a girl that I knew long ago,
Her hair was as fair as the snowgrass in summer,
Breaking my heart when she drifted away.

There are dreams in the twilight of long autumn evenings,
When the embers of memory still flicker and fade,
The tussock aglow with the deep golden sunset,
Gently caressed by the evening breeze.

These days I often describe myself as a singing historian, retelling our country's stories through song. My 'Ballad of James Mackenzie' is an example. I had always thought the story of Mackenzie and his dog quite properly belonged to Canterbury and Otago, little realising that Southland had a large part to play, and without that background maybe it all would have turned out differently. When I was commissioned to write a Mackenzie song telling the Southland side of the story, I found there was more to the yarn than first meets the eye.

After taking up land at Edendale in Southland, Scots immigrant James Mackenzie ascertained that he had to stock his small holding with sheep within three to four months, or forfeit the land. He obtained his first flock in Canterbury, droving them south to Edendale via the secret route and inland plain that now bears his name. However stock numbers weren't large enough to satisfy the current rules and regulations, so while making a further attempt to drove some sheep south, he was arrested as a sheep stealer and taken to Lyttelton, where he was farcically tried under the name of John Douglas in 1855. Mackenzie was later visited in gaol by a fellow Scot named McNab, who he alerted to the existence of some choice farming land in Southland — the town of Gore is built on that very same land today. After considerable public lobbying Mackenzie was pardoned in 1856 and returned briefly to Edendale to collect his belongings, before sailing to Queensland Australia in 1857.

Folk sing the praises from Farewell to Bluff,
Of a braw highland shepherd wily and tough.
Who owned a fine sheep dog, a half collie cross,
That was trained to find sheep that no one had lost.

Chorus Hero or villain, the court must decide,
If James Mackenzie is dead or alive.
Unjustly treated for no reason or rhyme,
They gave him hard labour for a trivial crime.

He was called a free-booter as history will say,
For leading a mob of Rhode's sheep astray.
The followed his nose as he'd done before,
To discover a track leading southwards to Gore.

From Lowburn to Kelso he blazed a new trail,
To that haunted bush growing round Edendale.
He planted potatoes on his wee plot of land,
But to stock it with sheep was his daring plan.

Mackenzie was hired to drove sheep again,
Over the plain that now bears his name.
Though captured and gaoled, twice he broke free,
On the fate of his dog no one could agree.

Their legend is known both far and near,
Though the myth keeps growing year upon year.
His droving deeds have outlived the rest,
To be remembered as simply the best.

While I was living in Australia, I heard a great song entitled 'I Am Australian', and even sang it on a few occasions around the traps with my band Bush Telegraph. When I returned home in 1996, however, I was reminded that the Kiwi cultural cringe was alive and well and still permeating all levels of our society. I thought about this for a while and after reaching the conclusion that as many other nationalities are not averse to singing about pride and patriotism, especially the Irish, Australians and Americans — why not us?

I decided to write a song which would help us put aside perceived differences as we join together in harmony to tell the world how proud we are to be Kiwis. I had hoped the resulting song, 'Proud to be a Kiwi', might make its way into the school system and with this in mind I arranged to have some children sing the chorus with me. It seemed to work well and soon after my *Sense of Place* album was released, I was being approached by schoolteachers and choir leaders wanting their charges to sing the song. For that I am eternally grateful.

I came from Hawaiki far across the sea,
I sailed in the first canoes to reach this sanctuary.
I'm a warrior, a chieftain, the mighty kauri tree,
The spirit of Tane is watching over me.

I'm Cook, a British Captain, who sailed the seven seas,
I'm Gisborne where the world's first sunrise can be seen.
I'm a sealer and a whaler cast upon these shores,
I am the fire-god speaking when Ruapehu roars.

Chorus I'm proud to be a Kiwi standing strong and tall,
The spirit of our nation unites us one and all.
Let's join hands together and sing in harmony,
Our land New Zealand means all the world to me.

I'm a settler and a pioneer, one of the pilgrim band,
I'm a farmer and a bushman, I helped to clear the land.
I am the snow-clad mountains, the mighty nor'west breeze,
I am the rugged valleys with the rivers running free.

I'm Gabriel Read, a miner and I discovered gold,
I'm a shepherd James Mackenzie, whose exploits will be told.
I'm Richard Pearse, inventor, the first man yet to fly,
I'm an ANZAC at Gallipoli, whose memory never died.

I'm Slattery 'the Shiner' my legend has begun,
I'm Hillary, a mountaineer, whose race is never run.
I'm an All Black and I wear the silver fern with pride,
I'm Footrot Flats, whose story is known far and wide.

I'm a woman and a mother, a companion and a wife,
I'm a child of the future, bringing dreams to life.
I'm a poet and an author, writing stories fresh and bold,
I am the nation's heritage, preserved for young and old.

In answer to numerous questions from listeners, I can reveal that James K Baxter was the poet referred to, and the author was Katherine Mansfield. Their names just wouldn't fit snugly into the song, so I used a little poetic licence in the hope that people would realise who I was singing about. Perhaps it didn't quite work out as I'd planned. I'll never forget the day I was singing 'Proud to be a Kiwi' at a Canterbury school and after I finished a young lad in the audience asked me what position I played in for the All Blacks. Needless to say I was truly flattered — if only it was that easy!

I have written a great many songs and each of them has a story attached, but that's something I'm going to save for another day.

XIII

SHANTIES BY THE WAY

Moonshine, malt and mash

How the Devil can a man keep sober,
In those shanties by the way!

Some of New Zealand's reputation as the most 'English' country in the British Commonwealth was well-earned, but one notable exception was the Kiwi pub. Our pubs evolved along different lines from their English counterparts and continue to do so today. Six o'clock closing influenced our way of life for many years, and trends created by that uncivilised era are still in evidence today.

> The bar is crowded, for the five to six rush-hour is in full swing. It's part of the ritual, the New Zealand way of life and I'm jammed into a corner, hemmed in by a talking, drinking throng. Glasses of beer jerk precariously above their heads to eager hands stretched up as if from the lineout, men push in and out with cries of "Mind ya backs" and "Make way for a naval officer." The glasses stand in platoons on the slopped bar and the barmen pounce about with plastic hoses browned with beer, squirting them full again from chromium beaks. "The same again" and "Fill 'em up Bill", "In goes your eye out", "Let's get crackin', "Fill 'em up." Those with a hard-won beach-head on the bar and a foot on the rail, stand firm, elbowing out and the rear files hem them in — the walls echo the talk talk talk, everyone stating his opinion loudly to defeat the tumult and drinking beer in the rapid round, New Zealand style.
>
> *Rush Hour in the Pub ~ Gordon Slatter*

Whereas the English inn incorporated a variety of folklore and architecture under one roof, our tradition has been one of 'survival of the fittest' — our earliest shanties or grog shops were makeshift, built to serve and not to last. As our population

236

spread and towns expanded, so did these buildings, and as times changed they were demolished and rebuilt.

They may have originally been rough-and-tumble affairs such as whaling grogshops, bush pubs, miners' calico shanties and coaching halts, but they helped give birth to politics and live theatre in New Zealand. They were among our first utilitarian buildings — often before houses, churches, banks and other trading establishments — serving as community meeting places and sporting centres. This is where interest lies, not so much in the heritage, but in their colourful differences. Despite a relatively short history beset by complex and baffling regulations, New Zealand has managed to produce pubs and publicans with a character and heritage that remain typically Kiwi. Barrett's Hotel, which opened its doors in 1840, became the hub of all social life in the Port Nicholson settlement for the next 15 years — and, as we've already discovered, many early goldfields hotels contributed towards the presentation of live theatre and entertainment.

This story begins with the oldest licensed house in New Zealand, the Duke of Marlborough, erected on the beachfront at Kororareka on a plot which was purportedly one of the earliest land purchases in New Zealand. The land was sold to one of the first Europeans to run an official business in the Bay of Islands. There is doubt as to who that first European was — Ben Turner, who opened the first grog shop, or Johnny Johnson the grogseller, described as a "dealer in liquid fire". Both men were time-expired convicts from Australia, and within a few years, seven of the eight businesses trading in the town were grog shops catering to whaling crews, who thought of Kororareka as the Cyprus of the South Pacific, whereas missionaries labelled it the "Hell-hole of the Universe". Where else could one find 30 to 40 vessels at anchor at any one time, while their crews enjoyed R&R with Pomare, a local entrepreneur who kept 95 Maori maids on call to satisfy the whalers' needs? There was a total lack of law and order — fights and smuggling were commonplace, rum '40% overproof' was regularly smuggled in, and whalers found Kororareka an ideal place for recreation or even settlement. The song 'Shore Cry' (in Chapter 2) captures some of the whalers' pleasures in the Bay of Islands.

The traditions begun at Kororareka in the 1820s spread throughout the country, especially to the goldfields of the West Coast and Central Otago.

In Christchurch the White Hart Inn was a lively centre of entertainment for many years. Some Canterbury pilgrims were prodigious drinkers, especially those like Trotman, who frequented the White Hart and was being sued for his beer account, as described by James McNeish in his *Tavern in the Town*:

"What's this ... five gallons a day?"

"Yessir."

"Is that true, Trotman?"

"I believe it is, your worship!"

"What, did you really drink it?"

"Yes, your worship and you give me a job at any time on the land and I'll do your worship justice and drink five gallons of beer — if you pay for it."

The Rev Joseph Twigger was another staunch patron. Twenty glasses of spirits a day was his quota, but while making his way home from the inn one night he slipped and fell into the Avon River. The inquest confirmed the deceased was "much given to excessive intoxication." Originally a picturesque wooden structure with three gables jutting from a steep slate roof, the White Hart in 1866 became a long, lean building crowned by an antlered stag. It changed yet again during its lifetime before finally succumbing to inner-city progress, but its name lives on as the White Hart Arcade.

Across the road Cobb & Co-style coaches left for the West Coast diggings, from a depot next door to the British Hotel, owned by John Birdsey who whipped up its reputation for fun, devilment and gambling. Evidence of this is in a song by local poet and satirist Charlie Martin, whose performances in the hotel were the only public amusement in Christchurch for a while. According to the Christchurch *Press* "his excessive use of the most detestable slang" was "calculated to amuse a public house auditory" but "was not fit for any drawing-room table."

I went into the British to get a glass of beer,
For what with dusty roads and all, I felt uncommon queer,
Says Birdsey, "Lad, what will you have? Mine's brandy pale," says he,
Says I, "I'm fresh from England but you don't get brandy on me."

I strolled into the billiards room to while away the day,
When Tomkins, that's the marking chap, asked me if I could play.
He let me win two half-crown games, "Play for a pound," says he,
Says I, "I'm green from England, you don't perform on me."

I've told you my experience since first I came on shore,
You would know as much as me, were I to tell you more.
When new chums land in Lyttelton their first ideas should be,
Athough I'm new from England you don't get over me.

from 'I'm a Young Man' – Charles Martin. These verses, slightly different from
Neil Colquhoun's previously published version, come from Dick Morris,
who recorded the song for Radio New Zealand in the 1950s.

There was a hierarchy among publicans, who were ranked according to respectability and profit. At the bottom of the scale were the 'grog shanty' keepers, who often owned nothing more than a mud hut, a tin shed or calico tent with a weatherboard façade. They frequently offered no facilities other than a bar, and if obliged by law to provide accommodation for travellers could only fulfil their obligation in a rudimentary fashion. One such shanty was described by Sir William Fox after he and his wife visited it in 1877:

We asked for a bed and something to eat and entered. All round the bar and in the house there were about 30 or 40 roadmen, Maoris, shepherds and other people in broad daylight, roistering, drinking and shouting — and this was a hostelry for the accommodation of travellers. Well in due time the dinner came and absolutely everything on the table smelt of rum. The roast beef smelt of rum, the potatoes smelt of rum, the water bottle smelt of rum and the very tea smelt of rum. The woman who brought the things into the room also smelt of rum and was so drunk that she could scarcely take them out again.

Goldminers expected more than just drink in their grog shops and shanties, so publicans featured actors and entertainers to draw in custom, something that became even more necessary for survival when other shanties opened and competed for business. I have previously mentioned Charles Thatcher, who performed in pubs and theatres for most of his time on the goldfields, and his name became closely linked with Bully Hayes by appearing at his United States Hotel in Arrowtown as it later became known.

Women were rare on the goldfields in the early days, but soon arrived in various forms and guises. One such was Mrs McLeod, who came as a bride and did not leave until carried out in a coffin 60 or so years later. She lived in a cottage halfway between Skippers and the Branches, and after her husband died she made a living selling whisky to passing miners. Despite being an unlicensed trader, she was a more than useful link in the lives of those hardy characters passing her door. Her whisky reputedly saved many a life — she used the old-style thick, heavy glasses and was renowned for pouring an excellent nip. She only charged one shilling but never gave any man or woman more than one drink.

> Big Poll the grogseller gets up every day,
> And her small rowdy tent she sweeps out.
> She's bringing in plenty of tin, people say,
> For she knows what she's about…
> For she knows what she's about.
>
> Polly's good looking and Polly is young,
> And Polly's possessed of a smooth oily tongue.
> She's an innocent face and a good head of hair,
> And a lot of young fellows will often go there,
> They keep dropping in, handsome Polly to court,
> And she smiles and supplies them with brandy and port,
> And the neighbours all say that the whole blessed day,
> She's grogselling late and early … she's grogselling late and early.
>
> Two sly grog detectives have come up from town,
> And they both roam about in disguise.
> And several retailers of grog are done brown,
> And reason to open their eyes … and have reason to open their eyes.

Of her small rowdy crib they are soon on the scent,
But Polly's prepared when they enter her tent.
They call for some brandy — "We don't sell it here"
"But," says Poll, "I can give you some nice ginger beer,"
And she adds, "Do you see any green in my eye?
To your fine artful dodge and disguise I am fly"
"For if Polly you'd nail, you'd have without fail,
To get up in the morning early … to get up in the morning early.

'Big Poll the Grogseller' - Thatcher

There is a story from the Dunstan goldfields about an Irish barman cleaning glasses with a handkerchief taken from his breast pocket. When asked if the customers ever objected to him using a hanky, he replied "Oh, it's quite all right, I don't use a clean one!"

Cardrona has a colourful goldfields history. The valley was originally explored by miners searching for Fox's elusive field. The Cardrona wasn't a rich field at all, with most miners in the area ekeing out an existence, enviously keeping an eye on the main commercial claim in the vicinity, the Gin and Raspberry mine. Two reasons have been advanced for this name: either the owners kept this drink on tap for miners who surfaced with more than a pennyweight a tub, or, more likely, this was the drink those same miners drank at the local pub. Whichever the case, it is a well-known piece of folklore in the district and inspired the song 'Gin and Raspberry' by local musician Martin Curtis:

While hunting for Fox we first came this way,
From Lake Pembroke's township took many long days,
We cut through the scrub, manuka and bush,
Till we found the Gin and Raspberry.

Chorus Oh, but it's hard, cruel and cold,
Searching Cardrona for nuggets of gold,
But an ounce to a bucket and we'll all sell our souls,
For a taste of the Gin and Raspberry.

The rumours went out and thousands poured in,
A handful grew rich and many stayed thin,
They all hoped to find their own patch of tin,
As rich as the Gin and Raspberry.

At first it was summer and we all thought it grand,
No shirts on our back as we sluiced and we panned.
But then came the snow and the southerly's blow,
Now there's ice down the Gin and Raspberry.

Panning for gold.
Harold Lowe

Now Jimmy McGrath worked hard and worked long,
Always ready to smile and to sing us a song.
But when he struck gold he was found dead and cold,
Down in the Gin and Raspberry.

So I'll serve out me time and I'll stay out of strife,
I'll save all me tin to send home to me wife.
And when the job's done, I'll leave on the run,
And to hell with the Gin and Raspberry.

We can't leave the Cardrona Valley without mention of the legendary Cardrona Hotel. Over the years this grand old lady has seen and heard stories of the Gin and Raspberry claim right opposite her front door — two of whose original sharcholders sold out and built the Wanaka Hotel with their proceeds. She recalls the one and only Paddy Galvin from Shingle Creek, who once put his foot through the floorboards while performing the Connaught jig. Paddy is well remembered for teaching music and playing for dances at the pub, where it was sworn that he continued to play even when asleep. After he was propped head-downwards in a corner, there he would rest, his fingers curled round the heel of the bow, fiddle tucked firmly under his chin with his bow-arm still moving across the strings of the upside-down instrument.

There are stories of the publican who would never give the driver of any vehicle more than one drink if they were crossing the Crown Range, but no problem for any of the passengers. Another publican kept very little beer in stock and once refused customers another round because he was down to his last. Perhaps a similar experience prompted James K Baxter to write 'By the dry Cardrona':

I can tell where cherries grow
    By the dry Cardrona,
Where I plucked them long ago
    On a day when I was sober.

My father wore a parson's coat
    By the dry Cardrona;
He kept a tally of the sheep and the goats,
    And I was never sober.

My mother sewed her Sunday skirt
    By the dry Cardrona,
They said she died of a broken heart
    For I was never sober.

O lay my bones till the judgement crack
    By the wild Cardrona!
The blanket swag upon my back
    Will pillow me drunk or sober.

241

I loved a girl and only one
  By the dry Cardrona:
She up and married the banker's son
  For I was never sober.

I courted a widow of forty-nine
  By the dry Cardrona,
She owned a stable and a scheelite mine
  But I was never sober.

All rivers run to the rimless grave,
  Even the wild Cardrona,
But the black cherry bent my way
  One day when I was sober.

GENERAL EDITOR John Thomson   New Zealand Playscripts

Jack Winter's Dream

James K. Baxter

PRICE MILBURN for VICTORIA UNIVERSITY PRESS

Jack Winter's song 'By the Dry Cardrona' is reproduced here as it appears in Baxter's playscript. Folksingers sometimes vary the orde of verses and end by repeating the first verse.
Price Milburn for Victoria University Press, 1979

The Cardrona, like many hotels, followed the tradition that guests could pay for the privilege of sleeping either on the floor or a billiard table (providing no games were in progress) if there were not enough beds available. No change was given in the bar — you put down your money and stayed until it was cut out. The custom remains today.

The miners' way of life was absorbed into West Coast tradition for fifty or more years thereafter and traces remain of the customs which began in the early days. One hotel in Hokitika used to offer a long beer to guests in bed instead of the usual morning cup of tea, or the licensee might deliver a glass of whatever you had been drinking the night before. The 'hair of the dog' tradition has died hard on the Coast and it was possible to get tipsy before getting out of bed for ablutions, let alone get out of the hotel in a reasonably sober state.

Beer, beer, I love thee, in thee I place my trust,
I'd rather go to bed with hunger, than to go to bed with thirst.

Vast volumes of grog were drunk in the goldfields towns, with a surprising lack of real drunkenness. Miners were fit and healthy after living and working hard and could drink large amounts without too much ill effect. They also had their own code of behaviour, considering inability to hold liquor a sign of weakness. This trait continues today: a man who can drink without showing intoxication is highly regarded, whereas one who gets drunk is not respected. My 'Ballad of Davy Gray' in chapter 4, 'The Golden West', alludes to one such occasion.

One West Coast Sunday morning after a particularly wild dance which had gone through till dawn, and with a few hours to go before booze would be available from the pubs, some miners were left with nothing to do. The Irish Orange and Green communities had gathered in separate groups. What fun, thought one of the Green community, if one of the girls was to wear a bright green sash and ride through the ranks of the assembled Orangemen. The deed was duly accomplished and the Orangemen suggested they had been ridiculed, so war was declared. There were smiles on both sides as they lined up, and thus began one of the finest fights ever known on the Coast. Fists and the occasional pick-handle were the main weapons, but the moment the nearest pub opened its doors the battle stopped and

everyone trooped inside together, nursing their bruises and discussing without any animosity the wonderful time had by all. The session that followed in the pub was described by both sides as one of the best possible endings to a notable social occasion.

Tom Bailey had the Full and Plenty Hotel in Greymouth in the gold rush era, and the following verses began life as a newspaper advertisement for his establishment. It was common for hotels or shanties to use rhyming ditties to advertise their wares. I obtained these verses from *The West Coaster,* compiled by Jenny Vidgen of Christchurch.

FULL & PLENTY
HOTEL
All meals 1s 6d Good Clean Beds 1s.
Pewter Beer 3d.
BOARD — 20s per week.
Board & Lodging — 25s per week.
FREE and EASY Every Night.
First Class Pianist
T. BAILEY
Proprietor

There is nothing on earth more inviting, productive of mirth or good cheer,
Or more to really delight in, than drinking a drop of good beer.
So if you will give heed to my ditty, a fact I will unto you tell,
The very best beer in the city is sold at Tom Bailey's hotel.

At threepence per glass it is offered and other drinks equally cheap,
If there you accept what is proffered, you certain advantage will reap.
And if you would really be merry, o'er claret or sparkling moselle,
Or brandy or whisky or sherry, just call at Tom Bailey's hotel.

A table well dressed is provided, of the best to be had in the town,
If you've tried I'm sure you've decided, to a better you've never sat down.
In Boundary Street there you'll see it — it's the corner house noted so well,
For pleasure for mirth or for glee is the old Full and Plenty Hotel.

Many of the pubs never closed on the Coast. After-hours trading was the norm and it was common to find an off-duty police constable drinking, or serving behind the bar. The usual etiquette was for the police to phone before raiding any licensed premises, advising all drinkers to leave. They did, and all would return after the visit to continue their drinking unchallenged. In this manner the police had been seen to fulfil their lawful duties.

For years drinking was illegal anywhere near a dance hall, as many a young man found to his chagrin, being charged and fined for his breach of conduct. Older readers may recall smuggling a hip flask into such social occasions, but as the authorities got wiser, security was placed at the door to prevent these activities.

> I had a schottische with the tart from the butcher's
> Had a waltz with the constable's wife
> Had a beer from the keg on the cream-truck
> An' the cop had one too, you can bet your life.

'Down the Hall on Saturday Night' ~ Peter Cape (the full song is on page 225)

In the 1950s and '60s it became commonplace to read about old pubs burning down around New Zealand. Irreplaceable, historic wooden buildings were gutted and destroyed.

> Pull up a stump and lend an ear and a story I'll relate.
> About a sinful waste of beer, I will elucidate.
> I'll tell of how calamity struck Wapakiwi town,
> And caused a dreadful tragedy, the day the pub burned down.
>
> Now the boys had gathered in the bar upon that fateful day,
> By horse and foot and motor car, they all had made their way.
> While listening to Manuka Jones, New Zealand's finest liar,
> They heard a cry that chilled the bones — "The flaming pub's on fire!"
>
> There'd been a drought for weeks and weeks, the wells and tanks were dry.
> No water flowed along the creeks, we had no town supply.
> The blazing sun without relent turned all the green to brown,
> Imagine our predicament, the day the pub burned down.

Through smoke and flame we dragged the booze to safety out the door,
Then thought of what we stood to lose and rushed back in for more.
"Stand by, the fire brigade is here, those men of high renown,
Oh fireman, fireman save the beer and let the pub burn down."

They bashed the tops of barrels in, while strong men knelt to pray,
They shoved their flipping hoses in and shouted "Pumps away!"
They fought with beer and lemonade that raging fire to drown,
And we fought and cursed the fire brigade the day the pub burned down.

Now moreporks haunt the old pub site round Wapakiwi town,
And shickers roam the hills at night and hunt the firemen down.
They curse the cash they cannot spend, their raging thirst to drown,
Dry horrors drove them round the bend the day the pub burned down.

'The Day the Pub Burned Down' ~ Bob Edwards

In the late 19th century the Northland gumfields population reached 7000 or more. Some diggers had the steadying influence of wives and families with them; not so others, hopeless itinerants and unlikely to become good settlers. Early letters and reminiscences tell of the wild life at diggers' camps, where wanderers from many countries met for a relatively short time — only a few ever making that lucky find. The diggers were a veritable League of Nations, including Russians, Finns, Germans, Dalmatians, French and sons of well-to-do English families, including remittance men. Among them were men as decent, honest and hard-working as ever you'd find, rubbing shoulders with runaway soldiers, sailors, rogues and vagabonds. Deprived of the amenities and social pleasures of town life, many sought relief in drinking bouts. But the diggers had their own code of ethics and it was uncommon to find robbery and violence; friendliness and hospitality were extended to all regardless of

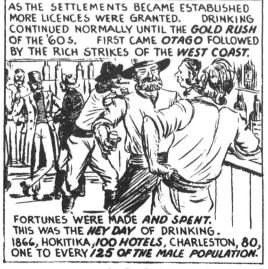

from Ross Gore's *It Happened in New Zealand*

245

background. A camaraderie existed, with no questions asked. The following song presents a fairly romanticised picture of it all:

We would roll our swags on Friday,
Leaving shanties near and far,
To spend our hard won silver,
With the diggers from the pa.
Then with Shorty, Carl and Scotty,
And the roving jolly tar,
We would gather round the barrel
In the old Gumdiggers' bar.

We would sing in happy chorus,
When the beer began to foam,
In billows on the tankards,
As it used to do back home.
Then our hardships were forgotten,
And with not a note to mar,
We found joy in harmonising,
In the old Gumdiggers' bar.

We would camp beneath the nikau,
If there wasn't room inside,
We were hardened birds of passage,
Truly tough in hair and hide.
So if the daylight found us,
Sleeping 'neath the paling star,
It was only as it should be,
Round the old Gumdiggers' bar.

THEN CAME THE *DEPRESSION* OF THE *80'S*. *BOOM TOWNS* BECAME *GHOST TOWNS*. MANY LICENCES *LAPSED*.

THEN THE *RECOVERY* OF THE *90'S* & SO ON TO 1914 & *WAR*. WARS ALWAYS BRING A *BOOM* IN DRINKING BUT *WORLD WAR ONE* BROUGHT SOMETHING ELSE, THE 6 O'CLOCK CLOSING & THIS WAR-TIME MEASURE IS STILL WITH US. SOME *LIKE IT*, SOME *DON'T*.

AFTER THE WAR THE LIQUOR TRADE ENJOYED A *PERIOD OF PROSPERITY*. THEN IN THE LATE 1920'S, *THE SLUMP*. BEER DOWN TO 5ᴰ, TO 4ᴰ THEN 3ᴰ, TEMPTING *FREE COUNTER LUNCHES*, DRINKS *ON THE SLATE*.

ON TO *RECOVERY* & TO *WAR*. THE AMERICAN "INVASION", RESTRICTIONS, SHORTAGES, *BLACK MARKET*. THE WAR OVER, WE SEEK BETTER DRINKING FACILITIES *COMMISSIONS* ARE SET UP, *TOURIST & CLUB* LICENCES GRANTED, *TRUST HOTELS* OPENED. PERHAPS ONE DAY SOME VISITOR MAY REMARK, *"NEW ZEALANDERS DRINK LIKE HUMAN BEINGS."* HOWEVER, IN SPITE OF INFLATION, BEER IS STILL 6ᴰ, SO, *ONE FOR THE ROAD*, THEN, *TIME GENTLEMEN!* COPYRIGHT. ROSS GORE

Now those days have long since vanished,
And the shanties far and wide
Have disappeared forever,
From the settled countryside.
Yet the memory still lingers
Of those distant days afar,
When we sang with voices mellow,
In the old Gumdiggers' bar.

'The Old Gumdiggers' Bar' ~ Dennis Hogan

The Depression of the 1880s and '90s saw countless men out of work. Many made their way north to the gumfields, while others took to the road, becoming swaggers. Some ended up as permanent wanderers, frequently blowing what little money they did earn at the nearest pub or grog shanty. This was a time when it was common to hear rough-hewn poetry recited in a packed bar instead of singing — epitomised in Dennis Hogan's 'His Master's Voice' (also known as 'Mason's Pub'):

Old Sandy was a bullocky, a local of renown,
Who hauled his logs to Mason's Mill, the sawmill of the town.
And often in old Mason's bar, a shanty on the hill,
His bullocks to a corner post, he'd hitch and drink his fill.

One day a rival of the clan, a breaker-out of note,
Contrived to start an argument, that got old Sandy's goat.
The pair grew heated as they glared and gave each other lip,
While Sandy bet his opposite, he didn't need a whip.

A fiver each on Mason's bar, they slapped a level bet,
While Mason, interested said "Drink up and have a wet"
But Sandy, riled, stood back apace and taking up his stance,
Yelled to his dozing team outside — "Wake up you loafers, dance!"

"Stand up there Captain, gee-off Prince, you mangy pair of goats,"
Old Sandy started bawling "Tighten up and earn your oats!"
The bullocks heaving moved as one as they were taught to do,
And hauling on the logging chain pulled Mason's pub in two!

With all this real and imagined debauchery going on amid mounting concern over alcohol abuse, the Women's Christian Temperance Union began lobbying for prohibition as early as the 1880s. Their crusade picked up considerable support, until successfully rendering the province of Southland dry for some fifty years from 1906. They later came within 3000 votes of national success in a special liquor referendum in 1919; only the votes of soldiers returning from the war kept the hotels open. Thirteen electorates were declared dry, however — notably Southland, Oamaru and some urban areas of Auckland. It took the establishment of community-owned licensing trusts to reverse that situation as recently as the 1960s and '70s.

Home-brewing beer and fermenting wine had been a pleasurable part of colonial life, and as the temperance cries grew louder, more people began to make their own. It wasn't illegal to make home brew, but it was to sell it, which is where distillers of whisky courted trouble with the law.

In *Puborama*, Ian Mackay describes a King Country bushmen's brew made by adding sap from matai trees to ordinary beer. For those tough enough to drink the concoction, it had a hefty kick. Mackay cites a 1912 Taihape newspaper:

> Matai beer … smells like an ancient bar room the morning after. It tastes like used machine oil, only a very low grade of machine oil. When a deep swig is absorbed, one has all the sensations of having swallowed a lighted kerosene stove. A sudden violent jolt of it has been known to stop the victim's watch, snap his braces and crack his glass eye right across — all in the same motion. If it must be drunk, drink it while sitting flat on the floor. Then you don't have so far to fall. …
>
> Those boastful Southerners will have gathered that their far-famed Hokonui is as ice cream soda to that virile product of the King Country palmy days.
>
> There was, some old-timers may remember, the classic yarn about the pioneer city angler engaged in prospecting one of the back country Ohakune streams. He was waylaid by an aggressive-looking bushman, who carried a bottle in one hand and a shotgun in the other.
>
> "Here, sport," said the bushman, "have a drink on me!"
>
> The angler protested that he didn't drink. Levelling his gun at him, the owner of the bottle ordered, "Drink!"
>
> The man from the city drank, then shuddered, shook, shivered and coughed mightily. "Well!" he spluttered, "That's horrible stuff!"
>
> "Ain't it?" agreed the bushman. "Now you hold the gun on me while I take a gulp!"

I have heard many variants of this yarn around the country, even set in rural Southland in the moonshine era. In the fifty years Southland was dry the notorious Hokonui Moonshine originated in the Hokonui Hills, thanks to the McRae family who made whisky in Scotland before emigrating in 1872. Mary McRae brought a still with her and her family became famous for their brew.

> My name it is McRae and from Scotland we set sail,
> Aboard the ship *Hydaspes* was her name.
> We landed at Port Chalmers all for to make our way,
> And we settled here among the Hokonui Hills.
>
> We learned to make good whisky on the island of Kishorn,
> And here we found people's needs were much the same.
> We set up a copper still not far from Dipton town,
> And soon our whisky trade was in full swing.
>
> *Chorus* If you want a drink of whisky that's bound to cure all ills,
> There's none like the moonshine from the Hokonui Hills.

Now moonshiners abound in the hills and in the glens,
And they sell their booze in buckets and tin cans.
But if you want a drop of the good old mountain stock,
Be sure to try the whisky from our still.

One day I was arrested and before the judge was taken,
For selling moonshine whisky at Springhill.
I was fined five hundred pounds as the law broke up the still,
And we had to watch the whisky poured away.

If whisky is the life of man, let's drink good whisky when we can,
We'll keep a welcome here for every man.
It doesn't matter hot or cold, we'll drink it new or drink it old,
That moonshine from the Hokonui Hills.

'The Hokonui Hills' ~ Phil Garland

'Discovering the Still on Saturday Morning' — painting by Janice Gill, who writes:
"The police sometimes saw smoke in the manuka scrub but couldn't find the
source. They went to the suspect's farm, mounted the horses standing in the yard
and, unguided by reins, the horses trod the familiar path to the still … covered
with tarpaulins stolen from the NZ Railways."
Telling Stories Steele Roberts 2009

Drinking has given us a strong legacy of poetry and song, but nothing beats the writings of 'Blue Jeans' (Ross McMillan) in capturing the atmosphere of the country pub and its drinkers. Many of us can recognise or identify with his observations:

> Now I've been around this land of ours — a roving man am I
> Auckland and Invercargill towns have seen me passing by.
> But there's a traveller out ahead in every place I know,
> No matter where, he seems to show
> The brown and empty Bottle-O.
>
> I climbed Mt Cook to take a look away up in the sky,
> The air was like a draught of wine and clouds were drifting by.
> I saw him gleaming in the sun before I turned to go,
> Up in the highest peak of snow,
> The brown and empty Bottle-O.
>
> I've sailed out with the oyster fleet that leaves the port of Bluff,
> I've shipped with mutton birders when the seas are high and rough.
> Beyond the twelve mile limit too where fishermen all go,
> I've seen him sinking down below,
> The brown and empty Bottle-O.
>
> By tracks out in the lonely bush, by huts out in the west,
> By shearing sheds and logging camps while on the roving quest.
> I've found him lying here and there — sent by a careless throw,
> In every place I care to go,
> The brown and empty Bottle-O.
>
> He's king of all the wanderers, he travels like a toff,
> By car and train and ship and plane — until his crown comes off.
> By horse and foot and motor bike in rain or sun or snow,
> He's found in every place I know,
> The brown and empty Bottle-O.

'The Brown & Empty Bottle-O' ~ Ross McMillan

(Thanks to James McNeish's *Tavern in the Town* for some material in this chapter.)

XIV

STRETCHING THE TRUTH

Collected yarns and tall stories

Buy me a beer and I'll tell you some lies,
of the wild backblocks where the bush hawk flies

Trevor Crabtree

A RICH STORE OF YARNS AND STORIES once flourished around campfires and in pubs after a long day's travel or work, and wherever Kiwis gathered to quench their thirst, reminisce and tell stories, you could guarantee one tale would lead to another. Yarns may be based on fact but often improve with the telling, with clever exaggeration and other ways of stretching the truth. Some stories recur widely, adapted for different settings.

In this young country folk yarns and tall stories have their origins in men's efforts to impress or be accepted by their peers. Our links with Australia are often reflected in shared tales and traditions found on the goldfields and in the high country. These traditions survive in remote country areas, where our culture has always valued a man for his prowess with a bullock team, the number of horses he could ride or the sheep he could shear. His feats and outdoor pursuits have become tales passed from man to man, acquiring colour and character along the way.

The old-time songs, ballads and yarns are slowly but surely disappearing as many Kiwis see them purely as colonial curiosities. Our language and habits have changed dramatically, generally influenced by other cultures, and the younger Kiwi generation know little about our pioneering heritage. The BBQ has replaced the old campfire and the television set the piano, but some form of home-made stories will stay with us forever, reflecting changing customs and traditions.

Collecting yarns and stories can be easier than collecting songs because there are hundreds more yarns than songs, and informants often know lots of them. On my travels I've come across many that are an integral part of Kiwi folklore and oral history. Most have been heard or collected in the South Island — many depict an ever-evolving society, where nothing is the creation of one man but has been added to and enriched by the people themselves. I'll share a few with you now.

Musterers, drovers and dogs

A bunch of drovers were camped just south of Hokitika. It was Saturday night and the camp was quiet, so one old-timer decided to head into town and ended up in a pub. There were few drinkers in the establishment, so the barman saw the old-timer sitting by himself down one end of the bar and thought that he'd go over and have some fun with him.

"Listen, I've got a riddle for you, see how you get on:

"My mother gave birth to three children — one was my brother, one was my sister, so who was the other one?"

The old-timer thought for a minute or two before replying. "Gee, mate, that's too tough. I give up."

"It was me!" the barman said and walked away, chuckling to himself.

The old drover finished his beer and headed back to the camp, rejoining his mates, who asked how he'd got on.

"Oh, she was pretty quiet in town, but while I was there I heard a riddle I couldn't make head nor tail of. Let's see how you blokes get on:

"My mother gave birth to three children. One was my brother, one was my sister, so who was the other one?"

The drovers pondered, then said, "Nah, that's too tough mate, who was it?"

"It was the barman I met in Hokitika."

***

An Australian visitor to New Zealand was watching television one Saturday night and was so captivated by a dog's performance in a sheepdog trial that he wanted to get one to take back home.

Next day he asked around where he could possibly obtain one of these marvellous dogs, and was told that Bill Wilson from down south was one of the better breeders. Off he went in search of his special dog.

As luck would have it, the day he arrived at the property, Bill was leaning on the gate with a couple of dogs by his side.

"G'day," said the Aussie visitor.

"Gidday," responded Bill.

"I'm looking to buy one of your champion heading dogs, if that's possible."

"Well," said Bill, pointing at one of the dogs, "you're in luck — this one here's for sale."

"Great," said the visitor. "How much do you want for him?"

"Oh, I reckon about $250," said Bill. "But I should warn you in advance that this dog can talk!"

"Don't be ridiculous, a dog can't talk, it's not possible," said the Australian.

Whereupon the dog spoke up. "Yes, mate, I can talk just as well as any human and what's more, I'm a bit of a hero round these parts."

The Aussie was amazed. "What do you mean you're a hero?"

The dog replied, "Well, last month I raised the alarm over a homestead fire in these parts and dragged the children to safety. The family love me and I can't do anything wrong — I'm a real hero! Then just a couple of weeks ago I saw two children drowning in the local creek, so I dived in and rescued them from certain death. Everyone's been making a huge fuss of me ever since, so you can see I'm a real hero round here!"

"That's truly amazing," said the visitor, turning to Bill. "If he's a champion dog who can talk and a real hero to boot, how come you're selling him so cheap?"

"Well," said Bill, "it's because he's such a bloody liar!"

***

Dogs are an important asset to farmers, musterers and shepherds in the high country, as can be seen by the statue on the shores of Lake Tekapo in the Mackenzie Country. Old Jack owned a fast heading dog that had become a legend by the time he was only three years old. This dog was reputed to be so fast that when he was working with sheep you couldn't see him with the naked eye.

One day a bunch of musterers out on the Mackenzie Country were finding it hard work to get some of the big merinos off the high country. They camped out overnight, but a couple of young dogs barked in the night and spooked the sheep. When morning came they had dispersed all over the plain.

The musterers were pretty upset, for it meant they'd have to start the job all over again. However, someone had a brainwave — to call in Old Jack with his champion heading dog and just maybe this could save them a heap of time.

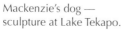

Mackenzie's dog —
sculpture at Lake Tekapo.

Old Jack gave the dog its orders, and there was a shower of shingle and dust as it took off in a hazy blur. Unfortunately someone had left a fence standard in the ground almost fully concealed by the long tussock and snowgrass. Before the dog had built up to top speed he hit the standard with full force and it completely split him in two. Jack didn't miss a beat, he was over there in a flash and grabbing the two halves, slapped them back together. Within a few moments the dog was off again.

Several hours later the dog reappeared with all the sheep, but to everybody's horror and distress they noticed that Jack in his haste had put the two halves together end to end the wrong way up and the dog was now running on only two legs, with the other two sticking up in the air.

You might have thought this would adversely affect the dog ... but no, it actually improved the animal. Whenever he got tired, Old Jack would simply flip him over onto the other two feet, which would give him a fresh dog every time.

***

Bill had been watching sheepdog trials and decided to purchase a likely looking dog for $200. When he returned home he called out one of his rousies and they took the dog out to round up a few sheep from across the river.

They arrived at the riverbank just below the bridge, so Bill sent the dog across the river to move the sheep towards the bridge. To his utter amazement the dog crossed the river by walking on water and began to work the sheep extremely well, which prompted him to say to his rousie, "He seems to be pretty good, Joe."

Joe replied, "You've been had, boss — he can't swim!"

***

High country farmers are proud of their sheepdogs, especially when they turn out to be truly remarkable animals capable of amazing feats.

One such farmer took his dog to town for a visit and as it was a hot day called into the nearest pub to quench his thirst. After a couple of drinks he boasted about his dog to the barman.

"Yeah, my dog's absolutely brilliant," he said. "There's nothing he can't do — back on the farm he does just about everything for me. He catches rabbits, yards the sheep, collects the mail from the post box and even fetches the newspaper for me. In the evening he delivers my slippers and pipe to me straight after tea. You couldn't wish for a better dog."

"Well," said the barman, "if he's so bloody good, why don't you call him in and I'll shout him a beer."

"I can't do that," said the farmer. "It just wouldn't be right, seeing as how he's got to drive me home!"

The barman was pretty intrigued by now and said, "Listen, mate, if I give him the money, would he buy me a paper, because I forgot to pick one up this morning on my way to work?"

"Certainly he will," says the farmer and calls the dog in, hands him the cash, gives him his instructions and off he goes.

A couple of hours go by and the dog hasn't returned, and the barman's been giving the farmer a real hard time. Embarrassed and a trifle concerned, he sets off to look for the dog. After lengthy searching the farmer meets the dog slowly returning, looking rather the worse for wear.

"Where the hell have you been?" he asks the dog. "I can't go back to that pub again after you've embarrassed me like this!"

"Well," said the dog, "on my way to buy the paper I met this lovely little bitch and we ended up having a real nice time together. But I knew I had to get back to you, so here I am on my way at last — better late than never!"

"Well I'll be damned," said the farmer. "You've never done that before!"

"No," said the dog. "That's 'cause I've never had the money before!"

***

The very same dog loved chasing rabbits and one day he came across a buck and a doe playing in the grass. Naturally he just had to chase them and they made for the nearest burrow.

Realising they couldn't stay in there forever, the dog waited outside for them to come out.

Inside the two rabbits were talking. The doe says to the jack, "He's waiting outside for us, what are we going to do?"

The jack replied, "It'll be all right, we'll stay in here for a couple of weeks, then go out and surround him."

Farmers and shearers

A bunch of shearers were drinking in a bar when a well-dressed bloke entered and ordered a large cold beer. Not wishing to appear standoffish, one of the group walked over, introduced himself to the newcomer, and asked what he did for a crust.

"I'm a taxidermist," was the reply.

"What's that?" asked the shearer.

"Well, I stuff things — generally animals, like trout, deer and native birds."

"What about sheep?"

"Yes, I'll stuff sheep as well, if I'm asked to," replied the stranger.

The bloke returned to his mates who promptly asked him, "Well, who is he and what does he do?"

Back came the reply: "He says he's a taxi driver, but I reckon he's a shearer just like the rest of us."

***

A cow cocky from South Westland got fed up with the incessant rainfall on the Coast and decided to get away from it all. After some research, he ascertained that North Otago was in the midst of a drought, so there wouldn't be any rainfall to contend with. He travelled across to Christchurch and caught the Southerner train down to Palmerston South. As he disembarked from the train, he glanced up at the sky and noticed a mass of threatening black cloud overhead. He stopped the nearest porter and said, "I thought it didn't rain over here."

"That's right," replied the porter.

"Tell me what are those up there?" He pointed to the threatening black clouds overhead.

"Oh, those are empties coming back from the West Coast," replied the porter.

***

A wealthy farmer from New Zealand was visiting London, where he received an invitation to lunch at an exclusive businessmen's club. On arrival he was introduced to a very British gentleman and naturally said, "Gidday, I'm from New Zealand — can I get you a beer, mate?"

The gentleman replies, "No, thank you, I'm teetotal. I did try it once and found I didn't like it."

"Well, how about a smoke, mate?"

"No thank you, I tried it once and didn't really like it either."

"That's okay, mate — would you like a game of snooker?"

"No, thank you once again, I don't play — although I did try it once and didn't like the game at all."

At this juncture a young man came in and the gentleman said, "May I introduce you to my son Julian — he might like to play snooker with you."

"Thank you very much, I'm pleased to meet you, mate," said the Kiwi. "I suppose you're an only son …"

***

A deeply religious cocky lived on a large station in Southland, close to where the river flooded frequently.

One year there was heavy flooding and all properties in the vicinity had to be evacuated, but this fellow stayed put on his land, repeating to himself over and over again, "God will save me!"

Eventually a boat arrived to rescue him, but he refused to leave, saying "God will save me!"

Another boat came and he refused to be rescued again, saying over and over that "God will save me!"

The land was almost under water when a helicopter arrived complete with a rope ladder and telling him it was his last chance to be saved. Once again the cocky refused to leave, saying "God will save me!"

The flood waters got higher and the cocky finally drowned.

When he arrived at the Pearly Gates he was angry, and as soon as he saw St Peter he bailed him up. "What's going on? God was supposed to save me. How come he didn't and I've ended up here?"

St Peter replied: "Well we tried our best to save you, but you ignored the two boats and helicopter we sent!"

***

A West Coast farmer was in court on a charge of cattle stealing.

The jury consisted of local farmers, all of whom had probably indulged similarly at some stage of their lives and therefore fully appreciated his predicament.

Once the evidence had been presented, the jury retired to deliberate and returned within minutes.

The judge asked, "Have you reached a verdict?"

"We have," they replied.

"Do you find the defendant guilty or not guilty?"

"Not guilty, your Honour, but he has to give the cattle back."

The judge pounded his gavel. "You can't deliver a verdict with stipulations attached — go back out and come up with a proper verdict!"

The jury duly retired again and returned forthwith.

Once again they were asked, "Have you reached a verdict?"

"We have, your honour."

"How find you?"

"We find him not guilty, your Honour, and he can keep the bloody cattle!"

***

I heard this story from an old South Canterbury cocky in Waimate a few years ago. Back in the 1890s, when a large number of South Island sheep stations were being overrun by rabbits, whole paddocks and hillsides were teeming with an ever-increasing number of bunnies. Station owners began hiring rabbiters to bring the plague under control. These men could make a reasonable living by shooting and skinning the bunnies, but every so often along came someone with a slightly different idea on how to get rid of the pests.

One of these blokes, a recent English immigrant, was holding court in the local pub and telling anyone who'd listen that he'd never seen so many rabbits in one place at a time and it was certainly proving a long and arduous job to get rid of them.

When asked how he went about the job of ridding the countryside of rabbits, he replied: "I use a team of ferrets when I'm working on most of the stations round here, but I tell you there's so many rabbits, I have to get down on all fours and put my hand into the burrow to pull a few rabbits out before my ferrets can even get inside.

***

Coaches & travellers

A Cobb & Co coach was travelling from Christchurch to Greymouth and there were four men seated inside. In those days it was common for people not to speak unless they had been officially introduced.

The coach had been travelling about an hour or so when one of the men put down his paper and said, "I say, chaps, my name's Johnson. I'm a retired big city banker, I'm married and have three sons!"

The man sitting opposite spoke up. "That's a coincidence, my name's Johnson, I'm a retired big city banker, I'm married and I've got three sons."

Up spoke the third gentleman in the coach. "By Jove, that is a coincidence, my name's Johnson too I'm a retired big city banker, I'm married with three sons."

The fourth man put down his book and said, 'My name's Smith, I'm a retired goldminer. I was never married but my three sons were all big city bankers!"

***

Another Cobb & Co coach was on the road from Westport to Greymouth and one of the ladies travelling inside was intrigued to hear the driver calling one of the horses 'Nightdress'.

At the first halt she disembarked and went over to the coach driver to ask, "Why do you call your horse Nightdress?"

Whereupon he replied, "That's because she's the easiest of the lot to pull up!"

***

A tourist was travelling around the North Island, driving from Auckland to Wellington, when he ran out of petrol in an isolated spot on the Desert Road. He got out of the car and flagged down a passing motorist, who turned out to be a recently retired Taranaki farmer.

"What's the problem, mate?" asked the farmer.

The tourist replied, "I've run out of petrol, can you possibly help me?"

Full marks to the farmer, who said, "That's okay, I've got a full tank, just follow me!"

The goldfields

I was at the old gold mining site of Bendigo down in Central Otago and clambering through the relics of this interesting township when I came across a large and deep hole in the ground, obviously a disused mine shaft. I picked up a large rock from the nearby mullock heap and tossed it down the shaft, listening to it clatter and bounce down the hole before culminating in a loud boom as it hit the bottom.

I thought I'd try something bigger and after a bit of searching found a bit of old railway sleeper, so I struggled over to the shaft and dropped it in.

As I stood there listening and waiting for the inevitable boom, I heard the sound of running feet behind me and turned round to see a large billy-goat charging head-down, straight at me. I narrowly managed to sidestep the animal, which kept running towards the shaft and leapt in.

While I was standing there recovering from the shock of this near miss, a local farmer happened by and asked if I'd seen his goat anywhere.

Still shocked by what had happened, I replied that I hadn't.

"Ah well," said the farmer, "I don't suppose he can go very far, because I've got him tied up to piece of old railway sleeper."

Swaggers

It was Show Day in a country town and sideshow alley was doing a roaring trade. Outside one large tent, the owner was exhibiting curiosities in the hope of persuading the crowd to part with their cash to view the display inside.

"This valuable object here is the skull of Shiner Slattery," he told the assembled audience.

There was respectful hush for a few moments, when a voice from the back of the crowd called out, "Rubbish, the Shiner had a much bigger head than that!"

Recovering quickly, the showman continued: "This here is the skull of the Shiner when he was just a lad!"

***

A young swagger called in at a station hoping for some leftovers and a doss-down for the night. He knocked at the back door and to his surprise the mistress of the house opened it, wearing just enough to excite the young bloke's imagination.

"Excuse me, Ma'am," he said. "I wonder if you can spare me a bite to eat and somewhere to sleep for the night?"

"Certainly," she said. "Come in and when you've eaten your fill, you might like to keep me company for the night, as my husband will be away for a few days."

The swagger couldn't believe his luck and duly complied with the lady's wishes. Only a few hours had elapsed, however, when the station owner returned home unexpectedly.

The swagger leapt out of bed, saying to the mistress, "I need somewhere to hide!"

She thought for only a moment before telling him to hide in the upstairs bathroom. "You should be safe in there, my husband hardly ever goes near it."

The swagman did as he was told, but the husband called out a greeting to his wife, saying he's off to the bathroom to clean up after an accident down the road.

He opens the bathroom door and to his surprise, the swagger is there pacing up and down stark naked and clapping his hands as he moves around the room.

"Good heavens!" said the husband. "Who are you and what are you doing?"

"I'm the pest exterminator," came the reply, "and I'm killing moths."

"But you've got nothing on!" said the husband.

"Ah well, they're vicious little blighters, aren't they!" said the naked swagger.

Australians

An Australian tourist visiting New Zealand was very keen to try fishing at Lake Taupo. He found himself a local guide and they rowed out onto the lake.

Now the Australian had recently purchased all the latest fishing gear with new rod, reel and flies, and was sitting in the boat without any sign of a bite.

His guide was sitting there hanging out the left hand side of the boat, using a piece of bamboo with nylon twine and a bent nail on the end and was catching a fish every thirty seconds.

The Australian was amazed but didn't say anything, lest he upset his host.

Next day they rowed out onto the lake again and the tourist was still having no luck with all the latest gear and equipment. His guide was hanging out the right hand side of the boat, using his piece of bamboo with nylon twine and a bent nail on the end and catching a fish every thirty seconds.

The Aussie could contain himself no longer. "Mate, how do you do it?"

"Ah well," he replied, "I work on a hunch."

"What do you mean you work on a hunch?"

"Well, when I wake up in the morning and look across at my wife, if she's lying on her left side, then I fish out of the left hand side of the boat. And when I wake up in the morning and look across at my wife, if she's lying on her right side, then I fish out of the right hand side of the boat."

"I understand," said the Aussie, "but hang on a minute, mate, what happens if she's lying on her back?"

"Well, then I don't go fishing!"

***

A Kiwi farmer had won a couple of tickets to a Bledisloe Cup rugby test in Sydney and flew over a couple of days early to see the sights.

The day before the match he wasn't feeling too well, so he went to the doctor.

"Hey Doc, I don't feel too good, eh," said Bill.

The doctor gave him a thorough examination and said he had bad news.

"What's wrong, Doc?"

"Well you've got a prostate problem, but we can cure it by removing your testicles."

"No way, Doc!" replied Bill. "I want a second opinion."

So Bill left the medical centre and found another doctor a few blocks away. The second doctor gave Bill a thorough examination, with the same result. He advised Bill that his prostate problem could be cured by removing his testicles.

Bill was absolutely devastated but still refused any treatment.

The next day as he was on his way to the big game, he came across an expatriate Kiwi doctor and decided to get his opinion on the problem.

The Kiwi had a look and said, "Yes, you've got a prostate problem all right."

"Is there any cure, Doc?"

"There is, Bill, but we're going to have to cut off your balls."

"Phew — thank God for that!" said Bill. "All the Aussie doctors wanted to take my test tickets off me!"

***

An Australian visitor drove his hired car into a ditch in a remote country area. Luckily a local farmer happened by and offered to help with his big strong Clydesdale, a horse named Hercules.

He hitched Hercules up to the car and yelled, "Pull, Captain, pull!" but Hercules didn't move.

The farmer yelled again, "Pull, Prince, pull!" but once again Hercules didn't respond.

The farmer shouted yet again, "Pull, Blackie, pull!" with no result.

Then the farmer quietly said, "Pull, Hercules, pull!" and the horse easily dragged the car out of the ditch.

The motorist was thankful but curious, so he asked why the farmer had called his horse by the wrong name three times.

"Old Hercules is blind," the farmer replied. "If he thought he was the only one pulling, he wouldn't even bother trying."

Travellers

Years ago I was travelling from Lyttelton to Wellington on the overnight ferry and found myself sharing a two-berth cabin with an attractive young lady.

During the night she woke and called out to me. "Excuse me, sir, I'm cold, would you mind fetching me a blanket?"

I replied, "Listen, you don't know me and I don't know you, so why don't we pretend we're married, just for tonight?"

She thought about this for a few moments. "All right, why not!"

So I said, "Well good, you can get your own bloody blanket then!"

Various

It was late Friday afternoon in the local butcher's shop and they were cleaning up after a fairly hard week. A customer came in asking for the last leg of lamb sitting in the window. The butcher weighed it on the scales. "That comes to fifteen dollars and ninety-five cents, madam."

The customer then asked, "Do you have a bigger one?"

The butcher picked up the leg of lamb and retired to the back of the shop for a couple of minutes and then returned with the same leg of lamb, saying "You're in luck, madam, this one is seventeen dollars and fifty cents."

The lady replied, "Thank you, I'll take both of them!"

***

A couple of rural lads had decided to join the army. They duly passed all the physical tests and were sitting in the waiting room to have their eyes checked by the army doctor.

The doctor came out of his office with a pair of glasses perched on the end of his nose. He pointed to the first lad and said "You! In here."

The first lad went in and the doctor fiddled with his glasses as he said "Read that chart on the wall."

The lad read the chart: "A-Q-R-B-N-W-S-G-X."

"That'll do fine," said the doctor.

"Am I in, Doc?" asked the lad.

"Not yet," he said. "I have to ask you a couple of questions to check your mental competence. If you should lose the sight of one eye, what would you be?"

"Half blind, eh," said the lad.

"Very good," said the doctor. "Now what would you be if you lost the sight of both eyes?"

"Totally blind, Doc," replied the lad.

"That's very good — off you go and pick up your uniform down the hall."

As he went out the door, the first lad called out to his mate: "Half blind, totally blind … you'll shit in!"

The doctor came in to the waiting room, still fiddling with his glasses, and called the next lad into the office. "Now read that chart on the wall," he said.

The lad read the chart: "A-Q-R-B-N-W-S-G-X."

"That'll do fine," said the doctor.

"Am I in, Doc, am I in?" asked the lad.

"Not yet, I have to ask you a couple of questions first. If I should lose one of my ears, what would I be?"

"Half blind, eh," said the lad.

This is a very strange answer, thought the doctor — I'll try again.

"If I should lose both my ears, what would I be?" he asked.

"Totally blind, Doc" replied the lad.

"Okay, this is very interesting" said the doctor. "I'm intrigued to know how you reach the conclusion that without both my ears I would be totally blind."

"Oh that's easy, eh — there'd be no place to hang your glasses!"

***

A man walked into the produce section of his large supermarket in London and asked for half a head of lettuce. The young man working in the department told him that they only sold whole heads of lettuce. The customer insisted that he ask his manager about the matter. Walking into the back room, the young man said to the manager, "Some old bastard wants to buy half a head of lettuce."

As he finished the sentence he turned to find the man standing right behind him, so he quickly added "and this gentleman kindly offered to buy the other half."

The manager approved the deal and the man went happily on his way.

Later the manager said to the young man, "I was impressed with the way you got yourself out of that difficult situation. We like people who think on their feet. Where are you from, son?"

"New Zealand, sir," the young man replied.

"Why did you leave New Zealand?" the manager asked.

"Well, sir, there's nothing but whores and rugby players there!"

"Really?" replied the manager. "My wife is from Christchurch!"

"Is that so?" replied the young man. "Who'd she play for?"

Politics

One day Michael Cullen and Winston Peters were discussing how to win the rural vote at the next election.

"How will we go about it?" asked Winston.

Michael suggested that they dress themselves in swanndris, gumboots and hats and take along a huntaway dog, so they would really look the part. "We'll go to a typical backblocks pub and show the locals that we really belong."

"Righto," said Winston. Some days later, all dressed up and with the dog in tow, they set off from the Beehive in a southerly direction. Eventually they arrived at a backblocks town, where they found the perfect little country pub. They walked into the bar with the dog at their heels.

"Gidday, mate," said Michael Cullen to the barman. "We'll have a couple of Speights, if you don't mind."

"Good afternoon, Mr Cullen," said the barman as he poured their beers.

Cullen and Peters leant on the bar drinking their beer and chatting quietly, nodding now and again to anyone who came into the bar for a drink. The dog lay quietly at their feet.

Suddenly the door from the next bar opened and an old stockman came in, walked up to the huntaway, lifted its tail and looked underneath, before shrugging his shoulders and walking back to the other bar.

A few moments later another stockman came in, walked up to the dog, lifted its tail, looked underneath, shrugged his shoulders and returned to the other bar.

Over the next hour or so, another four or five stockmen came in, lifted the dog's tail and went away looking puzzled.

Eventually Cullen and Peters could stand it no longer and called the barman over.

"Tell me," asked Cullen "why did all those old stockmen come in and look under the dog's tail like that? Is it an old high country custom?"

"Hell no!" said the barman. "It's just that someone told them there was a dog in this bar with two arseholes!"

Some examples of humorous verse

The frost we had the other day, really can't compare
With what they get in Central parts — oh, how it freezes there.
Walking through a paddock once, I saw a full grown sheep,
Start to jump a ditch and stop, halfway through its leap;
The frost had come all sudden like and as the creature rose,
Before it came to earth again, suddenly it froze.
And there it hung just six feet up, as stiff as any board,
And stayed there all the winter time, until the frost had thawed …
No, frosts we get in Southland aren't quite as bad as those,
It's rarefied Otago air, what does it I suppose.

FWG Miller — Invercargill

Frosts! I've seen some whoppers, the old campaigner said.
One winter for some ducks to bag, to Central parts I sped.
'Twas early in the morning and the ducks were on the lake;
Their wings they fluttered frantic'ly, but off they didn't take.

And why? I summed the situation up in just a trice —
Every single duck I saw was fastened in the ice.
And as I looked upon that lake, that frozen solid sheet,
The flapping wings began to make a harmonising beat.

I saw their purpose at a glance, some brainy ducks were there,
And presently the whole caboose rose slowly in the air.
And all them ducks still wedged in ice, and keeping perfect time,
Flew away with lake attached for some warmer clime.

And up till now, the old man said, I haven't told a soul,
But where that mountain lake once lay, remains an empty 'ole.

FWG Miller — Invercargill

We've already found that Ross McMillan, writing as 'Blue Jeans', has a way with words and he does it very well. He has a seriously good sense of humour too as I'll demonstrate with three of his poems:

I've Met Them All

I've met them all in the roadside bars where the thirsty congregate,
I've heard the tales that they swore were true, from them or a drunken mate.
I've met the man who outran Snell and the man who outshore Quinn,
While the man who outclimbed Hillary was drinking squash and gin.

I heard of the man who kept a great big bull frog as a pet,
How he taught it to leap the Molyneux for the sake of a dollar bet,
I listened a while to a cove who trained a kea how to speak,
And it whistled the tune 'Salome' from the corner of its beak.

I've met the man who mustered round the top beat on Mt Cook,
He hunted all before him from each snowy niche and nook,
When he penned his mob at nightfall he had quite a motley crew,
Ten sheep, six deer, some chamois and a skiing girl or two.

I've had a whisky with the man (a legend now they say)
Who rode the bull through Cromwell on a crowded festive day.
And met a man — Alf Brown by name — a son of Central loam,
Who found a moa in the Alps and tried to fetch it home.

I've met the gent who owned the best 'eye' dog in all the world,
With human mind and cunning brain and under good command,
It could head three mountain grasshoppers, drive them across a flat,
And hold them safely in the ring — or yard them in a hat.

In shearing shed and hut and bar, I've heard the tales they've spun,
The characters of Central — I've met them all but one.
And soon with luck I hope that I will find the ways and means,
To meet that cow from Wanaka, who claims that he's 'Blue Jeans.'

The Hang-and-Glide Birds

Today was fine and sunny as I went around the sheep,
When I saw movement in the hills — the Kakanuis steep,
I focused the binoculars — then I was stumped for words,
Like from some prehistoric age I saw two giant birds.

Now there are some about no doubt will think this yarn untrue,
And others will be sure to state that I'd been on home brew.
But I saw them in silhouette against the mountain side,
Caught by a balmy updraught, they seemed to hang and glide.

They didn't flash across the sky like sparrowhawks in flight,
Not like the oystercatcher or the duck or magpie might.
The skylark likes to circle, the pigeon likes to race,
But over the Endowment these big birds hung in space.

Far bigger than the heron or the goose and swan their span —
(The body underneath the wings somehow resembled man)
One had a very hairy face — the male bird I suppose,
Their beaks were red and shiny not unlike the human nose.

I thought of all the musterers to scale the mountain crest,
And wondered why some mountaineer had never found their nest.
The Maori killed the moa off — I guess he didn't know
About the hang-and-glide birds, that live up in the snow.

So when at last the lambing's done and I've got some spare time,
All through these rough and lonely hills I mean to probe and climb.
Round cliffs and crags and bluffs of rock — and I'll not spare my legs,
I want to be the first to find some hang-and-glide bird eggs.

Hedgehogs

I knew a lady years ago who owned a little farm,
She kept some cows, some hens, a dog, and came to little harm.
I still recall the tales she told, this one I'm passing on,
She vowed that it was true enough, so read and judge anon.

She sold butter and milk and eggs, a spot of loot to earn,
Each dawn and dark she milked by hand, would separate and churn,
But hard times came upon her head, the milk quota dropped low,
Though grass was high and water clean no cause was there to show.

Until one night, lantern in hand, around her sleeping herd,
She took patrol and in the dark great sucking sounds she heard.
And where the cows lay down to rest by bushes, bogs and logs,
Their milk was stolen as they slept by hordes of dry hedgehogs.

No doubt the shock she knew was sharp, but guile and craft had she,
She loosed her dog from off his chain, went on a hedgehog spree.
She mustered them into a mob (or so the story runs)
And drove them like a bunch of sheep, from old to baby ones.

Oh, what a sight it must have been to see that prickly band,
All sizes, shapes and ages too, strike westward overland.
I've mustered cattle from the runs and off the ranges wide,
And when they broke it was no joke as language testified.

I've driven rams and lambs and calves that made me 'do my scone'
I've mustered horses wild and free way back to hell and gone.
I've driven sheep through shingle slides and cursed my footsore dogs,
And though I've driven geese and hens, I *never* drove hedgehogs!

Though some will think this story odd, and doubt it, I'll be bound,
The best milk yield soon off her field then came for miles around.
I'd like to add a footnote here; I somehow think it's true,
A plague of hedgehogs struck Lauder — 'twas back in '52.

Men around a campfire: two rabbit carcasses hang from a log
GV Shaw collection, ATL PA1-q-269-47-2

XV

WHILE THE BILLY BOILS

Oral traditions, toasts & backblocks ditties

WHEN I WAS GROWING UP IN CHRISTCHURCH I was exposed to any number of rhymes, ditties and songs. Back then they were everywhere and I heard them from parents, relations and friends, never realising that they were all part of our rich tapestry of folklore. This treasure trove never truly registered with me until well after I developed an interest in New Zealand folk song and subsequent field collecting. I made a conscious decision to start at home by questioning both my parents in 1964, which immediately bore fruit. I obtained two songs from my father and a couple of fragments from my mother that she had known for years.

My ancestors from all sides of the family had migrated to New Zealand in 1823, 1839 and 1854, which certainly allows time for new traditions to develop and take hold, while some of the older ones were adapted to the new environment. My parents often recited:

> Red sky in the morning, shepherd's warning,
> Red sky at night, shepherd's delight

which originated in England, but I don't know where the next one came from. It was used to make us realise how much more we might learn if we kept our 'traps' shut and listened to what was happening around us:

> The wise old crow lived in an oak,
> The more he heard the less he spoke.
> The less he spoke the more he heard,
> Why can't we all be like that bird?

Dad's eldest brother, Lionel Heathcote Garland, had been in the army in World War I and returned home singing a song he'd probably learned from fellow Australian troops in the trenches. Dad couldn't remember the tune for 'Three Blackbirds' but seemed to think it might have been sung to an old hymn tune. It appears to be derived from the old British song 'Three Ravens', and possibly more closely related to the Australian song 'Three Black Crows':

Three blackbirds sat on a fence,
They were as hungry as they could be.
Said one blackbird "What shall we do?
For something we must surely eat."

They flew across a field of grain,
To where an old grey horse lay slain.
They sat upon his old backbone,
And pecked his ribs out one by one.

A farmer came out with a gun,
And shot those blackbirds all but one.
He flew away in such a fright,
That his black wings were turned to white.

That is why you'll often see,
Magpies perched high in a tree.
They wait until the time is right,
Before they eat a crop that's ripe.

Now one magpie sits all alone,
He's just a mess of skin and bone.
A scarecrow kept him thin and starved,
So he lay down and died, Yes he lay down and died.

My father claimed that this song explained how magpies came into being. I have never heard it anywhere else in the country.

Dad also told me about the Anzac camaraderie his brother experienced while on leave in London, which I wrote the next song about:

The year was 1916, I was serving overseas,
Along with mates from Maoriland, to keep the Empire free.
My name is Lionel Garland, from Christchurch I had come,
To fight the German enemy with bayonet and gun.

We fought alongside Aussies, who hailed from the bush,
While others came from Melbourne, or knew the Sydney Push.
As Anzacs from Down Under we were feared both far and wide,
I'm pleased to say the blokes I knew weren't on the other side.

The spirit of the Anzacs was unique and quite carefree,
But you'd never find a better case of hands across the sea.
The comradeship that blossomed there was lasting and true blue,
If ever someone needed help, they could always count on you.

When the war was nearly over, I was on leave in London town,
Looking for a good time and sinking poison down.
The night was getting shorter, when a little worse for wear,
I stumbled down the narrow streets to the barracks that we shared.

Two MPs tried arresting me and then as if on cue,
While dragging me towards the brig, two diggers hove in view.
They said "If you're a Kiwi, mate, we've come to lend a hand"
When the fight was over both MPs lay on the Strand.

They picked me up and carried me until they found the gate,
To where our lads were barracked and left me to my fate.
I never saw those blokes again, I never knew their names,
But I'll not forget to thank them should we ever meet again.

Now whenever diggers gather to review past memories,
You cannot beat the mateship that exists across the sea.
To us we were one country, a close knit family,
Let's hope our sons and daughters can preserve that harmony.

Whenever stone fruit such as cherries or plums were on the menu when I was growing up, my father would chant a rhyme at the dinner table as he counted and sorted through the stones, pushing them to the side of his plate. Once again, I have heard or seen no other reference to this rhyme since. Dad had learned it from my grandfather, who recited it in similar fashion at the table. It appears to be related to British rhymes such as 'Tinker, tailor, soldier, sailor, rich man, poor man, beggarman, thief' or 'She loves me/she loves me not/she loves me'. However, I found that it worked well sung to the tune of 'The old maid's song'.

One I love, two I love, three I love, I say,
Four I love with all my heart and five I cast away.
Six he loves, seven she loves, eight they love so true,
Nine he comes, ten he tarries, eleven he courts and
Twelve he marries.

This recitation alerted me to the possibility of more material out in the countryside, and this was compounded by what my mother was about to tell me:

Beer, beer, I love thee,
In thee I place my trust,
I'd rather go to bed with hunger,
Than go to bed with thirst.

She could only remember a couple of lines from the next one:

Beer, beer, glorious beer,
Fill yourself right up to here…

To her mother's dismay, Mum had learned these snippets from her father Harry Tully, who must have picked them up while fighting in South Africa in the Boer War. Mum also remembered a verse and chorus of 'The Tarpaulin Jacket' different from any Australian version I have seen or heard. The song, variously known as 'The Old Stable Jacket' and 'The Dying Stockman' usually goes something like:

A strapping young stockman lay dying,
His saddle supporting his head;
His two mates around him were crying,
As he rose on his pillow and said:

"Wrap me up with my stockwhip and blanket,
And bury me deep down below,
Where the dingoes and crows can't molest me,
In the shade where the coolibahs grow.

Mum's version had a couple of incomplete lines so I have filled in the gaps:

An old stable-hand lay a-dying,
A saddle supporting his head,
To his comrades around him still standing,
These were the last words that he said.

Wrap me up in my old stable jacket,
And let me go easy and slow,
With four stalwart comrades to carry me
To the place where I'm waiting to go.

This puts me in mind of the 'Musterer's Lament', a localised rewrite of the 'Dying
Stockman' which came from an informant in the Waimate district in the 1960s:

A high country musterer lay dying,
As in his whare he lay.
While his cobbers around him were yarning,
These were the last words he did say.

Chorus: Wrap me up in my oilskin and blanket,
And see the old beggar lies low,
Lay my faithful old dogs round about me,
'Neath the hills that we tramped long ago.

If I had the wings of a kea,
Far far away I would fly,
Back to the haunts of the red deer,
There I would lay down and die.

Then get two bonny young kowhai,
Plant them one at my head and my toes,
Then fetch a stout post and mark them,
Here lies an old shepherd below.

When the shadows of evening are falling,
And the sun on the ranges sinks low,
Pause there a moment just sometimes,
And think of the shepherd below.

When you're up on the tops at the dawning,
Or in camp when the firelight dies low,
You'll still hear my voice there a-calling,
Like a far echoed faint wayleggo!"

I have never considered myself much of a scholar or academic, finding it difficult enough at times for the 'folklorist' description to sit comfortably on my shoulders. Certainly I have spent many years collecting and researching folklore, some of which has become part and parcel of my stage performance. My interest in different aspects of folklore has developed through researching folk song and early woolshed dances, as I came into contact with the spoken word more and more on my collecting travels. The poetry, yarns, tall stories and toasts were originally just an adjunct to my main interest, that of trying to tap into Kiwi identity through song, but I kept everything that came my way and filed it away for future reference. As more and more gems came to light, I gradually realised I had stumbled onto a rich vein of Kiwi folklore and cultural identity. I found myself becoming increasingly interested in the yarns, ditties and ballads that had once been recited around rural campfires by the likes of farm labourers, stockmen, musterers, shearers, drovers and swagmen.

Not only had I discovered material that worked well when presented in the context of a musical performance, but also by incorporating this folklore into my concerts I was attempting to re-introduce it back into society. This combination of music and lore has enabled me to better understand and appreciate my own 'sense of place' as well as enjoying a closer relationship with my audiences.

Bush recitations have changed and spread in different directions, with the toast becoming one of the many variations — it is a four-line verse that may be used as a quip or sarcastic retort when an occasion demands. Some of these toasts have been written as such, or may have even been taken from longer songs, poems and recitations to eventually take on a life and identity of their own.

This piece has frequently cropped up in my travels throughout the South Island high country:

With a little bit of sugar and a little bit of tea,
A little bit of flour you can hardly see.
With hardly any meat between you and me,
It's a bugger of a life, by Jesus.

It appears to have originated in Australia and may have inspired the following piece found on the wall of the deer cullers' Wisely Hut in the Murchison mountains of Fiordland, and given to me by Sam Sampson on Stewart Island in 1994.

Where the keas call and the trees grow tall
And there's very little to please us.
It's here I've to stay till the end of May,
What a hell of a place, by Jesus.

The goldfields haven't turned up as much as I would have expected, except perhaps the following two or three. Among them, this piece lifted from a Charles Thatcher song and common to both Australia and New Zealand:

> Gold is the great friend of the masses,
> The mainstay of the classes.
> The grand, grand aim of the lasses,
> And the ruin of the asses.

Another ditty I've come across has been attributed to both Anon and Thomas Hood — it also makes an appearance in the book *Bright Fine Gold* by William Heinz.

> Gold! Gold! Gold! Gold!
> Bright and yellow, hard and cold,
> Molten, graven, hammered, rolled,
> Heavy to get and light to hold.
> Hoarded, bartered, squandered, doled,
> Price of many a crime untold,
> Gold, gold, gold, gold,
> Good or bad, a thousandfold.

These optimistic lines of positivity are attributed to Arthur Eversley in 1889:

> So to turn an honest penny, lead an upright life and free,
> Ere a man be wed to any, 'tis a digger he should be.

Followed by this one from the same source:

> There's ample room in the land of boom to make a mint of gold.

Jim Henderson mentions this unusual piece of verse, when talking about the mighty Buller River in his book *Swagger Country*:

> Buller River, silver grin,
> Haul the brash prospector in!
> Buller River, roar him home,
> Grind him down to skin and bone.

Sam Sampson gave me the following verses, which he'd originally collected from Ray Clarke at the Tophouse Hotel in the Nelson Lakes district. Apparently it was sung to the tune of 'My Bonnie Lies over the Ocean' on Maggie Terrace, a gold mining settlement at the junction of the Howard and Buller rivers in the 1930s' Depression. Sam recently informed me there was more in the form of a chorus, which I'll also include here in its unexpurgated form:

> They say there is gold on the Maggie,
> They say there is gold on the Maud,
> They say there is gold on the Louis,
> But it all sounds like bullshit to me.

Bull-shit, bull-shit, it all sounds like bullshit to me, to me,
Bull-shit, bull-shit, it all sounds like bullshit to me.

Along the way a variant of this verse found its way to a group of young four-wheel-drive enthusiasts in Canterbury, who thought I might be interested and gave me this:

We found no gold on the Maggie,
We found no gold on the Maud.
We found no gold on the Louis,
For it was all bullshit you see.

Still on the subject of gold, John A Lee remembers hearing about a big tough station cook and part-time swagger called Wild Bill McBeath, who would recite the following rhyme when he was out on the turps. These lines make for an interesting précised variant on the old West Coast song 'Shanties by the Way':

How in the devil can a man keep sober,
With pubs and shanties on the way,
Cards and billiards on the table,
And the landlord pressing you to pay?

Writer Mona Tracy recalls her mother singing a portion of the same song and mentions in her letters that her mother heard it frequently during her youth in Australia. After coming to New Zealand, she hadn't given it much thought or heard it sung in 50 or 60 years until asked about it by her daughter. But with her memory already failing, she could only remember the first verse. This verse is probably still in the process of transition from EJ Overbury's Australian bush ballad 'The Public by the Way' into what we now know as the New Zealand goldfields song 'Shanties by the Way.'

In the little outback sections, in each town and village street,
There shanties stand in all directions, dear to weary traveller's feet.
And should he for a moment linger, the die is cast — he's sure to finger
In those shanties by the way.

Here's another variant of the song collected in 1964 from Peter Sutton, who was head teacher at Greenhills School, just a few kilometres from Bluff. What makes this so interesting is the mention of shearers in the fourth verse of this Southland version, which manages to shift the character and atmosphere of the song from goldfields to pastoral New Zealand.

Chorus Rows of bottles standing upright, labels of bright blue and gold,
Beer's so cold it needs no ice in, for the cellars here are cold
To rest the weary traveller's feet, who has journeyed all the day,
Where four bush roads cross and meet, stands a shanty by the way.

Men and maids are dancing lightly to the music that they play,
Kerosene lamps are shining brightly in that shanty by the way.

Dice and darts upon the walls, cards and quoits stand in one bay,
Bagatelle and billiard balls, in that shanty by the way.

Hunched around a blazing fire, shearers who have spent their pay,
Waiting for another hire in that shanty by the way.

Penniless you'll have to wander, many a long and dreary day,
Till you earn another cheque to squander, in that shanty by the way.

Deer culling, farming, rabbiting, mustering, droving and other rural pursuits have all come in for their share of farewell toasts, many descended from 'Frank the Poet' Macnamara's famous Australian farewell to Van Diemen's land:

Land of lags and kangaroos,
Of possums and the scarce emus,
The farmer's pride but the convict's hell,
Land of bums, fare-thee-well.

This toast obviously struck a chord and has had wide circulation throughout both countries. Most of what follows has been gleaned from hut walls in the South Island high country. This toast is printed in John A Lee's book *Roughnecks, Rolling Stones and Rouseabouts*:

Land of rocks and rabbits too,
Rotten squatter, cockatoo,
Squatter heaven, swagger hell,
Land of rabbits, fare-thee-well.

Bruce Stronach quotes from the book *Musterer in Molesworth*:

Land of rocks and rivers deep,
Lousy with dogs and Merino sheep.
Squatter's paradise, musterer's hell,
Molesworth Station, fare you well.

Also writing about Molesworth Station, Peter Newton quotes a variant of this rhyme, which he says became well known: "… Squatter's glory, musterer's hell, Molesworth Station, fare thee well."

Jack Crump spotted this variant on the walls of the Iron Wool Store at Harper River in 1908:

Land of rocks and rivers deep,
Lousy with dogs and Merino sheep,
Squatter's hopes and musterer's hell,
Land of mountains, fare you well.

Jocelyn Logan from Auckland saw this version on the wall of a hut when she was tramping in the Waiau valley in 1968:

> Land of rock and rivers deep,
> Lousy with chamois and Stevenson's beef,
> Culler's heartbreak, musterer's hell,
> Waiau River Valley, fare-thee-well.

The next farewell toast adds a couple of extra lines to the standard format and was apparently popular with swaggers in the Mackenzie Country in the early 1890s. Evelyn Hosken quotes this in her 1968 book *Turn Back the Clock*:

> Land of rivers and lakes so deep,
> Mountains high and very steep,
> Plains as far as the eye can see,
> Nothing but tussocks and merino sheep,
> Squatter's glory, swagger's hell,
> Land of Mackenzie, fare you well.

The toast has developed and grown in length if the next piece is anything to go by, and the sentiments have changed considerably. Discovered on the back of a mountain picture painted on a scrap of paper, it was written by an anonymous boy leaving Algidus Station around 1939~40. In Mona Anderson's book *A River Rules My Life* it is quoted thus:

> Oh land of river, rock and spur,
> Of sun-kissed hills and skies so blue,
> I, a humble musterer,
> Will ever leave my heart with you.
> Tho' I dwell beneath some distant sky,
> My memory will ever turn
> To mates I knew in days gone by,
> And evenings when the camp fires burn,
>
> For I am leaving you this day
> To return again, but who can tell,
> For good or bad, I cannot say,
> Mount Algidus, I wish you well.

Here's Mona Anderson again, writing after her husband had nearly drowned in what was known as 'Old Man River' — the Wilberforce:

> Damn the nor'west, it brings rain,
> Damn the river, it's high again.
> Damn because we can't get mail,
> And damn because the bread is stale.

Damn the sleet and damn the snow,
And damn the mud wherever I go.
Damn the work and damn the sheep,
And damn because I want to weep.

"I've had this place" is what I say,
For two damn pins I'd give it away,
And yet I know with all this strife,
That damn it all, I love this life.

Completing a trilogy of positive goodbyes, let's take a look at my song 'Farewell to New Zealand.'

Fare thee well New Zealand,
Soon we'll be over the sea,
But I know in my heart that I will return,
To the land that's so dear to me.

Kia ora to you my country,
I must be on my way,
I'm off in the morning my fortune to try,
But you know I'll return some day.

Farewell to the snow-clad mountains,
That seem to touch the sky,
Your memory will haunt me again and again,
Until the day I die.

Farewell to the hills and valleys,
Where the rivers run so free,
And to your rugged sea-bound coast,
You'll always be home to me.

Farewell to the fern-covered bushland,
And the bellbird's sweet refrain,
The day will come when I know your sweet song,
Will call me home again.

The time has come for leaving,
To wipe the tear from my eye,
With my bags all packed, it's now I must
Bid you a final and sad goodbye.

The rainfall in South Westland and Fiordland has been known to depress more than a few hardy souls. This piece was found on the wall of a hut in South Westland:

Ashes to ashes, dust to dust,
If the mountains don't kill you, then the rainfall must.

277

This reminds me of a couplet I heard years ago:

> Ashes to ashes, dust to dust.
> If whisky don't kill you then abstinence must.

The next three examples take the toast as we have come to recognise it, but also precede it with a couple of lines. Which came first is anybody's guess.

> Mountains, rocks and river sand,
> All belong to Maoriland,
> To stay in thee, O land of mutton,
> I would not give a single button.

> Land of snow and rabbits too,
> Rotten squatter, cockatoo,
> Banker's heaven, swagger's hell,
> Land of rabbits, fare-thee-well.

Here we seem to have two toasts used in conjunction with each other, but the sentiments remain pretty much the same. The first four lines have also been collected on their own, while the term 'Maoriland' seems to give away the age and the approximate date of currency. Substituting 'Maoriland' for New Zealand was common throughout the 1890s and early 1900s, particularly in Australia, where they looked upon our shores as another state of Australia.

The next two are closely related and appear to have originated at an earlier time than the previous one — possibly in the 'Hungry Years'.

> Maoriland thou art a pest,
> To put us to so stern a test,
> No respite from recession's grip
> Our subsidies have been let slip,
> Banker's heaven, farmer's hell,
> Land of foreclosures, fare-thee-well

A similar version ends:

> … Our prosperity has been let slip,
> Banker's heaven, farmer's hell,
> Land of shylocks, fare-thee-well.

Despair became all too common throughout New Zealand with the 'Hungry Years' taking their toll. People left the country in droves during this Depression. Arthur Desmond was an eccentric political activist who also wrote poetry. His 'Exiles of New Zealand' written in 1891, expresses similar sentiments to the previous couple of ditties:

> We're off to bright Australia,
> Far o'er the singing waves,

Why should men live in Maoriland,
To be forever slaves?
To be forever slaves, to be forever slaves?
Why should men stay in Maoriland, to be forever slaves?

O Maoriland thou art beautiful,
As beautiful can be,
But what of all your coin and gold,
If there is naught for me?
If there is naught for me, if there is naught for me?
But what of all your coin and gold, if there is naught for me?

If pirates loot the ship of state,
If bankers steal the corn,
If Shylocks boss the worker's fate,
The commonweal must mourn.
The commonweal must mourn, the commonweal must mourn,
If pirates loot the ship of state, the commonweal must mourn.

So now to far Australia,
We steam across the waves,
Why should we toil in Maoriland,
As moneylenders' slaves?
As moneylenders' slaves, as moneylenders' slaves,
Why should we die in Maoriland, as moneylenders' slaves?

Australia has given us 'The Dying Stockman', along with its variants including 'The Dying Aviator', which was published in *Folk Songs of Australia* by John Meredith, who I met back in 1993 on one of my Australian tours. I had been staying with my sister in Mittagong, before heading down to the Illawarra Folk Festival at Jamberoo. The easiest way to get there was to catch a bus, which was due to stop on the outskirts of the township of Thirlmere — a ten-minute drive from Mittagong.

While I was waiting for the bus a couple of white-haired blokes came out of a cottage across the road, one carrying a concertina. They came over to the bus stop and it seemed we were probably headed in the same direction. They introduced themselves — the one with the concertina was Alan Scott, while his mate turned out to be John Meredith, whose work I knew by dint of his Australian folklore collecting, research and publications.

When I introduced myself, John Meredith exclaimed, "Bloody hell, I've been thinking about coming over to New Zealand to visit you and here you are standing right outside my door!" After the festival I spent a full day discussing folklore, collection and research with him at his cottage, which proved to be fascinating and beneficial. I was really pleased I had this opportunity to talk with him, albeit too briefly, because he passed away a few years later in 2001, just before I was due to perform again at the Jamberoo Folk Festival.

I have chosen this song because it follows the normal pattern for six verses, before continuing with the aviator's arrival at the pearly gates:

"What have you done," asked Saint Peter, "to be seeking admission up here?"
"Oh I was a young air-force pilot on earth, for well over a year."

The gate then moved open quite sharply, as Saint Peter touched a small bell.
He said, "Come in and take up a harp, lad, for you've had enough there of hell!"

This has become a relatively common piece of verse in its own right throughout both countries and it certainly crops up all over the South Island. I obtained the following two pieces from two separate sources — Sam Sampson on Stewart Island and Parish John in a hut near Hanmer Springs in 1969.

Before the gates a bushman stood, his face was scarred and old.
He stood there like a trembling tree, awaiting entrance to the fold.

"What have you done," St Peter asked, "to gain admission here?"
"I've been a bushman, sir," he cried, "for many a weary year!"

The pearly gates swung open wide, St Peter rang the bell.
"Come in, come in and choose your harp, you've had your share of hell!"

It cropped up again at a deercullers' reunion dinner in Christchurch back in 1975. I sang Peter Cape's 'Culler's Lament' ('Black Matai') to the assembled multitude and the song moved some old-timers to tears. In return I was handed this wee gem.

Before the gates a culler stood, his face was scarred of old,
He stood there like a trembling fawn, awaiting entrance to the fold.

"What have you done," Saint Peter asked, "to gain admission here?"
"I've been a culler, Sir," he cried, "for many a weary year!"

The Pearly gates swung open wide, Saint Peter rang the bell,
"Come in, come in and choose your harp, you've had your share of hell!"

Imagine my delight to later find a variant of this piece cropping up in a book about *The Moonlight Ranges* in Southland by David Milligan.

A carrier knocked on the Pearly Gates, his face was scarred and old.
He stood before the man of fate, for admission to the fold.

"What have you done," Saint Peter asked," to gain admission here?'
"I've been a carrier, Sir," he cried, "for many and many a year"

The Pearly gates swung open wide, Saint Peter touched the bell,
"Come in," he said, "and choose your harp, you've had your share of hell!"

Farm workers and labourers made a lasting impression on local Canterbury folk poet Joe Charles, influencing his body of work over the years. In the tradition of singing the praises of 'Black Billy Tea', comes a toast from Joe:

Mutton stew and rabbit pie,
Washed down by billy tea,
Bullocky's joy on hunks of bread,
Is just the thing for me.

As mentioned, swaggers have made a huge contribution to the rural economy and farming community of New Zealand, notwithstanding this verse quoted in *Swagger Country* by Jim Henderson:

The swagger is a lonely man,
And sometimes very old.
And every day he walks around
Like a lost sheep from the fold.
It's baccy here, hot water there,
Perhaps a drop of tea,
But if you say "Go chop some wood"
Then down the road he'll flee.

I collected the next piece in 1969 from Mrs Bateman in Christchurch. She was the daughter of John Fisher Dakers, who was born at Montrose in Scotland, coming to live in New Zealand in the early 1900s. He resided at the Crown Terrace and Arrowtown for many years, writing this in 1928:

Along the road the old man came,
Worn and weary, footsore and lame.
Stopped at the creek near the roadman's camp,
Laid down his swag on the tussock damp.
Took his black billy, went down to the creek,
And when he had filled it, I heard him speak,
For weeks I've been searching for work in vain,
Tramping alone in the wind and the rain,
Begging a meal or a crust of bread,
Sleeping out in the open, or in some old shed.

I received a letter in 1979 from Mrs E J Milligan of Invercargill. She was 88 years old and was responding to a request for old songs and poems I had made in the *Southland Times*. She decided to write something and this is what she sent me:

Oh, where have they gone, those men of the road,
Swaggers we called them as they trudged with their load.
They carried their swags in a roll on their back,
Their old billy dangling from a rope round their sack.

Some wore clothes that were worn and old,
Others wore clothes to keep out the cold.
If the weather was stormy they asked for a bed,
In a farmer's outhouse or maybe a shed.

Seldom they offered to do any task,
A meal met their needs, they had only to ask.
Perhaps one or two tried chopping some wood,
Showing their thanks for the gift of the food.

Some entertained with stories to tell,
Other slunk away once the darkness fell,
Now times have changed, no more do we see,
The men with their swags roaming the country.

Receiving a poem like this was the next best thing to interviewing this remarkable lady, who was in all likelihood committing her youthful memories to paper in a ballad form.

The origins of the next couple of ditties are unknown, having been sent to me by an anonymous informant. They are obviously closely related.

The days of hard luck swagmen seem so long ago,
When they roamed about the country, carrying their load.
The places where they camped beneath the open sky,
Are just forgotten places, ignored by passers-by

The days of hard-case swaggies seem so long ago,
When they roamed across the country, shouldering their load.
The shelters where they made their camps beneath a starry sky,
Are hardly ever noticed by people passing by.

Perhaps these ditties refer to some historic site or sites beside old swaggers' tracks that are never noticed by today's traffic speeding along life's modern highway.

John A Lee mentions the following rhyme in his *Shiner Slattery*, describing an ex-swagger remembering what he'd read on a woolshed wall. The swagger says:

"I'd walked about forty miles and got a job, one of the first I'd ever had and I'm sleeping in the shed — when I woke I noticed a rhyme above my head."

Away out back, upon the track,
I stayed one night with Clancy,
Of all the prayers he said that night,
This one took my fancy.
"May God above send down a dove,
With wings as sharp as razors,
To cut the throat of the dirty bloke,
Who lowered swaggers' wages."

I'll conclude by quoting a poem sent in a letter to Mona Anderson in 1963-64 after the publication of her *A River Rules My Life*. This poem extols the musterer's life and was written by an unknown man who signed himself simply 'Tinwhistle.'

I'm eighty years old and somewhat,
But I give to God the praise,
They made a shepherd of me,
In the good old mustering days.
Then men loved dogs like women,
And mustering the hills was more
Than signing on as a greasy,
Or scrubbing the cookhouse floor,
Or wiggin' or crutchin' or shearin'
Or crutchin' or wiggin' again,
In the days of mustering the high tops,
The hill was a place for men.

You could see our good dogs running,
With heart and limb like deer,
You could hear them bark like thunder,
As they cast out far and near.
And 'twas 'wayleggo' behind my lad,
When a dog had run his best,
And we spun full many a hairy yarn,
Ere we hit the hay for a rest.

Remnant of a bygone era: Molesworth Homestead in the Awatere Valley, Marlborough in the 1950s.
EP Christensen, ATL 34052 ½ AAQT 6401 A 17984;
Archives NZ/Te Rua Mahara o te Kawanatanga Wellington Office

New Zealand
Folklore Society

XVI

KIWI FRUITS

Harvesting folklore

THE NEW ZEALAND FOLKLORE SOCIETY'S AIM of encouraging modern composers
has been achieved on more than one occasion and thankfully continues today.
Long-time Auckland Society member and collector, Bill Worsfold, has recently
composed songs based in the tradition, while at the other end of the country Martin
Curtis has been doing this successfully since his arrival from England in the 1970s.
John Archer is another who has been writing vernacular ballads for many years and
is promoting local folk music via his Kiwi music website. Michael Brown, from the
next generation, is already making his mark by concentrating on in-depth folklore
research and study at Victoria University. The future for Kiwi folk music looks to
be in good hands.

While I was living in Australia, I returned home for a concert tour of New
Zealand in 1990 and met up with Roger Lusby on my visit to Christchurch. Roger
grew up in Roxburgh, Central Otago, and had began writing and adapting earlier
material to modern-day situations. He was acquainted with Arch McNicol, who had
written the poem 'Man upon the Track' which I had set to music and was singing
around the traps. Roger took the song and modernised it thus:

> Have you seen so many people down upon their luck,
> All the worldly goods they had, sold or taken back.
> Left without a dollar or a solitary bob,
> Trudging round the country just looking for a job.
>
> They sold off all our assets and we'll never get them back
> Didn't ask us for a mandate, we would never give them that,
> What about tomorrow, yes the future's looking black,
> Better take to walking 'fore they sell the bloody track!

There's something that is missing, it's our mana that we've lost,
Can't help our fellow Kiwi, without charging him the cost.
Nothing done for nothing and we've got to change it back,
Because the richest man of all was the man upon the track.

Roger also adapted and modernised the famous four-line verse, written on the wall of an Otago shearing shed and attributed to the Shiner.

Don't blame the struggling farmer for his luck it has run out,
Don't blame the little business man, he knows what he's about.
Don't blame the corner dairy if your children lack for bread,
But blame the Labour government for the reckless way they led.

Roger has recently moved to Nelson and continues to write and compose Kiwi-themed songs and humorous recitations. I'm sure we'll be hearing a whole lot more of his work in the coming years.

Sam Sampson was a member of Folklore Society in its early days before taking on life as a teacher of outdoor pursuits. He spent time at Lake Rotoiti in the Nelson Lakes district before heading south to Tautuku, then later to Stewart Island where he recently died after a long illness. While stationed at Rotoiti, Sam would often drop in for a drink at the Tophouse Hotel. When the Licensing Commission closed the Tophouse Hotel in 1974, despite it holding the longest-running liquor licence in the country, this was Sam's response. He originally sang it to the tune of Charles Thatcher's 'Wakamarina' but believed it could also be sung to 'The Dying Stockman'.

There is strife in the Province of Nelson,
Round the shores of Lake Rotoiti,
They've closed down the pub up at Tophouse,
'Twas too scruffy for them don't you see,
If you want a beer or a whisky,
It's a drive to the Wairau for me.

Wrap me up with the bits of my Rover,
And on my headstone with my name,
Say "He pranged driving home from the boozer,
The Commission's entirely to blame."

They said our pub was too scungy,
For people to drink there, a sin.
They think we should only be happy,
In a DB lounge drinking pink gin.
When the pressure inside us has built up
To the point where we feel we must burst,
They say we must use stainless troughs now,
Not just go out and use a fencepost.

The place must be built out of plastic.
Formica and chromium too,
An old wooden bar's unhygienic,
And beer out of kegs just won't do.
A bar that seats six is quite stupid,
It should take five hundred or more,
With plush padded seats and a carpet,
And a patented lock on the door.

The passing of Tophouse was something
I'm bound I shall never forget.
We used buckets to drink from — not glasses,
We all got skunk drunk you can bet.
Then from ten o'clock to the small hours,
Old Ray turned the grog on for free,
And by five o'clock in the morning,
There was hardly a bloke there could see.

I suppose they will take the pub's licence,
To give to some new city barn,
Where you're jammed in so tight and the noise is so loud,
You have trouble in hearing a yarn.
It's the same now all over the nation,
As the old country pubs are closed down,
The beer baron's business keeps booming,
As the licences shift into town.

John A Lee publishes a chorus only of the optimistic song 'I've Made Up My Mind' in his book *Roughnecks, Rolling Stones and Rouseabouts,* which I present here:

I've made up my mind to sail away,
Sail away, sail away,
I don't mean to waste another day,
I'll find luck somewhere.
In our colonies I mean to try,
Yes I'll try, do or die,
For some time I will say,
But I'll return some day,
And I may be a millionaire.

'Silence' is a poem from M Bennett, which is more art than folklore, but nevertheless captures the mood and deserves a mention:

Return now to silence,
The sounds of men are gone,
From river valley and ravine creek.

Mountains where the monitors roared,
And the iron-shod feet of the stampers
Followed the track of the prospectors,
To the secret places of the mother lode.

Dust returns to dust in the bush,
Where wealth and vanished dreams are one,
In the silence.

Geraldine shearer Dave York sent me his 'A Rousie's Life' song in the 1980s:

Out of school and you can't find a job,
Sign on the dole or join up with the mob,
Shift to a city, survive if you can,
Only thing left are the shearing gangs.

Chorus   Your rousie's life ain't no cup of tea,
Don't get much for the union fees.
Summer you bake and winters you freeze,
But it still beats working in a factory.

Fall out of bed at the crack of dawn,
Dry horrors from the night before,
Five-thirty another day begins,
Six-thirty then you press the pins.

A shed-hand's lot takes you interstate
But there's always wet dags and a shearer you hate,
Kicked in the butt or abused on the board,
Waiting for wages from the month before.

Gorse, matagouri, thistles and ticks,
Wrinkle stretchers, rained out, stuck in the sticks.
There's no sick pay or overtime,
But it sure beats manning the production lines.

A rouseabout's life ain't no piece of cake,
Sweat so hard for the money you make,
So after all this in a year or two,
Pack your bags and head for shearing school.

Alternative final verse:

A rousie's life ain't no pleasure cruise,
Counting out rams and Perendale ewes,
So after all this in a year or two,
You pack your bags and head for shearing school.

Staying with the rural life, here's a recitation from the ubiquitous Anon:

Wanted, a youth for a dairy farm,
Young Nixon saw the ad,
He packed his bag, grabbed his bike,
Jumped on and rode like mad.

He reached the farm at milking time,
"You'll do," the farmer said.
Young Nixon donned his dungarees,
And followed to the shed,

"Before we start," the cocky said,
"I want to make it clear,
Be careful how you treat these cows,
We'll have no rough stuff here.

Handle 'em gentle, treat 'em kind,
Or else you'll get the sack."
Thus speaking, he approached a cow,
To pat her on the back,
The cow let out a mighty kick,
That knocked the cocky flat.

The cocky rose and grabbed a stick,
That cow got more than ample,
With all the things the cocky said,
He set a bad example.

The timber industry appears to have produced little verse and song, other than 'The Dying Bushman' and 'Timber.' During my research I've picked up a couple more along the way. When I was browsing the library in Shantytown on the West Coast I chanced upon the words to 'When the Gay Tui Calls' in a book *In the Shadow of the Bush* by John Bell, published in 1869.

O give me the life in the forest,
Away from the crowd and the crush,
What heck though the work be the sorest,
There's no place for me like the bush.

Chorus For the ring of the axe and the tree as it cracks,
          And the earth shaking crash as it falls,
          Are the sounds that I love all others above,
          That are heard when the gay tui calls.

We are out when the first birds are singing,
And home as they settle to rest.
And each evening the whare is ringing,
With laughter and song and with jest.

Let clodhoppers plough then and harrow,
Let larrikins loiter at flax.
Let the navvy ply shovel and barrow,
But give me the swing of the axe.

Anon gives us this one as well:

Oh you bushmen of New Zealand,
How can you all agree,
When the rivers are running bank to bank,
You're bound to get on the spree.
The landlord laughs and jokes and smokes,
And to his wife he makes a bet,
Before sunrise, to their surprise,
I'll have them all in debt.

Musicologist Roger Buckton recently sent me a review of 'A Bush Concert' which had been published in the *Weekly News* of 1865, and I quote several excerpts from the article. This is yet another example of that great Kiwi tradition, the amateur community concert.

"Musical Bushmen," we think we hear one say. "Are there such men? Can they find pleasure in sweet sounds? Then melody indeed has charms to sooth the savage breast." Yes, bushmen, rough and coarse as they are, can be subdued by music and many will travel miles to hear a good song, Amongst them are men of real vocal and instrumental talent and they relieve the monotony of their lonely life by spending pleasant hours indulging in that talent. Sometimes they get up amongst themselves an entertainment and concert, at which their wives and sweethearts attend. We believe that these do a great deal of good. Everything is prepared beforehand. The room lent by their employer or borrowed from some neighbouring farmer is cleaned out; one with the knack of carpentry makes seats and arranges a stage; nikau and tree ferns are cut to relieve the appearance of white-washed walls; the programme is written and posted at the store and public-house …

… at last the night arrives. Those connected with it are seen in an intense state of excitement, bustling with importance. The company assemble for the occasion …

… Well might the storekeeper be pleased, for events of this kind caused a run upon handkerchiefs, neckties, hair-oil etc, to say nothing of the demand for lollies. Bushmen appear to have a childish passion for these things and on occasions like these invest largely — it did not look well for a beau escorting his belle to smoke anything but cigars.

Besides there were many who had come from long distances — settlers, bushmen and men of crafts. The stage had been set — the whole surmounted by the New Zealand cabbage tree … The bell is rung, however and we must pass onto the performance. "An overture by the whole strength of the band" — violin, concertina, flute and bones. Then a fierce rough-looking bushman told us in stentorian tones that he was the 'Pirate of the Isles' and his appearance almost led us to believe him … What a glorious encore did the sharp little Cockney comic obtain when he had sung one of the old hall stagers! … Of course there were some faults. Some broke down. One individual, doing this however made amends by starting another song — another forgot his and tried back, but could not recall the link to memory. One couldn't join in with the accompaniment … but to tell all would be impossible. How some were sent back to the 'land o' cakes' by the melodies of Tannahill or "softened by the strains" of Burns. How Irishmen grew excited over 'No Irish Need Apply' and Englishmen over 'The Tight Little Island. Christies Ministerails caused excitement with 'Sally Come Up' and 'Jordan' and how everybody was seized with an itching of the feet when the jig-and-reel dancer made his appearance, how the National Anthem was sung with one heart and voice and how everyone wished that, long as it had been, it wasn't over … The men seemed excited, but it was with pleasure, and we felt that it would be a relief to be able to use the words of a song composed expressly for that occasion and say:

I but a simple bushman am,
Yet who so gay as me?
Let others toil and wealth and fame,
Give me sweet liberty.

I would not in a city live —
I would not health for fortune give,
Those who do nought but toil and slave,
Are bound by fashion's rules.

Heeding not to gain and save,
I look upon as fools.
Oh no! I'll be free,
A bushman's life for me.

I am indebted to Mike Harding and Michael Brown for the next couple of deer culling songs. While Mike was researching his book *When the Pakeha Sings of Home: a source guide to folk and popular songs of New Zealand*, he discovered a song 'There's Culling to be Done', apparently sung to the tune of 'Blow Ye Winds in the Morning', and originally published in *The Deer Wars* by Graeme Caughley in 1983. Michael Brown zeroed in on this, found the publication and passed these lyrics on to me:

The word went round in Greymouth in the year of thirty-six,
Internal Affairs Department was in something of a fix.

Chorus So oil up your boots, my boys, and check your pack and gun,
　　　　The deer are far too numerous, there's culling to be done.

At ten bob for each skin you get, I can't see how you'll lose,
Or half-a-crown each tail you get, if that is what you choose.

The skipper was convincing, he didn't need to shout,
He said I'd have a thousand deer before I's three months out.

We shot the Dobson Valley to the limits of the ice,
And we'll shoot the halls of Hades if they raise the tail price.

We shot the face of Algidus, we shot the head of Haast,
We baled up at Harper's Rock as each nor-wester passed.

According to Caughley, the song got the date wrong but the rest is near enough. This is yet another example of the full truth being not necessarily important. It appears the Department of Internal Affairs was constantly complaining about its lack of funding and the scarcity of good men, despite there being no shortage of manpower after the Great Depression. Most aspiring cullers lasted no more than a month at best, because the work was hard, physically and mentally. Only those who proved themselves a cut above the norm survived, as they searched out new experiences and high adventure while exploring the wild and rugged countryside. Caughley mentions some further lines from yet another deer culling song in the same book:

I shot the Rangitata, the Cameron and the Clyde,
I shot the Whitcombe faces until I nearly died.
I shot the Hokitika, the Borland and the Blue,
'Cause they got me to sign on the dotted line
To see the season through.

I have come across the following ditty on a couple of occasions, a deer culler's one-verse parody of the old song 'South of the Border.'

East of the border, over Canterbury way,
There on a neighbouring block,
To boost my tally I did stray.
Nearby rifle shots told me, that I must not stay,
East of the border, over Canterbury way.

Further to my mention of toasts come a few more I've occasionally heard on my travels or stumbled across. How unique they may be to New Zealand is anybody's guess — I list them here, should someone like to research them one day:

Here's to a long life and a merry one.
A quick death and a painless one.
A pretty wife and a loving one,
A long cold drink … and perhaps another one.

It's raining it's pouring, the old man's snoring,
Thunder and lightning stop life being boring.

Make new friends but keep the old; new ones are silver, while old ones are gold.

Deer hunting, possibly in the 1920s.
Alexander Turnbull Library G100198 ¹/₂ NZ Free Lance collection

John Newsham of Gisborne sent me the following drinking toast, telling me that the first time he ever heard it used was in New Zealand, but attributed to officers in the British navy. However I have also heard it in New Zealand on a few occasions.

To our wives and sweethearts — may they never meet.

One colourful saying that tickles my fancy has obvious origins: "Mad as gumdigger's dog" — while others originate with axemen and shearers: "Wouldn't that gap your axe" and "Wouldn't that gap your shears."

Children's playground chants and skipping rhymes are a complete study in themselves and while only a few have come my way on my collecting forays, some still occasionally do so today. However, apart from discovering that 'Bright Fine Gold' had spent time as a skipping rhyme in school playgrounds for many years, none of the others appear to have had such wide currency, so I have forwarded them to Janice Ackerly, who has undertaken extensive research into children's rhymes, chants and playground games.

While I was looking for toasts and ditties I published a plea for help and received a few sports chants from around the country. Robyn Park of Hasting sent me two from her mother's schooldays at Petone Technical College:

The emu, the kangaroo, the wallaby, the wombat,
The blue and white, the blue and white, the blue and white cat,
Boom-a-langa, boom-a-langa, bish bam boo,
We are Petone, who the hell are you?

Robyn says she's not sure why the Aussie menagerie in Petone, but the blue and white cat refers to the school colours, at least in the 1930s and '40s.

Who are, who are, who are we?
We are, we are, Pe-to-ne
Are we it, I should smile,
We've been here for a helluva while!

Another version of the same chant came to light from Michael Brown of Wellington, who sent this Waihi Rugby Club version (circa 1940s), which he found in the book *Tales of Old Waihi — Dig This One*, written by Percy Allison in 1987:

Who are, who are, who are we?
We are the boys from Wai-wai-hi.
First in law [war?], first in peace,
First to be arrested by the Waihi police!

Another chant which had wide currency is:

Two, four, six, eight, who do we appreciate,
C-A-N-T-E-R-B-U-R-Y, Canterbury!

The team could be from anywhere — school, club, town, city or country.

While on the subject of sport, I have found the following song 'You Don't Get Over Me' (air 'Young Man from the Country') interesting, for it demonstrates a wider currency for the earlier 'I'm a Young Man Just From England' in 1862. This rugby version of the song was published in the *Paraekaretu Express,* Tuesday 20 June 1893, and can be found on microfilm in the Alexander Turnbull Library.

I'm a boy from Ohingaiti and Pat Larkins is my name,
They try to play at football there and faith I do the same.
The captain met me on the ground, "You'll join the club," said he.
Said I, "I'm Ohingaiti and that's just the game for me.

Said the captain, "On the dribble, I'm afraid we're rather weak."
"Faith," said I, "I larnt to dribble long before I larnt to speak."
Said he, "Your comprihensun isn't what it ought to be."
Said I, "I'm Ohingaiti and you don't come that on me."

We played a match, they called it scratch, the captain said "You're tough."
"I may be, but bedad," said I, "me fate's sore enough."
"We'll pick you for the match that's on Saturday," said he,
"I see you're Ohingaiti and you're just the boy for me."

"You play forward," said the captain. Said I, "Is that the scrum?
Do you want to break my collar bone or dislocate my thumb?
My skull is not the thickest!" "Faith it's thick enough," said he,
Said I, "I'm Ohingaiti, so don't poke your fun at me."

When I got among the forwards, faith I wished that I was back,
For they kicked the peelin' from my shins and both my eyes were black.
Said I, "It scarcely is the game that it's cracked up to be,
But I'm stuff from Ohingaiti, and they don't get over me."

At home, abroad, I don't care where, I like a friendly game,
But it's rough when both your legs are blind and both your eyes are lame,
I try to keep my temper and that same I like to see,
I'm the boy from Ohingaiti and you don't get over me.

Although we try to do our best, we cannot always win,
And we're just as game when we have done as we are when we begin.
A goal is not an easy thing to get, you will agree,
We are the boys from Ohingaiti and we're tough as tough can be.

So I come from Ohingaiti and Pat Larkins is my name,
They try to play football there and picked me on the team.
Although to play a forward game, I'm backward, as you see;
I'm the boy from Ohingaiti and you don't get over me.

The research and background information for this song has come from Allen Shaw, a Kiwi living and working in Mt Isa, Queensland.

I have deposited this information and accompanying photos into NZ Folklore Society archives for preservation. Allen's original hometown was Ohingaiti near Taihape and while doing newspaper research into the area's local history as part of an interest in the 1960s, he stumbled upon this rugby song, an 1893 parody on 'The Young Man Fresh from England'. What is important from my folklorist's viewpoint is that this latest variant helps show the original song was known throughout the country for nigh on a hundred years. Rona Bailey in *Shanties by the Way* mentions that she collected five verses of this song from a Mrs Wallis in Cambridge as recently as 1957, and another version was obtained from a correspondent on Waiheke Island. In Radio New Zealand archives in the 1960s I discovered a further version performed by Dick Morris and recorded in the 1950s. Dick sang it to the tune of an old music hall ditty 'As Green as Watercress'. It had interesting changes from Charlie Martin's original lyrics, which demonstrates a thriving folk process at work for almost a century.

It is particularly interesting that the name 'Larkins' has been retained from the original 'Young Man' song of 1862, as Allen sent me a photo of the winning Ohingaiti rugby team of 1893 and there is no mention of a Larkin or Larkins in the team.

Talking recently with David Koch (currently living in Newcastle, Australia) who grew up in New Zealand in the '50s and '60s, he recalled listening to Sunday morning children's radio in Auckland during this time and hearing these words:

> Good Queen Vic sent a fella with a stick
> To the land of the Long White Cloud.

He couldn't remember any more and wanted to know the rest. The search was on, and after drawing a blank from acquaintances in New Zealand the best result seemed to come from Michael Brown in Wellington, who suggested it might be due to memory loss or a mis-hearing of a couple of lines from Rod Derrett's 1965 'Puha and Pakeha', where he sings:

> Down by the mud pools, once upon a time,
> In the land of the Long White Cloud ...
> Good Queen Vic sent a man with a treaty,
> To the land of the old Kiwi.

The jury is still out on this one, and if anyone can help further I'd love to hear from you.

As I have described, I spent time chatting with Rona Bailey in Wellington before setting out on my collecting travels in 1969. She gave me the benefit of her collecting experience as well as the name of Haldy Ryan to contact should I ever make it to Bluff. Haldy had sung fishing songs to Rona back in the 1950s and one was 'A Trawlerman's Song', which later appeared in Neil Colquhoun's book of New Zealand songs as 'The Foggy Foggy Banks'. When I eventually arrived in

Southland, I was keen to record Haldy singing this song, among others, but I was unable to locate him.

Although I have always sung the tune that Neil published, there was a hint of British folk song about it and when the English folksinger Jez Lowe recorded 'Foggy Foggy Banks', his album notes mention that it was a New Zealand song, with an apparent British ancestry. He added a couple of verses from the English tradition, which fitted the song well.

Michael Brown showed me a further text of the song collected by Rudy Sunde from Hinga Clarke of Te Atatu in Auckland in 1972. Hinga originally came from Bluff and her uncle turned out to be none other than Haldy Ryan. Despite remembering only one verse and chorus, the tune she sang was a close relative of a country-style pop song 'The Blackboard of my Heart', popular in the 1950s and '60s. The lyrics in her version have changed to the 'doggy foggy banks', which places it firmly back in the British tradition, most likely referring to the Dogger Bank fishing grounds. The Kiwi lyrics still show traces of their ancestry, but the tune has been altered by those Bluff fishermen to sit more comfortably in a modern idiom, thereby losing virtually all other vestiges of their earlier connections. The version I sing today incorporates some of those same English lyrics, but varies slightly from those collected by both Rona Bailey and Rudy Sunde.

Out on the foggy foggy banks, we pitch and toss about,
And blow our frozen fingers when we hear our skipper shout.

Chorus Heave away on your capstan, lads, give a hand to heave the trawl,
When we get the fish on board we will have another haul.
Heave away on your capstan, lads, give a hand to heave the trawl,
In the middle of the night, heave ho ye all.

When I was but a lad at school, I would not stay at home,
Like lots of other foolish lads, I thought I'd sooner roam.
Soon I joined a trawler and there I quickly found,
There wasn't no plain sailing, when I reached the trawling ground.

Sailing on the ocean far from the port of Bluff,
The southern gale is rising and the sea starts getting rough.
When the waves are falling round us and pounding on the deck,
It's hard to keep your footing as you try to save your neck.

We work our guts out day and night, our backs are stiff and sore.
There's nothing more inviting than safe ashore once more.
When the work is finally over, hard up our tiller goes,
West by South to the harbour's mouth to the big jib on her nose.

There appears to be a very real shortage of quality Kiwi Christmas songs or carols apart from the frequently sung 'Te Harinui' written by Willow Macky (see earlier) and Kingi Ihaka's 'Twelve Days of Christmas':

On the first day of Christmas my true love gave to me
A pukeko in a ponga tree.
On the second day of Christmas my true love gave to me
Two kumara, and a pukeko in a ponga tree.
On the third day of Christmas my true love gave to me,
Three flax kits, two kumara, and a pukeko in a ponga tree.
On the fourth day ... four huhu grubs
On the fifth day ... five big fat pigs.
On the sixth day ... six poi a twirling
On the seventh day ... seven eels a-swimming
On the eighth day ... eight plants of puha
On the ninth day ... nine sacks of pipi
On the tenth day ... ten juicy fishes
On the eleventh day ... eleven haka lessons
On the twelfth day ... twelve piupiu swinging.

Here's a further version of the Kiwi twelve days of Christmas:

On the first day of Christmas my true love gave to me
A fantail in a kowhai tree.
On the second day of Christmas my true love gave to me
Two pukeko playing and a fantail in a kowhai tree.
On the third day of Christmas my true love gave to me
Three tui preaching, two pukeko playing and a fantail in a kowhai tree.
On the fourth day ... four penguins paddling
On the fifth day ... five tu-a-tara!
On the sixth day ... six bellbirds ringing
On the seventh day ... seven dolphins diving
On the eighth day ... eight weka waltzing
On the ninth day ... nine lizards lounging
On the tenth day ... ten kea clowning
On the eleventh day ... eleven weta walking
On the twelfth day of Christmas......................Twelve kiwi calling.

I'd like to inject a bit of humour into Christmas proceedings. Older New Zealanders will recognise the parody on the carol 'We Three Kings of Orient Are' as originally performed by Fred Dagg (alias John Clarke):

We three Kings of Orient are,
One on a tractor, two in a car,
One on a scooter, tooting his hooter,
Following yonder star.

Oh, Oh, Star of wonder, star of light,
Star of bewdy, she'll be right,
Star of glory that's the story,
Following yonder star.

I'll end with a Kiwi parody on the humorous Australian version of *Jingle Bells*, with apologies to Greg Champion …

Chorus Jingle bells, jingle bells, jingle all the way,
Christmas in New Zealand on a sunny summer's day.
Jingle bells, jingle bells, Christmas time is beaut,
Oh what fun it is to ride in a battered old farm ute.

Dashing through the bush in a battered old farm ute,
Kicking up a fuss, six-packs in the boot.
The kids are by my side, lighting Christmas candles,
It's summer time and we are dressed in
Tee-shirts, shorts and jandals.

Engine's heating up — we try to play it cool,
Backpacker climbs aboard, he is welcome too.
All the family's here, sitting by the pool,
Christmas day the Kiwi way, round the barbecue.

After Christmas lunch, Grandpa has a doze,
While the kids and Uncle Bruce go swimming in their clothes.
When it's time to leave, we take the family snap,
Pack the car and all shoot through before the washing up.

… and Yvonne Morrison's version:

Chorus Jingle bells, jingle bells, jingle all the way,
Christmas in New Zealand on a sunny summer's day
Oh, jingle bells, jingle bells, jingle all the way,
Oh what fun it is to have a Kiwi holiday.

Dashing to the bay in a Kombi campervan,
Christmas at the beach — the family's master plan.
Dad is at the wheel and mum sits by his side,
We kids are squabbling in the back as we go for a ride.

We stop off at the shops to load the chilly bin,
Hokey pokey ice-cream soon dribbles down my chin.
We jump into the van, heading for the shore,
Dad fiddles with the radio to hear the cricket score.

Soon we're at the beach, our rellies shout "Gidday!"
We swap our Chrissie pressies, a boogie board — hooray!
We change into our togs and to the sea we run,
What a joy to splash and swim, summer's so much fun.

The grown-ups call us in, they've laid out a spread,
Lunch is fish'n'chips and cheerios in bread.
L&P to drink, pavlova, pud and pie,
Anzac bikkies, choccy fish — it's cracker Kiwi kai!

The kids are keen to play, but the dads all want a nap,
The sunscreen starts to fly as mums go slip — slop — slap,
We race out to the sand to play a game of touch,
But all the cuzzies are too slow because they ate too much.

The barbecue heats up, the sun begins to sink.
Our tea's as good as gold we've scoffed it in a wink.
It's nearly time for bed, we've had an awesome day,
Celebrating Christmas time the real Kiwi way!

NZ FOLKLORE SOCIETY

Parts of this section were originally published by NZFLS (Wellington) 1969

This postscript highlights the general aims and objects of the New Zealand Folklore Society, demonstrating what it did to help create public awareness and interest in our folk culture and heritage. I hope to reawaken some of that original enthusiasm, by making a younger generation aware of a large body of collected material that needs a new lease of life today.

The New Zealand Folklore Society was formed in 1965 with the prime aim of creating a more widespread awareness of the part played by our folk culture in shaping our society. As society changed, with the old giving way to the new in successive overlays of culture, many New Zealanders were inclined to the belief that all of our history worth preserving had already been included in our history books. There was, however in the collective memory of people still living, a wealth of finer detail connected with the country's youth. Songs, stories and verse from the gold rush era, the whaling industry, the gum trade and farming, all graphically described the hardships, pleasures and sorrows of a pioneering people. They are an important part of the national heritage of New Zealanders and should be preserved.

The New Zealand Folklore Society tried to do this by assembling collections of songs, stories and anecdotes, to make them available in published form. There are numerous such collections in existence and the society had hoped to collate and centralise these, as well as augmenting them with the results of our own collecting. We had hoped that these collections would eventually form part of a national archive of folklore and to this end, intended to deposit our collections with the Alexander Turnbull Library from time to time. Before this could be done, many of the field collecting tapes were water-damaged beyond repair while in storage. This was a disaster and something that perhaps could have been avoided, given the amazing recovery technology available to us today.

The society also tried to encourage the formation of self-sufficient groups of people into branches around the country working together towards similar aims. As the years went by, however, there were fewer and fewer living links with the past, which made the society's job so urgent. The time was right for organised collecting and with various people's help and support much valuable material has survived to this day.

Original aims and objects of the society were to:

- Foster a more widespread awareness of New Zealand's folk culture and a greater understanding of the country's history as expressed in this culture.
- Collect songs, poems, stories and anecdotes relating to New Zealand's historical past.
- Record, collate, publish and preserve these collections.
- Encourage present-day composers of material in the tradition of New Zealand's folk culture.

Membership in the society was open to all who subscribed to its aims and objects. There were full members, who were actively engaged in the work of the society; associate members, who shared the aims and objects of the society and wished to support its work; and student members — full or associate members who were students at an educational institute.

People were asked to contact the society if they knew of any songs, stories or anecdotes or knew anyone who did.

The need for field collecting

These days, folklore field collecting or 'songcatching' has come to mean the audio-recording of songs, poems and stories in the homes of people who remember them. As such, it is still relatively new to New Zealand. Overseas, many people are familiar with field collecting and the results obtained by such luminaries as Cecil Sharp or Banjo Paterson in the days before recording machines and Bartok or the Lomax's since the advent of tape recorders. In 1957 Rona Bailey undertook an extensive field-collecting trip, unfortunately without a tape recorder, but for some time afterwards most of the known New Zealand songs stemmed from her groundbreaking work.

The New Zealand Folklore Society was founded in the belief that New Zealanders were basically no different from other English speaking peoples in that they had created and continued to create their own entertainment in the form of poetry and song.

That some New Zealand folklore existed was never in doubt and the initial work of the society consisted of assembling a body of information by collating material already known prior to 1966. This was done so that field collectors would gain an awareness of the type of material in existence, enabling them to become better equipped to locate previously unknown material.

Although the society didn't concern itself only with songs and poems from our historical past, at that time they were particularly interested in this type of material, because most of the songs from that period were in imminent danger

Phil Garland, Rona Bailey and Frank Fyfe in Wellington, 1969.

of extinction. When the only people who might remember them died, the songs died with them.

For what was basically the same reason, the society was largely concerned with one aspect of folklore collecting. The two main ways of locating previously unknown material were library research (sometimes referred to as 'dead' collecting) and field or 'live' collecting. Of these two forms of endeavour, the latter was clearly seen to be the most urgent. With each passing year, the living links with our historical past were rapidly diminishing.

It was particularly this, which inspired the sense of urgency and in turn determined the society's attitude towards other fields of endeavour. If it was to be collected at all, material had to be collected from live sources immediately.

The task of field collecting was made more difficult with each passing year. As New Zealand society became more and more complex, successive overlays of culture influenced our attitudes towards life and hence our way of life. Today, surrounded by radio, the cinema, television and digital technology, the 'common people' have much less need to make their own entertainment. Thus modern day shearers, for example, no longer find their relaxation swapping songs in their quarters at the end of a day. Today they are able to drive to the nearest pub or watch satellite or interactive television.

It was from more than forty or fifty years ago that the bulk of the material in which the society was interested had to come. For someone to have been involved in singing songs and reciting yarns and poems at this time, they were already sixty or seventy years old. The most pressing job was to collect from them and older age groups as soon as possible. The New Zealand Folklore Society believed that our tradition was a valuable one and that much of it was in danger of being lost, unless their activity was concentrated towards immediate field collecting. If our heritage of song and poetry was to survive at all, it had to be collected 'NOW'.

Early field collecting

Rona Bailey, Bert Roth, Neil Colquhoun and Les Cleveland all made extremely valuable contributions to the collecting of Kiwi folklore and music in the 1940s and '50s. Without their pioneering work, the country would be much poorer. Their work — particularly that of Rona Bailey, proved the catalyst for the formation of the NZFLS and a strong influence on both Frank Fyfe and Phil Garland.

Publications included:

Shanties by the Way (Bailey & Roth) 1967

New Zealand Folksongs (Neil Colquhoun) 1965 — reprinted 1972.

The Great New Zealand Songbook — Les Cleveland 1991

Considerable field collecting work was undertaken by various individuals and branches around the country in the 1960s, '70s and '80s, before the society began to gently slide into recession in the 1980s. From the beginning, the most active branch was Wellington under the guidance of the late Frank Fyfe, who later continued his collecting work in the Wairarapa, interviewing many people and recording very interesting material. One of Frank's first contacts was Samuel Barrett, who played a one-string kerosene tin fiddle, which he had built himself back in 1919. Fyfe went on to research and collect a great deal of oral history throughout the Wairarapa area and published numerous folklore and historical booklets, which are currently deposited in the local library archives. Frank Fyfe also researched articles on 'Bright Fine Gold' and 'Davy Lowston' which were first published in the *Maorilander* journals, and can be viewed in full at www.folksong.org.nz.

The Christchurch branch, of which I was chairman, was also active, undertaking a couple of visits to the West Coast in 1967 to interview and record individual members of the Kokatahi band. I became the society's first full-time collector, first visiting the Hocken Library in Dunedin for in-depth research, then travelling throughout Otago and Canterbury in 1969, generously supported by grants from NZFLS and National Folk Foundation in addition to funds raised by various clubs, firms and interested individuals. I collected first-rate material 'on the road' and have since travelled thousands of miles, continuing to collect on a more informal basis over the years. A great deal of my collecting work has been recorded by Kiwi Pacific Records and later published in a book *The Singing Kiwi* by Willy Wag Productions from Australia in 1996.

The Auckland branch also undertook a lot of research and field collecting with Rudy Sunde and Bill Worsfold to the fore. Both these entertainers have recently recorded albums highlighting their work. Rudy leads a highly successful Auckland

group, the Maritime Crew, who have recorded the songs collected and written by Rudy over the years, while Bill has recorded Kiwi material with his wife Kath via their Colonial Two-Step duo, lately branching out into the composing of original songs.

At the height of the society's popularity there were branches in Wellington, Christchurch, Auckland, Taranaki, Manawatu and Hawkes Bay.

Acknowledgements

Thanks are due to *Heritage* Magazine, which published articles and songs of interest to folklorists and folk enthusiasts around the country throughout their ten-year existence. The following newspapers also published feature articles on the work of the society: *Listener*, *Sunday Times*, *Evening Post*, *Manawatu Evening Standard*, *Daily Telegraph*, Christchurch *Press* and Christchurch *Star*.

Special thanks to TVNZ, for items in *Town & Around* (Dunedin & Christchurch) *On Camera* (Christchurch & Wellington) *Looking at New Zealand* (nationwide) and NZBC (Radio NZ) for numerous interviews conducted in Wellington, Christchurch and Hawkes Bay.

It would be remiss not to thank those early enthusiastic members and supporters from around the country, without whose help and generous assistance the society could not have achieved any of its original aims and objects: Jae Angwin, Angela

Annabel, Beverley Anscombe, Myles Armstrong, Rona Bailey, Joe Charles, Philip Calder, Peter Cape, Neil Colquhoun, Jim Delahunty, Curly DelMonte, Bob Edwards, John Flynn, Tony & Cath Ford, Frank Fyfe, Mike Garland, Peter Gross, Dave Hart, Howard Harris, Dennis Hogan, Hugh Isdale, Dave & Judy Knox, John Knox, Larry Lacey, Elsie Locke, Anne McGregor, Ian McGregor, Heather McInnes, Hugh McKay, Philip Maxwell, Bob Moore, Val Murphy, Chris Norris, Mitch Park, Alwyn Owen, Duilia Rendall, Sam Sampson, Tony Simpson, John Stafford, Sharyn Staley, John Steel, Libby Stuart, Rudy & Pat Sunde, Don & Arthur Toms, Julian Ward, Robyn Williams, Richard Williams, Bill Worsfold,

My sincere apologies to anyone I may have inadvertently overlooked.

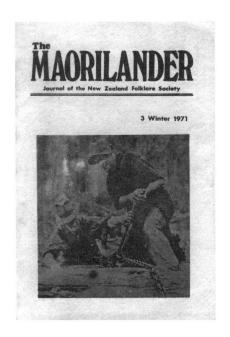

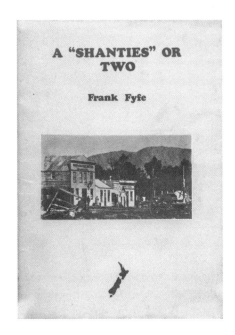

BIBLIOGRAPHY

PHIL GARLAND — DISCOGRAPHY

(for more information: www.kiwipacific.com)

One Hundred Years Ago
(1967: Action ACL 8001)

Tangiwai Disaster • A Hundred Years Ago • John Smith AB • The Old Scrub Bull • Down the Brunner Mine • New Zealand Whales • The Shearing's Coming Round • The Old Identity • The Shepherd's Dream • Banks of the Waikato • The Ships Sail In • Tuapeka Gold

Ah De Doo Dah Day
(1969: Odessa SDESS 14)

The Shearing's Coming Round • It's Raining, It's Pouring • Jamaica Farewell • My Dog's Bigger than your Dog

Down a Country Road
(1971: Kiwi SLC 87)

Wool Commandeer • Down a Country Road I Know • Snowed In • Smoko • Dug-out in the True • At the Mataura • Tuapeka Gold • Shanties by the Way •The Old Identity • Bright Fine Gold • Packing my Things • Farewell to the Grey

Song of a Young Country
(1972: Kiwi SLC 101/102)

Banks of the Waikato • The Day the Pub Burned Down

This is New Zealand
(1974: Ode SODE 038)

Culler's Lament • The Stable Lad

Colonial Yesterdays
(1975: Kiwi SLC 137)

Canterbury Jig • Culler's Lament • As the Black Billy Boils • Leatherman • Banks of the Waikato • The New Chum • The Shearing's Coming Round • Woolshed Dance Medley • When the Rainbird Sings in the Tea-tree • The Dying Bushman • Wool Away Jack • Across the Line • The Stable Lad • Black Billy Blues

Settling In
(1976: Kiwi SLC 146)

Run For Your Life • with the Bluegrass Expedition

The Old Station Days
(1976: Kiwi SLC 144; Canterbury Crutchings Bush & Ceilidh Band)

Bush Band in March Time • The Shores of Botany Bay • Five Miles from Gundagai • Retreat and Advance • In Slow March Time • All Among the Wool • A Billy of Tea • Davy Nick Nack/Soldier's Joy • Click go the Shears • The Drunken Piper/Staten Island/Mrs McLeod • The Dark Island • The Flash Stockman • Chief O'Neill's Favourite/Boys of Blue Hill • The Lime Juice Tub/Paddy on the Railway • Diddley Ah

Swags to Riches
(1979: Kiwi SLC 158; Canterbury Bush Orchestra)

Colonial Barn Dance • She'll Be Right • Country Pub • Susie's Delight • Springtime Brings on the Shearing • The White Cockade/Doc Boy's Jig/Durham Rangers • Charley Mopps/100 Pipers • Don't Blame the Wealthy Squatter • All for me Grog • Welcome to Erin • The Overlander • Brown and Empty Bottle-O • Sandy Grant/Angus Campbell • Rights of Man/Ballad of Ned Kelly • Bushman's Fancy

Springtime in the Mountains
(1984: Kiwi CD SLC 178)

The Hokonui Hills • Springtime in the Mountains • Scrub and Blackberry • Mason's Pub • Ballad of Stan Graham • Rocking the Cradle • Black Billy Tea • Kawarau Gold • Down in the Brunner Mine • The End of the Earth • Long and Friendly Road • Concertina Joe/Glenmore Jig • Hills of Coromandel • Farewell to Geraldine

Clear the Board
(1985: Kiwi SLC 182)

Canterbury Swing • Woolshed Ramble • Miss Kathryn's Wheel • Colonial Threesome • Supper Waltz • Shearer's Jamboree • Jacaranda Jig • Country Capers • BBQ Frolic • Charleston Galopede • The Magpie's Nest • Adieu or Goodnight Waltz • Nor'West Arches • Swagger's Farewell

A Homestead in New Zealand
(1986: Kiwi KML 6)

Wool Commandeer • Shearer's Jamboree • Billy of Tea • Canterbury Jig • Smoko • Bush Band in March Time

Send the Boats Away
(1986: Cityfolk CFR 014)

Faded Pictures

Hunger in the Air *(1987: Songs of Old New Zealand, Kiwi Pacific/Larrikin LRF 191)*

Hunger in the Air • John Smith AB • Bright Fine Gold • A Long Time Ago • Dug-out in the True • The Digger's Farewell • Come all ye Tonguers • Shanties by the Way • The Shearing's Coming Round • I'm a Young Man • Davy Lowston • Shore Cry • Man upon the Track • New Zealand Whales • Across the Line • Packing My Things • Leatherman

Wind in the Tussock
(1989: Kiwi Pacific CD SLC 200)

Wind in the Tussock • Yorky's Run • The Final Track • The Old Station Gate • Shantyman • Farewell to New Zealand • Greenstone Billy • Mother Nature's Children • Off to the Diggings • Hillsides of Bendigo • Faded Pictures • The Last Drop of Whisky • Driftwood

Phil Garland
How Are You, Mate?

SONGS OF A NEW COUNTRY

How Are You, Mate?
(1990: Kiwi Pacific CD SLC 212)

How Are You, Mate? • Boys of the Track • Homeless Drifter • When the Tui Calls • A New Chum out from England • In the Morning • Wheels of Arrow • The Old Forty-niner • The Kb Cannonball • The Latter End of Spring • Better Prospects • Gone to Maoriland • The Life of the High Country Shepherd • The Star Hotel • The Old Mud Hut • Full and Plenty • The Shepherd's Dream • The Dying Bushman • No Regrets

Waiting For News
(1993: Independent Australian Release; Bush Telegraph)

Click go the Shears • Raining on the Rock • Queen of the Murray • South Australia • Bright New Day • When the Rain Tumbles Down in July • The Diamantina Drover • Ballad of the Catalpa • The Band Played Waltzing Matilda • Home Among the Gumtrees • Shelter • Shores of Botany Bay • Water • Ten Thousand Miles Away • Sing Out Australia • Waltzing Matilda

Under the Southern Cross
(1996: Kiwi Pacific CD SLC 239)

Kawarau Gold • Old Station Gate • New Zealand Whales • Davy Lowston • In the Morning • John Smith AB • Lime Juice Tub/Paddy on the Railway • Last Drop of Whisky • Concertina Joe/Glenmore Jig • Wind in the Tussock • Mason's Pub • Wool Commandeer • Five Miles from Gundagai • Packing my Things • Boys of the Track • The Flash Stockman • The Dying Bushman • Farewell to Geraldine • Old Station Days

A Sense of Place
(1998: Kiwi Pacific CD SLC 250)

Take a Little Walk • A Sense of Place • Pelorus Jack • Walking off the Land • Gabriel's Gold • Proud to Be a Kiwi • Hands Across the Sea • The Roving Breeze • When I was a Young Man • Footsteps of the Miners • The Good Old Way/Shiner's Fancy • Old Jimmy Possum • The Gift of Life • Hokonui Whisky • So Long, Mate

Christchurch Acoustic 1998
(Christchurch Folk & Acoustic Music Club)

White's Hotel

Swag O' Dreams
(2001: Kiwi Pacific CD SLC 261)

Shores of Lyttelton • The Jewel of Whakaraupo • Age of Grace • Southward Bound • I'm a Young Man • Ballad of the Rakaia • Mackenzie's Ghost • Canterbury Jigs • The Shearing's Coming Round • Cheer Boys Cheer • White's Hotel • Come In Spinner • The Stable Lad • Farewell to Geraldine • Black Billy Blues • The Kb Cannonball/Kelly's Jigger • Beneath the Tussock

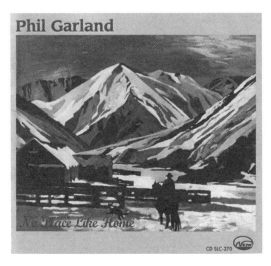

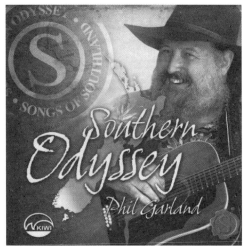

No Place Like Home
(2005: Kiwi Pacific CD SLC 270)

Bright New Day • No Place Like Home • The Big Smoke • Wool Away • The Moonlight Trail • At the Mataura • The Boys in the Band • Ballad of Davie Gunn • When the Rainbird Sings in the Tea-Tree • When the Country's Wet • The Tararua Acre • Winds of Change • And When They Dance • Time to Say Goodbye • One of the Blokes

Southern Odyssey
(2007: Kiwi Pacific CD SLC 265)

The Foggy Foggy Banks • Ballad of James Mackenzie • The Swag and the Shiner • Becalmed at the Bluff • The Drover's Song • The Hokonui Hills • Leaving Port Craig • Bring 'em On • The Kingston Flyer • Waikaia is my Station • Ballad of Davie Gunn • Ballad of Minnie Dean • The Tararua Acre • At the Mataura • McShane's Chained Lightning

For more information or to order music, contact Kiwi Pacific — www.kiwipacific.com

BOOKS

Acland, LGD *The Early Canterbury Runs*, Whitcoulls

Amodeo, Colin: *The Mosquito Fleet of Canterbury; The Summer Ships*, both Caxton Press

Anderson, Hugh, *The Colonial Minstrel; The Goldrush Songster*, Ramskull Press

Andrews, Shirley *Take Your Partners*, Griffin Press

Archer, John: *Home from the Hill*, 1990; New Zealand Folksong website

Bailey, Rona & Bert Roth *Shanties by the Way*, Whitcombe & Tombs 1967

Barker, Lady: *Station Amusements in New Zealand*; *Station Life in New Zealand*, both Wilson & Horton

Charles, Joe *Black Berry Pie*, unpublished manuscript; *Black Billy Tea*, Whitcoulls 1981

Cleveland, Les *The Great New Zealand Songbook*, Godwit Press 1991

Clune, Frank *Murders on Maungatapu*, Angus & Robertson

Colquhoun, Neil *New Zealand Folksongs – Song of a Young Country*, WEA 1965; Reed 1972

Courage, Sarah Amelia *Lights and Shadows of Colonial Life*, Whitcoulls

Elder, JR *Gold Seekers & Bushrangers in New Zealand*, Blackie & Son

Eldred-Grigg, Stevan: *A New History of Canterbury*, McIndoe 1982; *Pleasures of the Flesh,* Reed 1982*; A Southern Gentry*, Heinemann Reed 1980

Ell, Gordon *New Zealand Traditions & Folklore,* Bush Press 1994

Eyre, EL *Future Times & Other Rhymes*, Wilson & Horton

Forbis, John (ed) *Trail Blazers of New Zealand*, Duf Syndications

Foster, Bruce & Vernon Wright, *Stockman Country*, Broadcasting Corp 1983

— *Frontier of Dreams* TVNZ

Garland, Phil *The Singing Kiwi*, Willy Wag Productions 1996

Grady, Don *Sealers and Whalers in New Zealand Waters*, Reed Methuen

Gore, Ross *It Happened in New Zealand,* Digest Printing Co c.1950

Gross, Peter M *Some Colonial Verse*

Harrex, Wendy & Keith Sinclair *Looking Back*, Oxford Press

Heinz, William *Bright Fine Gold*, Reed

Henderson, J, *Open Country Calling*, Reed; *Swagger Country*, Hodder & Stoughton

Hobbs, Leslie *The Wild West Coast*, Whitcombe & Tombs

Hogan, Dennis *Billy Can Ballads*, WEA

Hosken, Evelyn, *Life on a Five Pound Note*, Timaru Herald 1964; *Turn Back the Clock* Reed 1968

Hoskins, Robert *Goldfields Balladeer*, Collins 1977

Keesing, Nancy & Douglas Stewart, *Australian Bush Ballads*, 1953; *Old Bush Songs*, 1957, both Angus & Robertson

Lawson, Henry: *The Complete Works; A Camp Fire Yarn*; *A Fantasy of Man*, all Lansdowne Press 1984

Lee, John A, *Roughnecks, Rolling Stones & Rouseabouts*, Whitcoulls; *Shiner Slattery*, Collins; *Shining with the Shiner*, Vital Books

Mackay, Ian *Puborama* Oswald-Sealy, 1961

Manifold, JS *A Book of Australian Folksong*, Penguin

Maning, FE *Old New Zealand*, Golden Press

May, Philip Ross *The West Coast Gold Rushes*, Pegasus Press 1962

McLintock, AH *The History of Otago*

McMillan, Ross: *In the Shade of the High Country*, Central Otago News 1970; *The Country Bloke & Other Verses*; *The Mountain Man*, both Otago Daily Times

McNeish, James *Tavern in the Town*, Reed; *The Mackenzie Affair*, Hodder & Stoughton 1972

Meek, George *Station Days in Maoriland*, Oamaru Mail 1952

Millar, J Halkett, *High Noon for Coaches*, 1953; *Westland's Golden Sixties,* 1959, both Reed

Milligan, David *The Moonlight Ranges*, Sycamore Print 1977

— *New Zealand Encyclopaedia*, Bateman

— *New Zealand Yesterdays*, Readers Digest

— *New Zealand's Heritage* Hamlyn House 1971

Owen, Alwyn & Jack Perkins *Speaking for Ourselves*, Penguin 1986

Park, Ruth *One a Pecker, Two a Pecker*, Angus & Robertson 1957

Paterson, Banjo – *The Complete Works; Singer of the Bush*; *Song of the Pen*, Lansdowne Press

Preshaw, George *Banking Under Difficulties,* Capper Press

Reed, AH: *The Gumdiggers*, Reed;
The Story of Northland, Reed

Reid, JC (ed) *A Book of New Zealand*,
Collins

Rickard, LS *The Whaling Trade in Old New
Zealand*, Minerva 1963

Roase, Maureen - *Making Melody: Puhoi
1863–2001*, Hibiscus Publishing

Scott, Dick *Inheritors of a Dream*, Ronald
Riddell 1962/Reed Education 1975

Simpson, Tony *The Sugarbag Years*, Alister
Taylor 1974

Slatter, Gordon *A Gun in my Hand*,
Collins

Solway, Robert *Station Ballads of David
McKee Wright*, Wright & Jaques Ltd

Steele, Roger (ed) *An Ordinary Joker*,
Steele Roberts 2001

Symons, Tod *I Know a Place*, Central
Otago News

Thatcher, Charles *The Goldfields Songsters*,
NZFLS archives & Canterbury Public
Library

Tod, Frank, *The Whale's Wake; Whaling
in Southern Waters*, both NZ Tablet
1982

Tracy, Mona: *Lawless Days*, Whitcombe &
Tombs 1928; *West Coast Yesterdays*, Reed

— *Trial of the Maungatapu Murderers, The*,
W Stiles & Co Nelson 1924

Willis, HA *Manhunt*, Whitcoulls

Winter, CH *The Story of Bidgee Queen &
other Verses*, New Century Press 1929

Wood, June *Gold Trails of Otago*, Reed 1970

Woodhouse, AE *New Zealand Farm &
Station Verse*, Whitcomb & Tombs
1950

OTHER SOURCES

— *Central Otago News*

Communicate New Zealand, Series 6401;
Archives NZ/Te Rua Mahara o te
Kawanatanga, Wellington Office

Cowan, James, 'Sailor Memoriess — The
Songs of the Sea' *Canterbury Times*
12 June 1912

Fyfe, Frank *Maorilander* journals, New
Zealand Folklore Society, Wellington

— *Heritage* magazine

Garland, Phil: *Clear the Board*, booklet,
Kiwi Pacific Records

— *Landfall New Zealand*, Replay Radio,
Radio NZ

Locke, Elsie 'Provincial Jigsaw Puzzle',
School Journal

Martin, Charles, 'Martins Locals',
Canterbury Public Library 1862

— New Zealand Folklore Society archives:
Wellington, Christchurch, Auckland

— *New Zealand Herald* 1893

— *Otago Witness* newspapers – Hocken
Library, Dunedin

Roth, Bert *Joy* magazine, 1958–59

INDEX

GOLD-DIGGERS OUT PROSPECTING

Shearing sheep at the Robinson farm
— Makara, Wellington, circa 1898.
ATL F58360 ¹/₂

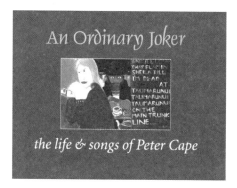

- Peter Cape's autobiographical sketch; family and historic photos.
- His 28 songs, words, music & chords.
- Notes and background on the songs.
- CD produced by Kiwi Pacific with all Cape songs for which the music is known — some previously unrecorded. Artists include Peter Cape, his son Christopher Cape, Pat Rogers, Don & Arthur Toms, Phil Garland, and others.

112 pp, hard cover book + CD $59.99

JAZZ AOTEAROA

- The first steps in documenting the history and great moments of improvised music in NZ.
- Classic performers, world-class events, livewire venues, fusion movements — including taonga puoro.

103pp, soft cover $29.99

COMING SOON in 2009
SONGS OF A YOUNG COUNTRY
New edition of Neil Colquhoun's classic

- Words, music & chords of 78 NZ folk songs.
- Revised and expanded from the 1972 edition.

108pp, hard cover — $39.99

info@steeleroberts.co.nz • www.steeleroberts.co.nz